Never Too Fast

THE PAUL TRACY STORY

PAUL FERRISS

ECW PRESS

NATIONAL LIBRARY OF CANADA CATALOGUING IN PUBLICATION DATA

Ferriss, Paul
Never too fast: the Paul Tracy story

ISBN 1-55022-469-7

1. Tracy, Paul, 1968– 2. Automobile racing drivers — Biography.
3. Karting — Biography. I. Title.

GV1032.T73F47 2001   796.72'092   C2001-900808-2

Cover and text design by Tania Craan
Front cover photo by Ian Smith/*Vancouver Sun* photo
Back cover photo by CP PHOTO/Kevin Frayer
Layout by Mary Bowness

Printed by AGMV

Distributed in Canada by
General Distribution Services,
325 Humber College Blvd.,
Toronto, ON M9W 7C3

Published by ECW PRESS
2120 Queen Street East, Suite 200
Toronto, ON M4E 1E2
ecwpress.com

This book is set in Minion and Eurostyle.

PRINTED AND BOUND IN CANADA

The publication of *Never Too Fast* has been generously supported by the Canada Council, the Ontario Arts Council and the Government of Canada through the Book Publishing Industry Development Program. Canada

Contents

Acknowledgements

I've heard it spoken several times: writing is a solitary occupation. For the person who is actually putting the words on paper, that may be true. But that's the only situation where the axiom applies. Writing a book requires not only the writer but the editor, publisher, proofreader, typesetter, graphic artist, promotional and marketing people. And, hopefully, readers. By the time they're all involved, the act of creating a book and telling a story is far from lonely.

So it's in that vein that I must thank many people who worked on the book you now hold.

Jen Hale at ECW Press for telling me to put together a proposal for this book and send it to her boss, Jack David. Jack, for liking the idea and then offering me a contract to get it done. Dallas Harrison for his careful and professional editing.

Paul Tracy for taking time between races, practices and personal appearances for interviews with me, a writer he'd never heard of. His candour was much appreciated.

For my parents, Marilyn and Paul for not telling me I was crazy to take this on when I already had a full-time job. As well, Stan Sutter at *Marketing Magazine* for taking an interest and for giving me the room to make calls and track down sources from my desk during that day job. As well, the rest of the editorial staff at *Marketing* for taking an interest in what I was doing and keeping tabs on my progress.

Among the interviews I did there were a few subjects who stood out with their contributions. Some for their candour, others whom I interviewed and then later hounded to fill in some gaps and still others for continuing to talk when I ran out of questions. Horst Kroll, Brian Stewart, Scott Goodyear, Ron Fellows, Scott Maxwell.

As well, there's Linda Fellows, Pat Caporali at Team Players and Dave Stevenson, Paul Tracy's business manager, for their extra help and for answering my repeated phone calls.

John Crowley of Quokka Sports and cart.com and Bill Frederickson of ESPN.com for showing me the ropes at Sneak Preview.

As well the several photographers who answered my (usually rushed) pleas for help, especially Ramesh Bayney, Bill Kistler, Peter Burke and Pat Cocciadeferro. Thanks also to Ralph Luciw, Ed Moodie at the Canadian Motorsport Hall of Fame and Aaron Irvine at Seventhgear.com.

But especially I owe a huge debt Sharon, my wife, best friend and writing coach. Only you know how truly daunting writing this book felt at times and only you know how difficult the deadline pressure became to work under. But you were my support through it all even as we (mostly you) prepared for our wedding and honeymoon. I truly, honestly, couldn't have written even one chapter without you.

CHAPTER ONE

The End and the Beginning

Suburbia, Karts, and Formula Ford, 1982–91

Even Hollywood would have been hard pressed to come up with a better end to the 2000 Championship Auto Racing Teams (CART) season. Five drivers were in the hunt for the Vanderbilt Cup and the cheque for $1 million that came with it. It was the season that Hollywood stepped into the world of CART. *Rocky* and *Rambo* superstar Sylvester Stallone and *Cliffhanger* director Renny Harlin had been hindered by Formula One's bureaucracy, so they turned to CART to make their racing movie *Driven*. They shot scenes at many of the CART tracks and in the process added some glamour to the world of speed and danger. During the 2000 season, 11 drivers won the 20 races, so it was only fitting that the season finale be something of a cliffhanger.

For the final race of the season, the CART teams returned to the California Speedway outside the small industrial town of Fontana, about an hour's drive from Los Angeles. In 1999, Adrian Fernandez won there, and Juan Montoya took the championship, but both of those victories were marred by the horrific crash that killed Greg Moore. Paul Tracy, Moore's 31-year-old compatriot, was now one of the five vying for the Vanderbilt Cup. During the previous season, Tracy placed third in the championship battle, behind Montoya and Tracy's teammate Dario Franchitti. Now Tracy and Gil de Ferran, Kenny Brack, Roberto Moreno, and Adrian Fernandez were the five drivers fighting until the end for the $1 million prize. Tracy was also keenly aware that another $1 million would be handed to the race winner. To further motivate himself and to let his fans and team know he was focused on winning, he dyed his hair green (also his team colour) and had dollar signs painted in green on his helmet.

October 31 began like many other California days in fall, with a cool but sunny sky above the packed racetrack near Fontana. The fans — not to mention the teams, sponsors, and CART management — finally had what they'd been waiting for. One Swede, two Brazilians, a Mexican, and a Canadian were taking the season down to the wire. Before the race began, one of the Brazilians was knocked out of contention. It was the end of the championship line for the affable 41-year-old Roberto Moreno. He'd spent the better part of his career as a journeyman in various open-wheeled racing series on both sides of the Atlantic, and he was now out of the running because he'd failed to grab pole position and the single point that went with it. So now it was down to four.

Coming into the final race, Tracy was tied with Brack for third place in the standings with 134 points, 20 points behind the leader de Ferran and 14 behind the second-place Fernandez. A maximum 21 points were up for grabs during the race (in addition to the point given for pole position), with 20 going to the winner and one to the driver leading the most laps.

As Tracy said before the start of the race,

> *We really have our work cut out for us, but it's great to go into the final race of the season still in contention to win the championship. You can't be concerned about what the guys ahead of you in the standings are doing. It wouldn't serve any purpose, anyway, because my championship hopes rest on winning the race. Fontana is tough on both cars and drivers, and it really comes down to survival of the fittest. If anyone has a good chance to be there at the end, it's Team Kool Green.*

Tracy started in ninth position, in the fifth row, plagued once again by the qualifying gremlins that had dogged him for the season, but he was higher on the grid than he'd managed in other efforts on superspeedways, with a fast lap at 30.293 seconds around the two-mile track. De Ferran, meanwhile, easily placed himself at the pole, picking up the extra point and the world closed-course speed record of 241.428 mph for a single lap in an open-wheeled race car, breaking the record of 240.942 mph set by Mauricio Gugelmin at the same track in 1997. If Tracy was to take the championship, he'd have to win the race, and de Ferran would have to drop out or at least finish lower than 12th, where he couldn't pick up any points. Of course, Brack was in a similarly tight spot. As he told the Associated Press before the race, "De Ferran obviously needs to bring his car home, Adrian needs to finish in front of Gil and I need to finish in front of both of them and lead the most laps. That's the plan. Easy, huh?"

When the green flag dropped that Sunday afternoon, the

race immediately showed the potential to be one of the best battles of the season, with the two Penske teammates, de Ferran and Helio Castroneves, battling for the lead and swapping it wheel to wheel five times during the first 22 laps around the banked two-mile oval. If de Ferran was nervous about wearing out his car and tossing away the championship, he didn't show it. And if Castroneves was at all concerned about risking the championship for his teammate by such close racing, he didn't show it. It promised to be a good fight — one that wouldn't end for over 24 hours.

Tracy got off to a good start, driving his Honda/Reynard hard from his ninth starting position to sixth on the first lap. Then disaster struck. With a decisive boom, Tracy's season and championship hopes came to a sudden and catastrophic end. His engine exploded, destroying it and the car's carbon-fibre engine cover and sending chunks of aluminum and carbon fibre onto the track. One of those pieces struck Cristiano da Matta's car, breaking his front suspension and sending his car into the wall. Both da Matta and Tracy were unhurt, but their racing day was over.

"I don't really know what happened. There was no warning," said Tracy after the incident.

> We were just cruising, kind of taking it easy, and all of a sudden we lost the engine. I looked at the car when I got out, and the top of the engine was gone. It's a disappointing day, but I can't complain. There's no reason to be upset, everyone involved in Team Kool Green has done their best, and you can't foresee something like that happening. We had a good season, we've got a lot to be proud of, and we've got some good momentum to carry into next year.

His calm demeanour was a change from that of seasons past, but it was in keeping with the attitude he'd begun to display in 1999 and 2000.

Honda spokesman Dan Layton told ESPN after the incident that the plenham — the metal engine cover — had blown off because of pressure in the engine. The plenham had then torn through the bodywork, scattering shrapnel around the track. "It was an internal engine failure," said Honda Performance Development General Manager Robert Clarke at the end of the 2000 season. "There was no way we could have prevented that one. What happened at Fontana was pretty scary." The problem with Tracy's engine was traced back to the pop-off valve.

The race continued for 10 more laps until the rain began. Like Formula One drivers, CART drivers continue to race in the rain on road and street courses, but racing on a wet superspeedway is nearly impossible. The red flag came out on lap 33, and the race was halted. While Tracy's broken car was already in the pit when the race was called, he might have made it back into the race on the restart. According to sources at the race, his team manager, Barry Green, lobbied CART officials to restart the race completely, thereby putting Tracy back into the competition. That plea was ignored, and Green's idea of putting the Canadian into his teammate's car was scuppered as well after officials said that, if Team Green did so, whatever points Tracy scored wouldn't be allowed. His misfortune was a windfall for Brazilian Christian Fittipaldi, who won the race and the U.S. $1 million purse.

While Tracy's season ended with a bang, but not of the type he would have wanted, the manner with which he handled it showed he was well on his way to becoming a more mature driver and person, at least in public. Since signing with Team Green, he'd begun to show a much more publicly friendly persona, although to some fans he still seemed to be aloof and even somewhat arrogant. During practice sessions, he'd not usually hesitate to step out of his car, hand his wife his helmet, hop onto one of the team motor scooters, and cut a path through the milling crowds to his trailer. But during the 1999 and 2000 seasons, he seemed to be much more aware of being constantly watched — by the team, by the sponsors, and most often by the media and his fans.

It wasn't always that way. When Tracy was growing up in the Toronto suburb of Scarborough with his two older half-sisters, Debbie and Leigh Ann, from his father's first marriage and his younger sister, Anne, just a few people noticed his interest in go-karts. One of them was his father. Tony Tracy is a big Englishman with the hint of an accent, some red hair that's given way reluctantly to grey, and an often brusque and always opinionated manner. He's still a strong believer in his son's talents and abilities, but it's clear he feels slighted by having been replaced as Paul's personal manager following the years and money he spent guiding his son from karts to champ cars, with a Formula One test and an F1 job offer along the way.

It was Tony who raced motorcycles as a youth and passed his love of cars and motorcycles on to his son. And it was Tony who bought the young Paul his first go-kart. While his father is listed as the greatest influence on his life in a profile of Tracy on his team's web site, it's apparent their relationship is that of a determined parent who constantly pushed his equally determined son. Tony is not unlike the stereotypical

Canadian "hockey dad" who both cheers and harangues his son and other players and coaches from the bleachers. But one of the differences between him and many parents who have high hopes for their children in sports is that he had enough money to get his son started in racing go-karts.

In the early 1980s, the Tracys met an aspiring racer and go-kart enthusiast named Scott Goodyear. His family ran a motorcycle, snowmobile, and go-kart shop in Toronto and provided parts for and helped to prepare go-karts. Tony Tracy asked Goodyear to teach his 10-year-old son some go-kart basics, and, so Goodyear could explain what they'd be up against when they began racing, he invited him to his house for dinner. "I remember Paul being at the dinner table and listening," Goodyear recalled in 2001. "I don't even think he really asked a question, and after dinner was over he was off to play outside, and I sat with his parents just to sort of explain to them what go-karting was all about."

Paul began racing karts in the junior levels and moved up to the senior level, ahead of his time, at age 13. He won the junior title. By the time he was 16, he had 74 wins in 82 kart races. There were some, however, who wanted the young racer to stay where he was. "After the first race, the race director wanted to put him back in juniors again. But they had to keep him, but the drivers didn't want him there," says his father. "They figured he was just a junior. But they figured 'Let him in, he's not going to do any harm.' When they raced him, they found out different."

Different indeed. In his first full season as a senior-level karter, Tracy won 91 of 94 races. While he quickly showed he could win races, he also showed a trait that would come back to haunt him. "He was a lot more aggressive than he is now," says his father. When asked whether the other drivers on the circuit welcomed that aggression, he replies, "If you're a winner, you're never the most popular person on the block, eh?" Whether or not Paul was the most popular driver, he was definitely a winner. He won both the senior national and international karting titles. Tony says his son remained quiet despite his success and didn't make many friends during that time, and he attributes his son's introspectiveness to rivalries among young drivers who were unwilling to hang out with the guy who was beating them on the track every week.

Still, for the boy who was already beginning to make a living from driving things fast, life wasn't all business. Tony Tracy, who has a vast collection of sports and vintage cars (including Aston Martins, Jaguars, Bentleys, and Rolls Royces), let his son take the wheel of his E-type Jaguar one night returning home from a kart race, several years before Paul had a driver's licence. As father and son rocketed along Markham Road on the outskirts of Scarborough, they soon attracted the attention of a police officer, who stopped the car. Considering there was a 12 year old at the wheel, the cop let them go with a warning. "We've been friends ever since," said a smiling Tracy of the police officer.

At age 14, in 1982, Tracy was asked to join the Team USA karting team under the leadership of George De Mannick. Paul competed against another racer, whom he'd later join on the CART circuit, Scott Pruett. Paul stopped racing karts when he was 15, in 1983, finishing two more seasons and winning the senior championship both times. Although he was a clear winner in the series, his father points out that the races were no cakewalks and that Paul was fortunate to be part of a skilled team aided by his father's money, which helped to buy him good karts. "It's not very easy. Most of the people out there were good racers. You could say possibly Paul had a slight edge because his equipment was always better than other people could afford," says Tony. "There were always good racers out there, and they'd come to race, and, you know, they had one engine and the same karts. Couldn't afford a new set of tires or a paint stripe."

The next time Scott Goodyear met with Tracy was in 1983 when the young driver attended the Canadian School of Motor Racing at the Shannonville racetrack east of Toronto, at which Goodyear was both manager and instructor. He describes Tracy's performance at that time as "head and heels over everybody else." "It became very evident that the first time in a car he had astounding car control, and it was to a point where, for the time that he had in the seat and the experience in the car, he was driving it faster and driving over . . . what he probably should have been doing, but the ability to . . . retrieve the car when it got all sideways was remarkable."

While Tony was still pushing Paul to be aggressive, he was also willing to step aside when he found a capable instructor, such as Goodyear, to point Paul in the right direction. "I think he had a big influence on . . . Paul," said Goodyear. "And he probably relieved Paul about having to worry about going out and looking for sponsors all through those grass-roots years. . . ."

Goodyear found Tracy to be an attentive if somewhat headstrong student.

> *Getting through all the one-on-one instruction with Paul over the three-day course, you could certainly see, even sitting there talking to him in the car, that he's listening to*

what you're saying, and he's absorbing it. But when the shield went down, and he went out on the race track, and the only thing that was of interest to him was putting his foot into it, and maybe [he was] missing some of the fundamentals along the way, but he was just interested in going fast, you know, which he did very well. Although it was spectacular, it was sideways. He was fast, but he never crashed or hit anything.

It was about the same time that Tracy met another up-and-coming Canadian driver, Ron Fellows. Paul was treated to a test in his Formula Ford 1600 car, which Tony was interested in buying. While never a CART competitor, Fellows has established a solid reputation as an excellent road racer in the Trans Am and Sports Car Club of America (SCCA) endurance series, he has driven in NASCAR on a regular basis for the past few seasons, and in 2000 he co-drove a Corvette to victory in the gruelling 24 Hours of Daytona. Fellows remembers Paul as a quiet, bespectacled, pudgy, "geeky little kid" whose driving style belied his looks — and his years. It was 1983, and Fellows, about 25 at the time (10 years older than Tracy), had already begun paying his dues in racing's minor leagues.

They met at Goodwood while Fellows's brother was also competing in karts, in a different division than Paul's. Tony Tracy had arranged for Paul to try out the car in a two-day test, and after the season was over Tony bought the car from Fellows to give the young driver some time to get used to driving open-wheeled cars. Fellows was impressed right from the start by Paul's ability.

It didn't take him long to adapt. I'd certainly seen a number of guys from karting, and sometimes they don't switch on right away. Even a lightweight formula kart, because it does have a suspension, it'll feel a bit lazy. And with the lack of precision, because you have suspension movement, oftentimes they don't quite find the edge, but Paul was there right away. I think the first time he drove the car the track was slightly damp, so it was pretty fun to watch. He wasn't that far behind, and I certainly had a lot more experience than he did at that time, but he wasn't very far behind me.

In his first few drives around the track, Tracy "absolutely destroyed" any lap record at the time.

He was incredibly aggressive. Obviously, he'd learned some of his technique in Europe. It was interesting to watch somebody drive a kart the way he did. Using his body in the kart, I'd never seen it before. It was just the kid's commitment — not his commitment to the sport but his commitment to the driving part. . . . [He was] very, very aggressive, and he was just a joy to watch.

Fellows compares Tracy's karting with that of some of the world's best F1 drivers, including Emerson Fittipaldi and Ayrton Senna. Like them, he believes, Tracy has a natural ability and is at his best when he's most aggressive.

At the time, Fellows believed Tracy was already ahead of most of his contemporaries, thanks in large part to his father's bankrolling his fledgling career.

He was . . . wasting his time competing here, and his dad made sure he had real good equipment. You couple that with the kind of aggressive driving style that he had, and the quality car control that he had, and that's a pretty tough combination. He needed to compete at an international level where there was a lot more competition. He was certainly one of the kids recognized as being special and . . . had a father who was also committed and had the financial resources to help him.

Tracy admitted during a Trillium Communications TV documentary on him in 1992 that it would have been a lot harder to learn to handle a full-blown race car if he'd "just jumped in the car and tried to go fast" without the benefit of proper instruction at Goodyear's school and trying out cars used by actual competitors, such as Fellows's Ford. Along with teaching the basics of driving and handling a race car, Goodyear's school went through the finer points of race car set-up and allowed young drivers to work their way up to a competitive speed.

Goodyear later found his generosity repaid by Tracy's father at a time when he needed it most. In 1984, Goodyear had been out of competitive racing for about a year and was working to pay off some debts. He was offered the chance to race a Formula 2000 car at Trois Rivières in Quebec but needed money for tires and some other expenses. Tony Tracy heard about the driver's plight and bought tires and invested in the car so that Goodyear could race, and he's always been grateful because the race allowed him to get noticed in the United States.

Looking back, Goodyear said he understood the father's and son's desire to drive fast and to become successful at racing, almost in spite of the cost. "My friends would say, if you work as hard at something else as you do motor racing, boy, you'll be very successful in life. But when you're growing up, there's nothing else in the world that matters, you just want to go race cars, which is what Paul wanted to do. Paul's life was just eat, breathe, and sleep motor racing — which is what you have to do." Goodyear also understood Tony's plan to let his son stay in any given series only for a short time, just long enough to make a mark.

Paul moved on to the Formula Ford 1600 series in 1984. He finished third in the standings, was named rookie of the year, and won the final race. This was all at the age of 16, when most of his peers were happy just to get a driver's licence and drive through Scarborough in their parents' cars. Formula Ford has been the first competitive car-racing series entered by some of the world's best race drivers. The late Ayrton Senna, Nigel Mansell, and current Formula One stars Michael Schumacher and Mika Hakkinen all cut their teeth in the series. Drivers compete in small open-wheeled formula race cars powered by identical 1,600 cc Ford engines capable of producing slightly more than 140 horsepower. They and other open-wheeled cars that give rookie drivers a taste of the big leagues are essentially scaled-down versions of CART champ cars. While other drivers also moved up the ladder of the usual racing development series — from small, stock-model touring cars such as Hondas and Fords to more powerful Porsches to Formula Fords and then on to the larger cars of the Formula 2000 and Formula Atlantic series (now powered by Toyota engines able to produce 240 horsepower)

— Paul drove in several series according to his father's plan, not necessarily spending an entire season in each. Tony's challenge was to expose Paul to as many different series and types of racing as possible — in both North America and Europe — while he could afford it. Then the plan was that Paul would enter Formula One or Indy-style racing and have someone else foot the sizeable bill. "We blew everybody away; then we went to Formula 2000," says Tony. "Had a few races. Won a few races. Then I said, 'All right Paul . . . now,' because I'm only a working stiff, so I've got a limited amount of cash to support him. So, if I'm gonna get him there, I've gotta advance his program, before it puts me out of business."

In 1986, Paul moved on to Formula 2000, where he drove a car with a three-litre engine but, contrary to many expectations, won only one race. He then made the jump to the Formula Atlantic series, also the training ground later for Jacques Villeneuve. "In a three-year period, he'd gone from Formula Ford . . . to Formula 2000, Formula Atlantic, and Formula Three [in Europe]. Now the next job was the U.S., so that's where we went."

Tracy estimates his father spent at least $3 million getting him started in racing and supporting his career until Penske signed him. While that amount is high, Tracy said his father's business acumen probably saved him quite a bit of money. He'd try to get sponsorship from companies he was working with in his various painting contracts. For example, as Paul approached his second-last season of Indy Lights racing in 1988, Tony was buying vast quantities of paint for an industrial job. He bought about $500,000 worth of paint and then asked Sherwin-Williams to sponsor his son's race car. Tony still runs the Toronto-based painting business that he ran while Tracy was coming up through the racing ranks.

Of course, Paul still had to attend school while away racing. He says his marks weren't the greatest, but he passed all his courses and graduated from high school. His teachers knew he was planning to pursue racing as a career and tended to look the other way when it came to his absences. A timely co-op placement helped him to get the best of both worlds near the end of his high school career. "I kind of pulled a bit of a scam," he says. "At one point, I convinced the principal to let me take a mechanics course at the Van Diemen factory in England and was actually racing for the factory team." It was while on the Van Diemen team that Tracy met Ralph Firman, the owner of the race car company. Tracy says that it was an honour to drive for the team considering the other drivers who'd passed through. "All of the best drivers in the world drove there — Senna, Prost, Mansell."

For Paul's racing in the United States and Europe, Tony Tracy again looked up Firman to work with the young racer. To this day, Tony recalls Firman as one of the few honest people in racing, someone who not only took Paul under his wing at a pivotal time in his racing career but also took him into his home, letting him stay with his family while he raced. Their relationship continued even after Paul wrecked Firman's wife's car and was caught speeding while driving the family car in Germany. Still too young to legally drive, he showed the officer his go-kart racing licence.

At one point, Irishman Eddie Jordan, owner of the F1 Jordan team, was interested in signing Paul but, according to the elder Tracy, took too much time to make a decision, so the Tracys walked away from the deal. But Tony's dismissal of

Jordan's interest doesn't include one important fact. Jordan wanted Paul to drive but couldn't round up enough interest from Canadian companies to sponsor the young driver's spot on his team. Despite sponsoring many drivers who've competed in various series internationally, Canadian companies aren't quick to get involved in Formula One unless they're international tobacco companies. Or, if they do become involved, racing sponsorship is often one of the first casualties of corporate realignments. Witness Teleglobe's pullout of its sponsorship of British American Racing in 2000. But such a lack of interest may be to their corporate peril. As Toronto *Sun* motorsports writer Dan Proudfoot noted in the TV documentary in 1992, "I believe in time there will be companies like Labatt and Molson that will regret that they didn't link themselves with Paul Tracy at that time."

So Tony took his son back to the United States and rented an Indy car for Paul to run at the Long Beach Grand Prix. It was the last race of the 1990 season. Tony paid $40,000 for one weekend's worth of racing. "I said to Paul, 'This car ain't gonna fuckin' finish. It's not quick enough to get to the pole. Do the best you can, get it up front somehow.' So he got it up as far as Mario Andretti" before the car broke down, Tony says. "That's one thing Paul was always good at. He could put the show on." It was important to Tony that his son blast into the race against some big-name drivers and, knowing the car wasn't likely to finish, put on enough of a show to get noticed. It marked the first time the champ car world got a glimpse of the "Sturm und Drang" style of driving that was to define Paul Tracy for much of his career.

CHAPTER TWO

Can-Am, Indy Lights, and the Nod from Penske

From Mosport to Long Beach

If Can-Am race cars were living creatures, they'd be freaks of nature. Part formula car, part endurance sports car, and part Le Mans-style racer, the powerful cars growled their way around the tracks of Canada and the United States throughout the 1980s. Luminaries such as Mark Donohue, Peter Revson, Danny Sullivan, and Bobby Rahal raced Can-Am cars before the final series of 1986, when its last champion, Canadian Horst Kroll, was crowned. Following that season, Rahal and company began a new series that would feature open-wheeled cars driving on ovals, speedways, and road and street courses. That's how CART was born.

Kroll, a genial German Canadian with a love of Porsches, now runs a garage in the east end of Toronto that specializes in German cars. He's also a member of the Canadian Motorsport Hall of Fame. In addition to being the final Can-Am champion and a well-regarded name in Canadian racing, he gave a rising Paul Tracy a taste of what was to come in open-wheeled cars by letting him drive one of his Can-Am cars in the final race of 1986. While Kroll no longer competes, he still attends the Molson Indy every year — making his way around the paddock on his homemade motor scooter — and keeps in touch with many of the friends he made in his racing days.

The car Kroll campaigned in that series can be found at the Canadian Motorsport Hall of Fame in Hamilton. It carries the names of not only Tracy and Kroll but also Jacques Villeneuve (the uncle of the current F1 driver), who drove the car just after it was built at an event on Quebec's Sanair track. At first glance, it resembles a futuristic hover-craft that would more likely float on air instead of scream across pavement. Can-Am cars make champ cars and F1 cars look positively malnourished in comparison. They were big and noisy, with 13-inch wheels on the front and 15-inch wheels on the back, fenders (some covered the rear wheels completely in an effort to improve aerodynamics), and a giant air intake above the cockpit.

Kroll first saw Tracy race in a Formula 2000 event at Sanair in 1986. While it was an uneventful race for Tracy ("He started dead last and ran out of gas," said Kroll), it nonetheless impressed the veteran. After the race, Kroll, who was both managing and driving for his own three-car Can-Am team, was looking for a third driver for an upcoming race at Mosport. He spoke to Tony Tracy, told him of his favourable impression, and asked him if Paul would be interested in driving in the last race of the 1986 season on the Mosport track and the last race ever for the big Can-Am cars. Paul accepted the offer and took the third spot on the team. This was a big step for him, although he wouldn't admit it at the time, attempting to cop a youthfully cavalier attitude. The Formula 2000 cars the 18-year-old had been driving put out about 200 horsepower, while a Can-Am racer produced about 560 horsepower and was bigger and used much more of the track.

At the time, the Tracy family lived in Scarborough across the road from Kroll. When Paul agreed to drive the car, Kroll had to make some adjustments to the pedals to accommodate Tracy's larger frame. But once that was done, the car was ready to drive. Kroll, his small crew, and Tracy took the car to the Mosport track, about 90 minutes east of Toronto, on the Friday of the race weekend for Tracy's first test. While the young driver was eager to show what he could do, he'd have to wait another day because a typical September rain hung over the track, and Kroll didn't want an eager young rookie taking one of his cars out on the slippery pavement. Kroll was protective of his cars not just because he was a mechanic and a driver but also because he funded his own racing operation with very little outside sponsorship. He made repairs himself. "I gave this opportunity to Paul in a car that is worth a quarter of a million dollars," Kroll told a TV documentary crew in 1992. "Driving around Mosport at 170 mph is quite impressive. A jump of 400 horsepower from one car to the other, and he handled this very impressively." Tracy agreed. "It's just real strange driving this 140-horsepower F2000 car to jump into this big, huge, wide-tired beast at 700 horsepower. It was just real strange, and it was a great opportunity for me."

When the sun came up on Saturday, Kroll took the car around the track himself and after four laps decided to give Paul a try. Mechanical problems back in June seemed to have been fixed. "After four laps, I'm smiling — this car works.

Whatever I did was perfect. So I said to Paul, 'I would like you to drive behind me, and we'll get faster every time.' He thought, I found out later, I was treating him like a child or as a teacher," said Kroll. He was forced to show the young driver how to handle the Can-Am car and qualify for the race all in one day because of the lost Friday practice. He himself was preparing to enter the race in a position to win the championship.

A calm and experienced driver, Kroll had driven the Mosport track many times before. Close to Toronto, it had become his "home track," and its layout lent itself to the big Can-Am cars. Kroll was aware of the young driver's reputation for on-track aggression, but he was shocked when Tracy showed he was more than ready to take the challenge. "After four laps, I said to myself, 'Paul, goodbye, I'm gone,' and I put my foot in it and did one lap, and I look in my mirror, and this kid is behind me!" he said. "Well, gee, I thought, so I put it up a notch [Kroll's best time in qualifying at Mosport was 1:13.4], so we're going in the 1:16s, and I couldn't believe it. So I went up another notch, and he's falling back a little bit but not to the extent I thought. And I thought, Jesus, Paul, what the hell are you doing? Right then and there was when I knew the kid had talent."

"The kid" had talent all right, but did he know when to hit the brakes? On the next lap, Kroll was heading through turn eight and entering turn nine when a hard crosswind caught his car in its path and lifted it up, causing him to lose control and slam into the guardrail. An unhurt Kroll swore and quickly jumped out of the car just before Tracy came hurtling around the corner and slammed into it, effectively driving across its nose. "So then my car is finished, and Paul's car is finished, two cars on the very same lap."

It wasn't so much the rookie mistake, which may have caused the accident, or the fact that the cars now had to be repaired before Sunday's race that upset Kroll; it was what happened next — or, more correctly, what didn't happen — that upset him. Kroll made his way back to the pits and wanted to talk to Tracy about what had taken place. But he was nowhere to be found. "They towed the cars in, and my main concern right now is to get both cars fixed for the next morning," Kroll said. "I expected him to stay there and discuss things like 'What happened to you, and what happened to me?' But he's gone; he's nowhere to be found. I asked Tony, and he said, 'Oh, he's gone home.' Jesus Christ, I would have liked to talk to him. He drove right over me! Something must have happened, because he drove over my front, my nose, and smashed up his nose." Tracy's disappearance and apparent lack of concern following the crash illustrates for Kroll a central element of the young driver's character: Paul is aloof and doesn't always seem to care about those around him. To Kroll, it was almost as if Tracy was thinking "I've crashed, everybody's okay, but the car is now someone else's problem." For Kroll, the incident is as fresh today as it was then, and he's disappointed that Tracy didn't take responsibility for it. Plus, at the time, Tracy told reporters that he came upon Kroll's car in the middle of the track and couldn't avoid it. "I've never pinned him down on this, but he said that I was sitting in the middle of the road, and he had nowhere to go. But I have pictures, somebody was standing there," Kroll said. "I hit the guardrail, and I was standing there, I was off the track. Why would he say that? I guess he was trying to say 'It was not my fault.' But this is the character that I am talking about. But I didn't call [him] up and say 'Look, you've got it wrong.' But that's Paul."

With two damaged cars and less than 24 hours until the race that would decide the Can-Am championship, Kroll had plenty to do. He worked on the cars until midnight, drove back to Toronto for about three hours of sleep, and then headed back to the track the next morning. He still hadn't spoken to Paul. His mind was on his most immediate challenge — finish the race ahead of Colorado racer Bill Tempero to claim the championship. Given the previous day's incident, he also had to stay out of Tracy's way.

The start of the race foreshadowed many other starts for Paul during his career. It was loud, fast, and reckless. Kroll, who saw Tracy rocket ahead from his vantage point two cars back, could only watch in disbelief. "He's leading the race. Tempero is second, and I'm running third. I'm watching him. Paul is just going off the track, through the cars, bits are flying," Kroll said with a laugh. "They're exchanging the lead. I'm sitting back because my oil light is coming on going into the corners. I thought, 'Oh, my God, there goes my championship.' He's ahead of me, and he's going like stink with Paul." The wily veteran hung back while the other two fought it out, hoping his oil pressure would remain patient and let him finish the race. He got his wish.

Five laps from the finish, Tempero dropped out, and Tracy took the lead, with Kroll sliding into second. And that's how they finished. Kroll was obviously pleased, and Tracy's drive didn't go unnoticed. "I was very impressed with his maturity," said Dan Proudfoot to the Trillium crew. "He wasn't some young hotshot who went out and drove the wheels off the car; he was a young hotshot who, when his tires started going away, had the maturity and judgement to back off and sit in second or third for a while until the tires came back, and he went on to win. He showed that he could think that day."

"Paul and I finished one-two. It was one of the greatest moments in my racing career," said Kroll during the documentary. "Having your cars finish first and second and a driver who is now making it on the pro racing circuit."

Tracy won his first (and only) Can-Am race, the youngest driver ever to do so, and Kroll won the final Can-Am championship and stood next to the young rookie on the podium. They smiled for the cameras and waved to the cheering Mosport crowds and accepted their awards. After the trophy presentation, Tracy left again. "I thought, man," Kroll said, "just hang around a bit, and I'll clean up my stuff, and we'll go have a drink or a coffee or something. Nothing. Paul is gone."

Tracy had his mind on moving ahead. In keeping with his father's plan, he was driving in as many racing series as he could, and almost as soon as he accepted it the Can-Am trophy was just another to add to his collection. His next racing move would take him to a series whose cars were closer to Indy-style racers and Formula One cars. And it would introduce him to a veteran team owner and Canadian who would prove to be instrumental in further shaping his career.

In 1985, Brian Stewart, the owner of the team for whom Tracy would eventually drive in Indy Lights, was campaigning for the Ontario Formula Ford championship with a Canadian driver, Scott Maxwell. The Ontario region is the largest in Canadian racing. "I was 21, and Paul was 16, at the time I was looked at as this young guy, and all of a sudden here's this 16 year old," said Maxwell. "I had heard his name, but I didn't know much about him, all I knew is he was a hot karter."

Stewart is a plain-spoken, serious man whose team's home base is in the small community of Pefferlaw, Ontario. He's proudly Canadian despite the fact that most of his business and racing is carried out in the United States. At times, Stewart displays a dry sense of humour, but he has the manner of a veteran hockey coach whose feistiness comes from knowing he has the best players on his squad. He staunchly defends Tracy's driving and relates an argument he got into with a fellow golfer during a game in the summer of 2000. The player, a member of Stewart's foursome, criticized Paul and promptly received a stream of invective from Stewart, who sprang to the defence of Tracy, whom he says is one of the best drivers alive. As well as fielding a car for Paul, he's had drivers P.J. Jones, Gualter Salles, and current CART drivers Bryan Herta and Cristiano da Matta on his team.

In 1985, the buzz around the paddock focused on Tracy, says Stewart, as he was entering the Formula Ford series. But Stewart had never heard of him. Maxwell won the first race of the season, and the always-combative Tony Tracy then paid Stewart a visit. "So he comes over to me, I didn't know him either, and he says, 'Listen, mister, don't even show up next week. I've done a deal with Quicksilver for the best motor that they can build,'" Stewart said. "I said, 'Who the fuck do you think you're talking to? The only thing you'll cost me is lack of sleep lying awake trying to figure out how to beat you, but I will beat you.' So at the next race he had his big motor, and we beat him again."

Maxwell and Tracy battled for the rest of the season, usually head to head and sometimes taking each other out of a race. The championship came down to a race between them, which Maxwell won. He said that, despite the limited budget he and Stewart had, they were able to put together a very competitive car. Yet they thought of themselves as the underdogs, looking upon Tracy's team as the "money team." Plus, while all Tracy had to do was drive, Maxwell was expected to work on the car. "We probably had a quarter of the budget Paul had, and he probably wrote off a couple of cars throughout the season," he said. "He did a lot of damage, but that's how Paul was, he was 16, he was fresh out of karts, and he was super, super fast, but you pay the price for that sometimes." Tracy, Maxwell said, was at the stage in his career where he hadn't learned to harness his speed, whereas he himself had already moved beyond the crashing phase. And neither he nor Stewart had the luxury of a big budget, so they couldn't afford a lot of crashes.

Maxwell added that Tracy didn't look like a racer with his quiet demeanour, husky build, and thick glasses, but his appearance didn't mean much when he was blasting around the track. Maxwell said the season was intense. He and Tracy battled it out on the track while Stewart and Tracy Sr. battled it out in the pits. "I love talking to Tony, but he was a shit disturber at the time. I was fortunate that I had Brian on my side, and Brian and Tony used to go head to head." Plus, during that summer, Paul dated Maxwell's sister. "I'd come home greasy from working on the car, and he'd be sitting in the living room," Maxwell said with a laugh.

The Tracy-Maxwell battle was heartily encouraged by Tony, and their on-track sparring garnered a great deal of media attention. Tracy didn't say much about the rivalry at the time, and off the track the two became friends and remain friends today. "I don't think we had one conflict outside the car," Maxwell said. "There was never a point when we were pissed off at each other. It pushed me really hard. If Paul wasn't around or if I wasn't around, one of us would have just walked away [with the championship] and probably not come out of the season as good a driver as we probably did because we pushed each other really hard." Maxwell and Tracy shared a similarly aggressive driving style. They were young and hungry enough to take more risks than some of the other drivers. "After the first couple of races, it was obvious that it was going to be between the two of us. A lot of the other guys were in a different position. A lot of them were not maybe as intent on making it a career, and some were a little older, more mature, and were just not going to take the chances we were taking," Maxwell said. "We just didn't know any better — that's all we could think about. A lot of these guys are working nine to five, Monday to Friday, and are putting every penny they've got to go racing. So they're not going to stick their noses in places Paul and I would."

The two raced again in the Rothman's Porsche Cup in 1986, but the cars were more evenly matched, and their driving wasn't as competitive because they had several other drivers to beat in the series. "I don't think his heart was in it. He was into formula cars, as I was," Maxwell said. "Paul's direction was always clear cut. They had the money to do karts, Formula Ford, 2000, Atlantic — whereas for me the next year I didn't know what the hell I was going to do. When I was given the chance to run a Rothman's Porsche, while it wasn't what Paul wanted to do, for me it was a lifeline to keep my career going."

Although the two didn't race much together after the Porsche series, their careers continued to dovetail. In 1986,

Tracy was the Van Diemen driver, and when he moved on to Reynard in 1987 Maxwell replaced him.

Following Maxwell's Formula Ford championship, both Stewart's team and Tracy moved on to Formula 2000. Stewart wanted to sign Maxwell as his driver, but the two were unable to put a sponsorship deal together. Stewart spent the next three seasons in Formula 2000 and did one Indy Lights race in 1988 under the Landford Racing banner with a part-time driver. While he continued using Landford as the team name until 1993, he added Irishman Tommy Byrne as a driver in 1989 and spent a full season on the Indy Lights circuit. Stewart was happy with Byrne's four wins that season — including the first race they entered at Long Beach and the storied Mid-Ohio course — but he still wanted to field Canadians.

The Mid-Ohio race in 1989 proved to be a turning point in the relationship between Tracy and Stewart and showed that, in the age of high-tech racing, cooperation between teams could still happen as if they were just amateurs in a Saturday-night, dirt-track competition. While Stewart's team had done well with Byrne at the wheel, Tracy had won the first Indy Lights race he entered in 1988. He struggled, however, in 1989. Until the Mid-Ohio event that year, Tracy and Byrne were "bitter enemies," said Stewart. Byrne was fighting for the championship, and while he won four races there were several he didn't finish. Tracy was faring well, but in the morning warm-up he crashed. The crash left him in a difficult spot — he'd already qualified and so was able to race if he could get his car fixed in time. Stewart pondered the situation. His driver, Byrne, was on the pole but would have to outrace his closest competitor for the championship,

Mike Groff, who had qualified behind Tracy. "We had to put as many people as possible between ourselves and Mike Groff," said Stewart. "And I knew for a fact there was not a snowball's chance in hell that Groff could get by Tracy. So we fixed his car."

Including Stewart, his team had 12 mechanics. Tracy's had two. They all began working furiously to repair the damage in time for the race. And, because CART was a more casual operation back then (CART is the governing body for not only the champ car circuit but also the Indy Lights series), the teams even managed to convince officials to delay the start of the race by 10 minutes. Stewart laughs when he recalls the story: "Of course, all the people who were behind Tracy were complaining, but they [track officials] were using all sorts of excuses, like they had to clean the track and all sorts of bullshit like that."

The race finally got under way, and Tracy beat Groff and helped, however inadvertently, Byrne to get the win. But a championship for Stewart would have to wait one more season.

Tony Tracy, as usual, had been at all his son's races, and because of their past acrimony Stewart had "avoided him like the plague." By the end of the 1989 season, Stewart once again wanted to take on Canadian drivers, so he raised the subject with Tony. By this time, Stewart was well aware of his reputation as a rabble rouser (Stewart described him as "obnoxious"), but he thought he had a deal that the senior Tracy couldn't refuse. "You know what, Tony?" Stewart said to him. "I don't like you, and I know you don't like me, but what we're talking about here is getting the job done, and you know we can do the job." The offer was this: Stewart would get the $250,000 from Paul's current sponsor, the Sherwin-Williams paint company, make Paul his driver, and keep all the prize money. The only condition of the deal was that Tony couldn't go to the races, except for the Toronto Molson Indy and the final race of the season at Laguna Seca. If he did go to a race, his son's car would be black flagged and withdrawn from competition. Stewart admits that the conditions were harsh, but he'd witnessed firsthand Tony pushing his son to win at all costs and knew that he would only be a further distraction to Paul if he were at the races. Stewart believed that while he was running the team Tony would try to undermine his authority, and he wasn't willing to tolerate that. With the millions that go into the top levels of auto racing and the number of sponsors involved, Stewart is not just taking part in a sport but also running a business, and his preventing Tony from attending his son's races was a business decision. Tony wasn't happy about the terms, but, according to Stewart, he truly wanted what was best for his son. And he knew that joining Stewart's team at that time in his career was one of the best moves Paul could make. As Stewart is fond of saying, "He went from me to Penske." Tony eventually agreed, somewhat reluctantly, to Stewart's terms, but he refuses to talk about it now.

Once 22-year-old Paul was signed to the team, he and Stewart were ready to begin the 1990 Indy Lights season, and they immediately got down to business. Tracy won seven of the first eight races of the season. Stewart said he was on his way to the eighth race when CART once again changed the rules. He maintains that race officials thought the team was cheating because Tracy was doing so well, so they instituted a new system of restarting the race following a yellow flag.

Under a yellow caution period, which occurs when there's an accident or obstruction on the track, drivers are not allowed to pass. Under Indy Lights rules, drivers restarted the race in single file, but to take away the unfair advantage that Tracy supposedly enjoyed they had to restart the race side by side, presumably to increase passing. The logic appears to be that since Tracy was usually out front he would stay out front after a restart because the cars were single file. Putting drivers alongside him would, in theory, make it more difficult for him to continue leading. Drivers communicate with their pit crews during races via two-way radios. They allow a driver to report an ill-handling car or the pit crew chief to notify the driver of an upcoming hazard on the track. Because of different track configurations, drivers don't usually know when a race has been restarted, so the pit crew watches the starter's stand and lets the driver know when the green flag comes out. If a driver isn't quick to hit the throttle when the flag drops, he loses precious seconds and potentially allows another car past. During the off-season, and with new drivers, teams often practise restarts on a track to improve a driver's reactions.

During that season's race in Detroit, CART instituted the new rule. In that race, Tracy had a healthy lead going into a caution period, and on the restart Byrne got a jump on him and took the lead as the Stewart team's radio malfunctioned. "Our radio fucked up, and we're yelling green, and he couldn't hear us, and Byrne got a jump on him, so Paul was pissed off, and we had a crash," Stewart said. "But anyway we had a great year, and CART did everything to impede us. Anyway, they only did it for one race, and then they said, 'Maybe this guy is a star, maybe we should start building something like a star system,'" which is what CART did when it later formalized the development series for open-wheeled cars from Formula 2000 on up to Indy Lights. Many of these series run their races as support events for regular champ car races. Stewart also maintains that, because of Tracy's wins, the series engine suppliers were told to give the team the least powerful engines. While all the cars use the same engine, some may have minor flaws that prevent them from reaching optimum performance. Those slightly underachieving engines were what the team got for Tracy's car, but they still didn't keep Paul from winning.

Stewart had a skilled veteran on his team serving as chief mechanic. Burke Harrison is a transplanted Canadian who now makes his home in California and works as a chief mechanic for Dorricott Racing. That Indy Lights team won the 1999 series title with driver Oriol Servia, who's now driving in the CART champ car series. Mechanic Grant Fitzpatrick and veteran engineer Alec Purdy joined Harrison on Stewart's team.

Harrison recalls that Tracy was an excellent driver to work with, one full of raw speed and natural aggression, but also one who could communicate well with his pit crew and mechanics, a skill that Roger Penske would value when he added Paul to his team. But Harrison also remembers a different kind of person — one who was growing up quickly in a high-speed world. "Just a young kid who could drive a race car" was how he described Paul. "I'd watched him race in Formula 2000, and you'd know when he was out racing because he was always quick. He was a little wild; he had a reputation." Tracy was recognized in previous series, says

Harrison, partly because he was always trying to get to the front of the pack. In doing so, he usually drove an inferior car and left the track almost as often as he stayed on it. He was concerned with beating the track record regardless of the kind of track. When he went to practise at the ageing Big Springs track in Texas, he wasn't even in the car before he wanted to know what time to beat. "You'd know the car was only a fourth-place car, and he'd try to win with it and crash," Harrison said. "All we did was give him a . . . set-up that suited him." Testing, testing, and more testing decided that set-up, which the mechanics didn't stray from much; they became confident that Tracy could do the job on the track if they gave him the right car. "I don't think a guy like Paul ever had a bad day," Harrison said. "I thought he was that much better than the rest, so if we did our job the car would always be in the front row. If we didn't do our job, then he'd be in the second or third row."

Harrison also found something other than the crash-and-burn reputation when he started working with Tracy. He found a driver who was always ready to get in the car and drive but didn't suffer from the pretentiousness of some drivers who lacked his skills. Tracy even lived with Harrison at his house in the team's home base of Phoenix. When Tracy signed on with the team, Harrison heard the usual remarks from other teams about having to prepare, and inevitably repair, a car for Paul. "Be prepared to put on spare parts" was one of the comments he heard, but he recalls that, in all the testing the team did, Tracy never bent a wheel and was remarkably mature for his age. He also had an excellent ability to "read" a racetrack — to see exactly where the right line is to make the fastest turn, to see differences in the surface that others would not. While that may seem like a trivial skill, consider that drivers must understand a track while driving on it at 150 mph. And some tracks are always better than others, and temporary street courses can be among the worst because the track conditions change from year to year. Champ car and Indy Lights drivers race every year at the Burke Lakefront Airport in Cleveland, Ohio. The rest of the year, the track is an airport. While the track has been a favourite of racing fans because of its openness and good sight lines, it's notorious for being tough on race cars and drivers. The runways and taxiways are much wider than any other track, but they also alternate between pavement and concrete. That transition can be difficult for drivers because tires with no treads can be slippery on concrete. As well, the course is bumpy thanks to the seams used to repair the concrete. So getting the right line into any turn at Cleveland takes a good eye to read the track. Harrison recalls watching Tracy qualifying at the Cleveland track and being pleased that he and his mechanics had set the car up to ride over one of the larger bumps where the cars crossed over the different runways. "You could see the car's movements as he's travelling over this bump, but Paul's was very subtle, and Alec and I thought, man, we got our shocks right, I mean we're pretty clever," Harrison said. "When Paul came into the pit, I mentioned this to him, and he says, 'I don't drive over that bump.'" In the middle of the track, at speeds over 150 mph, Tracy was able to shift his car inches away from the bump that every other driver was going over and take the best line through the turn, saving precious seconds as well as mechanical damage to the car.

Despite that natural ability, Tracy still made some rookie mistakes. One gave him what Harrison called his one "unforced error" of the season. During qualifying at the Portland International Raceway, Tracy was trying to pass a slower car on the outside of the last turn while trying to maintain momentum in a hot practice lap. Even the most skilled and experienced drivers rarely try to pass on the outside of a turn. Tracy couldn't make it and crashed heavily into a tire barrier. He escaped unharmed, but his March racing machine didn't. Not only did the move put an end to his practice run, but it also added a lot of work for the mechanics. Harrison, while frustrated by the daredevil passing attempt, gently reminded Tracy that he could just as easily have made the pass on the following straightaway. The driver reluctantly agreed.

Harrison and the team mechanics had to hustle to get the car ready for qualifying. While Tracy didn't outwardly apologize for causing the extra work, he sheepishly hung around the garage trying to lend a hand, but he was generally in the way. "Then he says, 'You guys want a drink? I'll go get you a drink.' We say, 'Sure, go get us a drink,'" said Harrison, glad the driver had something to do. "Then he says, 'You guys got any money?' He was basically just a young kid. He was basically a young, kind of pudgy, potato-chip-eating, video-game-playing kid."

But it was tough to keep this "kid" off the track. For instance, the team installed a new engine ring and pinion before a race at the Nazareth Speedway in Pennsylvania. Once installed, the car is supposed to be driven gently, accelerated and then decelerated in order to break in the new parts. Harrison told Tracy to take the car for a few laps around the track's inner "ring road" and then bring it back into the pit. Because of the pit wall location, Harrison could only see the top of the roll bar above Tracy's helmet and the rear wing going by on the ring road. They went by once. The next time Harrison saw the car, it was on the track, and Tracy was going at full speed. "He only did one lap, and of course everybody else is at speed, and I think he just had to get it out, and he burned the ring and pinion all up," said Harrison. It led to another late night while Fitzpatrick and Harrison repaired the car. Still, he preferred Tracy's driving style to that of a driver with less aggression because, and Roger Penske agreed with him, it was easier to reel a driver in than to tell him he had to go faster. It was also easier to tell whether or not a driver had any natural ability.

Harrison believes that Tracy was shown how a race team could be a professionally run operation during the season with Stewart's team. While Tracy had what all considered to be real talent before he joined the team, he saw firsthand how a car was put together and how a team worked together. Harrison wanted to make sure that the team stayed together, especially when Tony Tracy urged Paul to move on to another team during the season. Harrison was worried that all the work that had gone into keeping Paul a winner would then be lost, but he knew that Paul had to make the decision on his own, and, if he wanted to go, no one would stand in his way. Harrison credits fellow driver Mark Smith for influencing Paul to stay with the team. At the time, Smith was driving for Evergreen Racing, which, although a rival team, had struck a deal with Stewart to get the same set-ups on his car that Paul had. Harrison said that, because Paul was so confident in his ability to win, he didn't mind. Smith and Tracy then became friends, hanging around away from the track, making bets to see who could set the fastest first lap. Smith's counsel was what made Tracy stay with Stewart's team and win the championship that was to grant him entry into the CART kingdom.

And some of the few people who held the keys to that kingdom (and its chariots) got a close look at one of the young knights whom they believed would help them to win CART's racing crown. During a practice session at the Mid-Ohio Sports Car course, some observers from Team Penske stopped by to watch Tracy drive. The young Canadian was fast, he was winning races, and he was getting a lot of attention. But Harrison recalls that they were looking for more than speed. They were also looking for a driver who could conduct himself well off the track, provide good feedback to a crew, and handle times when the car wasn't running well and things weren't going in his favour. They didn't ask about his speed, they could see how fast he was, and Harrison had nothing but good things to tell them about Paul.

One incident sticks in Harrison's mind as capturing the kind of race car driver Tracy is. It took place at Mid-Ohio, and Tracy was in the process of clinching the Indy Lights championship. The race went ahead in heavy rain, and Tracy was doing well, but he had never fully tested the March in rain, and he was getting heavy pressure from rival Robby Buhl (Harrison now works with Buhl in the Indy Racing League). Tracy led early in the race and decided that, if Buhl made a run for the lead, he'd let him by, because he could still win the championship by placing second. This decision showed that he cared more about finishing the race than about getting into a battle with Buhl and potentially damaging the car and knocking himself out of contention. The race wore on, and with Tracy still in the lead Buhl continued the pressure. Harrison came on the radio and reminded Tracy of his decision. "Okay, Paul, if he really makes a run up the inside or dive-bombs you, let him go. Don't let him take you out," he said. A couple more laps went by, and the end of the race was near. Tracy came back on the radio. "Fuck that deal," he said. He'd worked too hard — he wanted not only the championship but that race too. Buhl's team owner later came into the pits and asked Tracy over the radio, "When are you going to give us a piece of the pie?" "It's my pie, and I'm eating it all" came the reply.

It was a great season for Tracy in 1990, one that held the promise of much greater success. He won the Indy Lights championship by winning 9 of 14 races. He set the single-season record for poles (seven), and in the process he set four race records and six qualifying records. His four consecutive wins were a series record. And Tracy was awarded the Bruce McLaren Trophy by the British Racing Drivers Club for being the British Commonwealth's most promising driver. The trophy is named after the famed Can-Am and Formula One driver whose F1 team still bears his name.

Despite Kroll's disappointment and his lack of understanding of Tracy's motives in 1987, first for leaving Mosport without a word after their crash and then for clearing out without even discussing or celebrating their mutual victories, Kroll concedes that Tracy is a different man today. Back then, he was a quiet kid who didn't like being surrounded by crowds and didn't like being the centre of attention. He was at the track to drive fast and win races, not make friends. And he carried the added pressure of being the son of a domineering father who pushed him to succeed.

Kroll and Tracy went their separate ways after that final Can-Am season. When Tracy drove for Stewart's Indy Lights team the following season, Kroll was on his way back from a race and stopped in the Dublin, Ohio, race shop of former Indy driver and team owner Bobby Rahal and his partner at the time, Steve Horne, who operated the Truesports Racing Indy car team. The conversation came around to the subject of Paul Tracy. Kroll promised that Tracy was sure to make his mark on the champ car circuit if not the F1 world circuit. But, he added, Tracy desperately needed a mentor. Without one, he'd continue to have times of struggle between flashes of brilliance. He related the Mosport stories, and an intrigued Horne later gave Tracy a test in his Truesports Racing car, during which Tracy easily beat the time posted by the team's driver, Raul Boesel, a CART and F1 veteran. Horne signed the young driver to a three-month testing contract. The time Paul spent in that car allowed Tony Tracy to rent a car for his son to drive at the Long Beach Grand Prix, a race that caught the eye of Penske. "Steve came to me afterwards and said, 'If you ever find another kid like this out there, please let me know,'" Kroll said.

CHAPTER THREE

Penske

A Test Drive and a Drive to Test, 1991–94

In every professional sport, there's one team that appears to have the magic touch, a team that has all the right training and discipline and whose will to succeed is far greater than that of any other team. It's a team that exudes competition and discipline whenever the players walk onto the field or enter the stadium. It's a team that can proudly speak in terms such as "dynasty" and "tradition." In the National Football League, that team would be the Dallas Cowboys, and in the National Hockey League it's the Detroit Red Wings with its string of Stanley Cups and the Edmonton Oilers during the high-flying Gretzky years. In Formula One, the teams to beat are usually Ferrari, McLaren, and Williams; the mantle usually passes between them from season to season.

In CART, the golden team is Marlboro Team Penske, led by Roger Penske. One of the few current team owners who has had as much success as a driver as a team owner and manager, Penske has always managed to attract the top drivers and personnel to his team. That's not to say he and his team haven't had their struggles. Before the 2000 season, the team was held at 99 champ car wins thanks to a Paul Tracy victory at Gateway in Miami in 1997. In 2000, the late Greg Moore was to drive for the team in the hope of giving it victory 100. But Moore was killed in the final race of the 1999 season and didn't get the chance to watch the green flag fly from behind the wheel of an orange-and-white Penske Honda-Reynard. The team struggled with engines and changes in personnel before Gil de Ferran gave a revamped Penske team its 100th victory in April 2000 at the Nazareth Speedway. De Ferran later added to the Penske legend by winning the 2000 CART championship at California Speedway in Fontana. His eight CART championships, along with his 10 Indy 500 wins, make Penske the winningest team owner in CART.

And he was no slouch as a driver. Penske began his racing career in sports cars in the 1950s and 1960s and was named *Sports Illustrated*'s Driver of the Year in 1961. In 1966, he formed Penske Racing and campaigned the Can-Am and Trans Am circuits with driver Mark Donohue. He also founded and owns the Penske Corporation, a transportation services company that has annual revenues of U.S. $6 billion. Sometimes known as "The Captain" — and sometimes seen in a Rolex ad aboard his yacht — Penske can be described as the quintessential American success story. Polished and professional, he is smooth and cool with the media, discussing on-track events with the calm of a man who has weathered many storms and will weather many more. With his stable of employees in their starched white shirts — complete with the Marlboro and Hugo Boss logos — and black pants, Marlboro Team Penske looks as if it would be just as comfortable flogging software at a high-tech trade show as getting oil and rubber under its collective fingernails preparing to race some of the world's fastest cars.

So why would Roger Penske hire a wild young kid like Paul Tracy?

Near the end of Paul's championship-winning Indy Lights season, Tony Tracy wanted to make sure his son got a chance to show what he could really do with a race car. But all was not well in the Tracy camp. Paul and his family had spent nearly everything they had during his three seasons on the Indy Lights circuit. Paul would have to get noticed by the champ car establishment or face the prospect of leaving the sport altogether. But even after winning the Indy Lights championship in 1990, he had no offer from a champ car team and no offer from a big-money sponsor. In short, his dream of making it in the top ranks of racing seemed to have hit a wall.

In a desperate attempt to get his son noticed, Tony rented a car, at a cost of $40,000, from the Dale Coyne Racing team for the Long Beach Grand Prix on April 14, 1991. Coyne and his team have entered cars on the CART circuit since 1989 but have had limited success. Observers of the sport, though, have lauded Coyne's ability to survive season after season with a lack of steady sponsorship and sometimes less than spectacular drivers. Throughout the life of the team, Coyne has fielded cars for Roberto Moreno, Michel Jourdain Jr., Memo Gidley, and Hiro Matsushita. Before the start of the 2000 season, Coyne's partner, NFL great Walter Payton, died of cancer, and Coyne was back to running the team on his own.

Tracy didn't have a long race in his first champ car run at Long Beach, but he pushed the car as hard as he could, knowing that his chances of winning were slim, doing just what his father had told him. He took the wheel of the car, painted a bilious yellow-green that was unsullied by sponsors' logos, and put on a show with his aggressive driving and his brief hounding of esteemed veteran Mario Andretti before the car's engine gave out. (Tony had taught his son not to be intimidated by famous drivers such as Andretti or to treat them with awe, as any fan would. When Andretti, one of the greatest drivers in the history of the sport, was out on the track, he was just another driver to get around.) "Going into that race in Long Beach," Paul told *Maclean's* in 1993, "I was thinking, 'why are we wasting this money? We have no chance to do anything with this team.'" But that team would open some important doors for him. He finished 24th overall in the race, earning $19,000 in prize money.

The first paycheque Tracy earned in CART wasn't enough to allow him to enter the next race in Phoenix. Still, Coyne, used to struggling, knew it wouldn't take long for other teams to notice Tracy. "We knew Paul was a tremendous talent," Coyne said in the 1992 television documentary *Paul Tracy's Big Test: Racing with the Big Boys*. "I think he's probably the best driver to come out of North America since Al Unser Jr., maybe he's going to be better than him. Time will tell." Tracy still looked like he belonged behind a school desk instead of behind the wheel of a race car. His round face, gold-rimmed glasses, and neatly parted hair displayed his youth. But he'd already learned how to display a game face, speaking in the documentary like a seasoned veteran as he described plans for his future with Coyne's team.

Going into this year, what I really need to do, even though it's not a top-notch team like Truesports or Newman/Haas or Penske, we've got a good opportunity to finish in the top 10, it's a building thing. The team's new — they've only been on the circuit for a year. If the sponsors aren't there, we just have to keep finishing races and try to finish in the top 10 and get as much prize money as we can to go on to the next race.

Tracy compared his situation to that of the Formula One world champion at the time, Ayrton Senna, one of his racing heroes, who was commanding $1 million per race in salary. "I'm not in the position to go to a team and say 'I want to drive your car, and I want to be paid a million dollars.' The position I'm in now is 'Hey, give me a chance. I'll drive for free, just give me a chance.'"

Despite the inauspicious beginning to his CART career, it was doubtful that Tracy would ever have to drive for free. And soon enough he didn't. "I've been asked what did I see in Paul Tracy? Why did I pick Paul Tracy?" Penske told a press conference in Toronto in June 1991. "He was a young fellow that wanted to go racing, [and] we needed someone to do testing. We sat down with him and were able to work out a situation where he would drive for us at Indianapolis and two other races in 1992. So he made a commitment to us, and we made a commitment to him. He's a fine young driver."

Indianapolis is the place every young driver wants to race, and Tracy was certainly no different. Being offered a job by Penske was a dream realized for the young driver, akin to a rookie relief pitcher being called up from the minor leagues to start for the New York Yankees. Brian Stewart said it had the same significance for Canadian sports as Wayne Gretzky's departure for the Los Angeles Kings from the Edmonton Oilers. Few drivers could afford to turn down an offer from Penske, and Tracy wasn't about to. He was facing a return to Scarborough or a trip back to the minor leagues if an offer didn't come his way. Penske was also well aware what he was getting with Tracy. Despite his youth, Paul had gained a reputation as a perceptive test driver. Because he always drove hard, he was able to squeeze all the horsepower out of a car, and he knew how to get it to perform the way he wanted. It was the ability to avoid the bumps in the track at Cleveland during his Indy Lights days that Penske was banking on.

As he would mention in his announcement about hiring Tracy, Penske was impressed with the young driver when he saw him drive the Coyne car at Long Beach. "I was sitting on a curb in the pit area when Roger Penske rode by," Tracy later said to *Maclean's*. "He said we were doing a good job." Whether or not he truly has a magic touch and a saving grace, Penske has a history of managing to pluck a good driver out of obscurity or bring one back from career doldrums when he needed a new start. He helped Emerson Fittipaldi to make a successful return to racing and won the Indy 500 with Fittipaldi driving in 1989. When Greg Moore was killed at Fontana in 1999, Penske immediately offered ebullient Brazilian Helio Castroneves Moore's spot on the team. At the time, Castroneves had no other options since Carl Hogan had pulled the plug on his CART operation. Castroneves also became a winner under Penske's tutelage.

Luring Tracy to Penske's team was a large blow for Coyne, who clearly knew that Paul was destined to win races, even in an underperforming car. A disappointed Coyne heard of the deal from the media while he was in Milwaukee. While Penske offered the deal to Tracy a week after his Long Beach drive in April, Tracy was told to keep it quiet until it could be announced in Toronto in June. At the time, Penske was attempting to do, in his own way, what the Indy Lights series had failed to do: create a succession plan of drivers who would eventually earn spots on the CART circuit. Although Tracy was the Indy Lights champion in 1991, no team came forward to offer him a ride. Nor did teams for many of the previous champions. Penske knew that Tracy could be an asset to his team, and he believed he could shape a driver to fit the Penske mould. He'd be doing himself a favour as well. "We met during the middle of May; he had decided not to run at Indianapolis this year," Penske said at the Toronto press conference.

> We sat down and said, "Paul, here's what we'll do for you. We'll sign a multiple-year contract with you on this basis: in 1991, all we're going to do is guarantee you some testing"; in fact, last week he tested with Emerson Fittipaldi at Mid-Ohio and was very competitive.
>
> We've got to spend some time going forward developing a driver who can drive for us at championship quality. Today testing has become a major part of success and a major part of the program. Emerson and Rick [Mears] don't have the time to do all the testing.
>
> Today I said, "Paul, we hired you, you don't have to prove a thing." Someday he's going to show us what he can do. We're excited about it; we think he's young, he's energetic, [and] we're going to put him on a program of working at the shop — he might drive a pickup truck

one day, and he might be working out at the gym the next day. We think it's going to be a complete commitment for him for the future. Again, an opportunity, but it's going to be a challenge for him. We're glad to have him on our team.

It's doubtful that Tracy ever drove a pickup for Penske, or even that he was asked to, but he did begin a fitness program at Penske's behest, and he began to build muscle and drop some extra weight. People around the race paddocks started to notice a trimmer, more fit young man.

But, as Brian Stewart told the TV documentary, they also noticed that Tracy was a Canadian who had signed on with the most American of American teams. There were some complaints that Penske had passed over several American drivers and instead hired a "foreign driver." Tracy recalls that

Mike Groff and his parents were upset because he didn't get the ride because he had won the Indy Lights championship and was struggling to find a ride. He won the year before I did, and I guess Penske talked to them and talked to me, and he was much older than me. I don't know exactly what his age was, but for whatever reason I got the job. They didn't get the job, and his parents said some things to some journalists, the journalists that cover the races all the time, Gordon Kirby and some people that are always at the races. Like, you know, "That's not right" and blah, blah, blah. I didn't really get any of it personally, but they complained that it wasn't right because at the time it was an American team, it was a Penske team, and they had me and

Emerson. No American drivers. There was Rick and then Emerson and me. They felt it was unfair that a young American didn't get the opportunity.

Penske dismissed the criticism, insisting he'd looked around and hired the best driver for the job. He said Tracy was getting the same treatment Mears got when he signed on with the team. Tony Tracy had helped his son in his dealings with Penske and when it came time to sign the contract. "Basically, there wasn't anything to do, you know, they presented us with a contract and said, 'This is what we are offering you. Take it or leave it,'" Paul said. "So there was really nothing to negotiate. There was no 'We want more money.' It was 'Here's what we're offering you. If you want to drive for us, sign it; if not, there's another guy who wants to drive, so sign it now or go on your way.'" What Tracy was signing for was U.S. $30,000. It was much more than he'd been making, and it was all Penske was willing to pay for an unproven driver.

Tracy's critics were surprised that Paul was hired by Penske given his reputation as an aggressive driver. Penske, while he didn't state it publicly, believed that it was harder to get a driver up to speed than to reel one in. There's not much anyone can do with a race car driver who doesn't have the desire to go as fast as possible.

In addition to testing cars for the team, Paul would drive in at least two races, one being the Indianapolis 500. "When I joined the team, there was no limit on the amount of testing you could do, and both Rick and Emerson were at the height of their careers, and they had a lot of appearances, and they were scheduled to do a lot of things outside of racing. They both had businesses going," Tracy said.

We were testing 90 to 100 days a year, and they just physically couldn't do all of it, and, you know, it was almost impossible. So I think the first couple years I tested 70 days for them, which is a lot.

We'd go from a race to a test for like two or three days and then go straight to the next race, not even get home. At that time, both of those guys were older, and they had a pretty busy schedule with stuff that they had to do personally as well, so they just couldn't do it.

Tracy began working with Mears, the four-time Indy 500 champ, in a year-old race car, the PC19. Penske wanted Tracy to have the experience of high-speed driving on ovals so he would know what to expect when he got to Indianapolis, and there was no better teacher than Mears. They trained at the Michigan Speedway, an unforgiving, high-banked oval track that has led to some of the best high-speed slicing and dicing between champ cars in the past few years. Mears and Penske were impressed with how well Tracy gradually came up to speed. During one day-long testing session, the young driver reached speeds of 220 mph.

Penske had only guaranteed Tracy some testing time, but he decided to speed up his progress by letting him loose in a CART race on the Michigan track. Tracy had sampled the speed that the oval could produce, but that wasn't enough to calm the rookie's nerves on race day. In his first race for Team Penske, Tracy met the wall at Michigan. Coming out of the last turn and heading back onto the straightaway at nearly 200 mph, Tracy lost control of the car and smashed into the wall in a flash of fire and a streak of black rubber. His car, shedding bits of carbon-fibre bodywork, rolled lazily down off the bank and settled in the infield. In a rush of adrenaline, Tracy tried to yank himself out of the twisted machine as safety crews rushed to his aid and tried to keep him from further injuring himself. They gave him oxygen and took him away on a stretcher. Luckily, Paul suffered just a broken left leg, but it would keep him out of competition for six weeks. "If it had been later on just coming out onto the straight, I would've been all right, but it was just at a point where you're just making that final point of the turn before you come onto the straightaway, and it just shot me up into the wall, and that's that," he related in the TV documentary.

> *I just remember hitting the wall real hard with the front end of the car and sliding down the front straight-away and trying to get out of the car, but my leg was trapped. The brake pedal and the clutch pedal were clamped on my leg, my foot went in between, and the pedals clamped together and broke my leg. I was trying to get myself out of there, but I couldn't get my leg out.*
>
> *It was the classic rookie mistake, but it shouldn't have happened, but I got myself into that position, and I can't do anything about it now. These are the things I need to learn before the Indianapolis 500, before I start doing a full season. It was just one of those mistakes where at a track like that you're not going to get away lightly, and this happened, and it could've been a lot worse, and hopefully this injury's not that bad.*

Tracy was back in time to place seventh on the storied oval speedway at Nazareth, Pennsylvania, ahead of both

Mears and Fittipaldi, and notched a 14th-place finish on the road course at Laguna Seca, California, in the final race of the season.

During the break between the 1991 and 1992 seasons, Tracy got a taste of the business side of racing. He joined Mears in appearances at the Toronto auto show and learned how to handle media interviews and fan requests with a smile, decked out as always in the white Penske shirt and black pants and the fire-coloured Marlboro Team Penske jacket. "I'm pretty excited about doing this," he said during a media and autograph session at the show. "It's something I've always looked forward to being able to do. I guess if you're Rick Mears and you've done this for 14 years it could get a little tedious."

In 1992, Penske's plan for Tracy included racing on the oval at Phoenix and in the Indy 500, as well as more testing at Michigan. Indianapolis is home to many racing teams, which keep offices and garages there. With all Team Penske's success there, Indy has become its "home track." Penske had high hopes for his newest team member, whispering in his ear that he'd be the guy to beat in the 500 miler. Knowing his protégé's desire to drive fast and hard, Mears had some cautionary advice: "That place can kind of make you or break you," he said during the TV documentary. "You put your foot in the wrong place at the wrong time [and] it can come back to haunt you. My advice to him is to take your time, work up to it, he's not out there to prove anything to anybody; he's got the job." Tracy fared well at Phoenix, qualifying a respectable sixth and finishing an even more respectable fourth. He was beginning to show that he could be both consistent and blisteringly fast.

At Indy that year, Tracy began to understand the meaning of the word *pressure*. Before the split within CART that led to the formation of the Indy Racing League (IRL) in 1996, Indy was the crown jewel of American motorsports. It consistently drew the biggest crowds and the biggest single-day television audiences. Teams prepared for the race for an entire month, and Team Penske was no exception. Had Tracy been superstitious, he would have seen the good omens around him as he entered the race. At age 23, he was the youngest driver in the field. He was driving the car that Mears drove to victory the year before, the Mobil 1-sponsored PC20. The car bore the number seven, Paul was one of seven rookies in the field, and he qualified in the seventh row. But none of that potential good luck could keep Tracy's gearbox intact for the entire 500 miles. It self-destructed on lap 96 as Tracy sat in seventh place. Mears crashed during the race and broke his wrist, so he was out of contention for much of the rest of the season.

While Tracy sat out the rest of the 1992 Indy 500, it was not without some drama for Canadians. Scott Goodyear, Tracy's driving coach years earlier at Mosport, nearly became the first Canadian to win the race when he streaked across the finish line a nosecone's distance behind Al Unser Jr. in the closest finish in Indy history.

Tracy was called on to replace the injured Mears. Now occupying a more prominent place on the Penske team, Tracy went on to the streets of Detroit for the next race, in which he ran 33 laps wheel to wheel against Michael Andretti until his gearbox again failed. Paul had a much better result on his return to racing at Michigan, where he became half of the first Canadian CART one-two finish, taking second place behind Goodyear for the best result of Tracy's fledgling career. Paul even led the race for 67 laps. As he mentioned in the TV documentary,

> *I think Michigan was one of the best races for me; after having the first year there and having the accident and breaking the leg, it was kind of a sore point, so I was a little bit nervous, but — to get through it and lead a whole bunch of laps and be in a position to win it and still come out with second in my third 500-mile race — I think that was a great accomplishment for me.*

Yet gearbox gremlins continued to haunt Tracy's car, and at the next race in Cleveland it failed before the start. Tracy was forced to start from the pits five laps after the green flag had dropped. He didn't finish the race.

Tracy was finding mechanical problems, most of which seemed to be beyond his control, somewhat difficult to deal with when talking to the media. Some reporters assumed that the gearbox problems were a result of his hard driving, but the team didn't want him to talk openly about any mechanical work they were doing. So Paul learned one of the first things that all athletes have to master: how to speak about problems without really saying anything about them. And he learned to make sure that he mentioned the sponsor: "The Marlboro Team Penske car. . . ."

Of the 11 races that Tracy entered in 1992, he finished five, posting two seconds, a third, a fourth, and a pole at Elkhart Lake. He ended the season in 12th spot in the championship standings with 59 points. Tracy was pleased with his results considering that he'd competed in fewer than half of the races. He'd had his first taste of champ car success, and he was not only gearing up to grab his first win but also eyeing a place for his name on the championship trophy.

Paul spent the time during the off-season attending to personal matters. During the 1992 season, he'd bought a house in Phoenix and asked his girlfriend and high school sweetheart to marry him. On February 13, 1993, they were married and moved into the new house. Tara Cormier, a petite blonde whose innocent appearance matched her husband's perfectly, had done some scoring and timing in the Penske pits during the previous seasons. She described her future husband for the TV documentary in 1992:

> He's a really great guy. He's always there for me, and he cares about who I am, not for what I look like and what I have, and that's the way he's always been. He doesn't take this racing thing, this thing with Penske, he doesn't think of it as he has to be the top and he's going to have everything. He's just a basic guy, and he knows as long as he has me by his side and there to help him out he doesn't need anything else.

In May 1993, Cormier gave birth to their first child, Alysha.

While Tracy was settling into his new home life, Mears surprised fans and drivers alike by announcing his retirement from racing. But Tracy would continue to receive coaching from the veteran, who decided to still work with the team. Paul would now be thrust into the spotlight.

In 1993, Tracy was offered a full-time spot on the team, and his rough edges were still being smoothed by the Penske influence. During the Vancouver Indy that year, Penske said he wasn't fazed by Tracy's youth. What he wanted was a fast driver and a consistent winner who could handle the demands of sponsors off the track, demands such as personal appearances at banquets and barbecues, product launches, and photo ops. "Paul has really fit those criteria," Penske said. "And from now on, he's going to get better through experience." Tracy wasn't entirely comfortable with those off-track duties, but he was assisted by Penske public relations staff and often reminded that his responsibilities included being a public personality. Almost as soon as he signed on full time with the team, the business aspects of racing began to play a bigger role in his life. Paul met some of the marketing people from No Fear, at the time a fledgling sports apparel firm based in Carlsbad, California. (It continues to make sports clothing and has developed a motorsports arm that makes driving gloves, sunglasses, and racing shoes.) Jim Hancock, vice-president of marketing at No Fear, had done promotional and marketing work with a number of athletes, including Mears, and had built a relationship with the Penske team. He'd become familiar with Tracy from his days in Indy Lights. No Fear's Jeff Surwall had introduced Hancock to Tracy. Surwall was a former motocross racer who'd met Tracy in Canada at a motocross event and then reintroduced himself when he went to California to work at No Fear. Hancock says he became something of an advisor to Tracy — although not on a professional or full-time basis — and was entrusted with trying to draw the young man out of his shell, increase his profile as a racer, and get him more comfortable with promotional work. In short, he was to make Paul more media and sponsor friendly. What was diagnosed as inexperience by team PR people when Tracy balked or seemed ill at ease at sponsor events Hancock says was really a display of a bad attitude and insecurity, along with a dose of immaturity. Paul was competing in a dangerous and glamorous sport, a husband and father at the age of 24, making more money than he'd ever seen, being pulled by the often competing interests of a powerful and influential team owner and a strong-willed father. Tracy disputes Hancock's assessment.

So 1993 was the year that Tracy really began to leave his mark on the sport of Indy car racing. He was now in a position that any young driver would envy. He had a spot on one of the most successful teams on the circuit, a young wife, an expensive new house, money in his pocket, and fast sports cars and motorcycles to play with. And, thanks to some coaching, Tracy was beginning to show that he had the skills necessary to compete against some of the biggest names in racing, such as Danny Sullivan, Bobby Rahal, Mario Andretti, and Al Unser Jr. Paul was still as aggressive as he'd always been, but the 1993 Penske car was an improvement over that of the previous year, and it was serving him well. He was able to respond to the pressure that he placed on himself and the expectations that fans, teammates, and supporters had placed on him from the beginning of his career.

Tracy notched his first CART win at Long Beach on April 18, 1993, the only race of the first five that season that he finished and one during which he survived two flat tires. He took part in the full 16 races of the series, and by the end of the season he'd added four more wins and garnered 157 championship points, good enough for third place in the standings. But it was the win in his hometown that he'll remember for the rest of his career.

After crashing at Phoenix and Milwaukee, Tracy enjoyed a dominating win at Cleveland and was feeling confident heading into the Molson Indy in Toronto. But it was a race that came with a lot of baggage. Several Canadians had contested the race before Tracy, but none had won it. Fellow Torontonian Scott Goodyear had a great season in 1992 but was having a much tougher time at the Budweiser-King team in 1993. He had finished sixth in Toronto in 1992, two laps behind winner Michael Andretti. Andretti, incidentally, has made the Molson Indy his personal playground, winning there six times. In the first Molson Indy in 1986, Jacques Villeneuve — uncle to F1 driver Jacques and brother to Gilles — crashed on the first lap while making a run from his seventh-place qualifying spot. Former sports car endurance racer Ludwig Heimrath Jr., also of Toronto, took part in the 1987 Molson Indy but dropped out after 16 laps. John Jones placed seventh as a rookie in 1998, and it proved to be his best finish in Toronto and on any other CART track. So, carrying the weight of Canadian racing history on his shoulders, on July 18, 1993, Tracy wanted to storm home in style and take the checkered flag.

Penske teammate Fittipaldi edged the 24-year-old Tracy for the pole, but the youngster pulled away from the wily veteran in the closing laps to take the win. "It's still the biggest win of my career," Tracy told the Toronto *Sun* in 1997. "In the last lap I could hear the cheering over the top of the car and the last couple of corners it just grew. A great feeling. But Toronto's great — even finishing second this year they were cheering louder for me than for the winner. So it's a great feeling when you do well at home." During the race, which was largely uneventful until the end, the capacity crowd cheered wildly when Tracy passed Fittipaldi for the lead 15 laps into the 103-lap race. When the Brazilian got out of the pits first following the first round of pit stops, Tracy was in second place until he took the lead and held it for the final 31 laps following a fast second pit stop. What further endeared him to the hometown crowd, as if it needed more motivation, was his waving of the Canadian flag from the victory podium. "There was a flag on each side of the stage," he said.

> *I heard some high school friends calling me from that side of the stage, they were congratulating me through the fence, and I kind of had my hand on the flagpole as I was leaning over toward them. I looked up and saw the flag and pulled it out of the stage. What can I say? It was the greatest moment in my life.*
>
> *Most certainly it changed my life. It instantly made me a household name in Canada, made me more recognizable. Everywhere I go now in Canada, people know who I am.*

Tracy's next win came at his favourite track, Road America in Elkhart Lake, Wisconsin. Heading into the next race on Canadian soil, the Vancouver Molson Indy, Tracy was in third place in the championship standings, within striking distance of leader Nigel Mansell. Mansell, with his trimmed moustache and straight brown hair, looked every inch the British schoolmaster away from the track. While in appearance he was the opposite of Tracy, in reality he was smooth, very fast, aggressive, one tough competitor. Like Fittipaldi, Mansell, 40, was a Formula One world champion, but he had turned his back on the politics of F1 to try North

American-style open-wheeled racing, and he'd become the first driver to win the Formula One world championship and the CART title consecutively.

Goodyear, whose dismal 1993 season was continuing, had some high praise for Tracy and his championship chances. "He seems to have the fastest package right now," Goodyear said of his former student to the *Vancouver Sun*. "Being around Rick Mears, Emerson Fittipaldi and Roger Penske has accelerated his learning curve by five years. He's doing a veteran's job. He's thinking like a winner and a leader." He added, "I think motor racing would be very quiet right now if Paul wasn't doing what he's doing. I take great pride in the fact that when Paul wins a race now, it's front page news across Canada."

With four races to go in the 1993 season, Tracy trailed Mansell by 38 points, with a total of 88 points still up for grabs. Although Tracy had already won three times, and had led the most laps (617 compared with Mansell's 169), he had trouble finishing consistently, mainly because of mechanical problems and tangles with other drivers. He knew he had to work on finishing races if he was going to beat Mansell, let alone teammate Fittipaldi, who had second spot in the standings in his grasp. The British driver had had some bad luck in Toronto, crashing twice in practice and dropping out of the race altogether. Yet up to the race in Vancouver, Mansell had two wins and two third-place finishes and had missed just one race because of an injury.

Recalling the lesson his father taught him, Tracy told the *Vancouver Sun*, "It's nice to be racing wheel to wheel with the current world champion and being able to beat him, but once you're out there racing, he's not Nigel Mansell the world champion; he's another driver and guy we have to beat." Heading into qualifying for the Vancouver Indy, Tracy had his second Canadian win on his mind, and in early qualifying he seemed to be headed toward that goal as he took the provisional pole with his 109.046 mph run around Pacific Place. Goodyear qualified a respectable fourth, Swede Stefan Johansson — another F1 refugee — slid into second spot, and Fittipaldi clocked in at 108.046 mph to sit in third spot. Bad luck in Canada continued for Mansell when he clipped the wall and didn't finish his qualifying run. He was also angry because he had to hit the brakes during one of his qualifying laps to avoid Tracy, who was trying to coast back to the pits after running out of fuel. Mansell ended up qualifying ninth. By the time the green flag dropped, Goodyear had bumped Tracy out of the pole position and was off to a good start, leading for 13 laps before being slowed by transmission problems. He settled for fourth spot, while Tracy managed to lead just one lap before he was sidelined with electrical problems. While Tracy's hopes for his repeat Canadian win were dashed, his championship hopes remained alive though diminished. Paul was still in third place, behind Mansell and Fittipaldi respectively, but now he was 46 points behind. It was fitting that veteran and crowd favourite Al Unser Jr. notched his first win in nearly a year and a half in Vancouver. Unser finished ahead of Bobby Rahal by just over 11 seconds.

The following race at the Mid-Ohio road course, near Lexington, was a raucous event that saw both car parts and accusations flying — between Mansell and Tracy, Unser and Fittipaldi, and Tracy and Pruett. Fittipaldi crossed the finish line first, but Unser questioned what he called the Brazilian's "win-at-all-costs attitude." Tracy started from second place on the grid and took the outside of the track on the first turn. Because of the lack of grip and the usual assortment of rubber bits and loose gravel on the outside edge, heading immediately to the outside is usually left to daredevils such as Tracy. He tried to get around Mansell, who claimed in the *Vancouver Sun* that Tracy "chopped me right across the front of my car. It's very unprofessional, isn't it? I just hope he didn't do it on purpose." Tracy said he got ahead of Mansell, whose left front tire touched his right rear tire. Mansell headed to the pits to have his nose wings replaced and ended up at the back of the field. He finished the race in 12th spot. Tracy led for about 15 seconds until he slid into a tire barrier to avoid a collision with Scott Pruett. Pruett, who would later move into the NASCAR stock car series, seemed to need a car with fenders that day. As Tracy said to the *Vancouver Sun* after the race, Pruett went over a hill with his car sideways and then braked much too early for a turn, leaving Tracy with little room to get past and sending him to the sidelines to catch his breath. His championship hopes would soon be over. Later in the race, Unser attempted a daring pass on Fittipaldi, but the Brazilian refused to give way. The two cars bumped wheels, Unser headed for the grass, and on his trip back onto the track he collided with Scott Goodyear's rear tire and lost his front wing. Goodyear, for his part, was enjoying one of the best drives of his difficult 1993 season. He finished the race in third spot, behind Californian Robby Gordon, after a lengthy duel with Raul Boesel.

After such a wild run at Mid-Ohio, the 1993 championship came down to a duel between the two Formula One veterans: Mansell and Fittipaldi. Mansell was in the lead with 170 points, but Fittipaldi was gaining on him and had 156. Tracy had 122 points but no chance of winning the championship with two races remaining.

Coming into the final race, at Laguna Seca, Tracy took a page from his Indy Lights days. He broke the track record on the first day of qualifying for the season finale on the winding course situated in front of mountains and cypress trees near Monterey, California. Tracy was still up against Rahal and Boesel for third spot in the championship, and he fought for it like it was first spot. Tracy grabbed the provisional pole with a lap of 1:11.140 at a speed of 112.039 mph in his Penske Mercedes. He beat the previous track record of Michael Andretti, who'd lapped the course at 111.967 mph. Fittipaldi would edge Tracy off the pole during Saturday's qualifying, but Tracy would still start from the front row, albeit in second place.

The race turned out to be one of the strangest Tracy ever drove — he now knows what it's like to be weightless. With about 25 laps to go, he had caught up to some traffic and somehow managed to hit his seatbelt release. Laguna Seca is a challenging course with several elevation changes and very fast turns, and Tracy had to drive the rest of the race while trying to keep himself from being bounced around inside the cockpit. And there weren't any caution periods during the race, so there was no chance for him to duck into the pits and get rebuckled. "It was horrible," he told the *Vancouver Sun*. "I never realized how hard it is to drive like that because I never had my belts off. With all the elevation changes and fast turns here, it really throws you around inside the car, and I was doing everything I could just to keep my body inside the car." Yet Tracy showed no restraint throughout the race, charging ahead of Fittipaldi at the start and leading all but

3 of the 84 laps. New champion Mansell collided with two different rookies during the race, spraining his wrist in one incident, and didn't finish. Fittipaldi took an excursion backward through a sand trap while trying to pass perennial back marker Hiro Matsushita. The Brazilian finished a distant second to Tracy.

Tracy ended his first full season on the Indy car circuit in almost as wild a fashion as he entered it two years earlier. It ended with not just car parts flying but also seatbelts flapping. His third-place finish in the championship standings and his five wins showed that he could more than hold his own against veterans and other rookies alike. He was now regarded as a fixture on the circuit, and his name was spoken in the same breath as Fittipaldi, Unser, Mears, and Andretti. Tracy's aggressive nature seemed to mesh perfectly with Penske's disciplined, almost militaristic, operation despite their different backgrounds and Tracy's lack of experience. Paul had done just what Penske had hoped he would do. He added some spark to a team that had seemingly lost a star when Mears retired. And Fittipaldi, although still competitive and highly skilled, was nearly twice Tracy's age and was in the twilight of his career. As well, Penske hadn't had to reel Paul in as some critics had anticipated. Despite the mechanical breakdowns, Penske was generally able to give Tracy a competitive car that he could drive at the limit. His learning curve was still on the upswing, but the wins had come much quicker than almost anybody, including Tracy, had expected.

Paul was now a father himself, but his relationship with his own father had become strained. Shortly after Hancock and Surwall from No Fear met Tracy, they introduced him to Dave Stevenson, who'd managed motocross racers. They believed that Tracy needed a higher profile, and they wanted to work with him in promoting their products, so they encouraged him to sign Stevenson as his manager. They saw that Tracy much preferred to drive than do anything else, including making personal appearances and attending sponsor functions. At the time, Tony Tracy was still working for his son, but many began to see how much of a distraction for Paul his influence was. Paul told *Racer* magazine in December 1999 that his father was

> *always trying to be a mover and a shaker. He listened to all the rumours; and when I first started with Penske, I was getting fired every week for something — whether I crashed or wore the wrong shirt to an appearance — and my dad got caught up in that stuff. He was looking out for me, in his own way, but you get to an age where you're an adult and you don't want your father to be doing all your business for you — but there was a period when he didn't want to let go.*

Without his father's help, Paul wouldn't have been able to make the leap to Indy cars, but increasingly it was beginning to look like it was time for father and son to part professional ways. The senior Tracy believed he still knew what was best for his son, but Paul wanted to surround himself with people who were experienced in the racing business. He said later that his father really didn't trust anyone, whereas he himself was almost the opposite.

While his personal drama began to play itself out, Paul may not have noticed the Hollywood-style drama at the start of the new season. Hollywood has been no stranger to the racing world, and the sport has inspired many movies but few great films. John Frankenheimer's 1966 epic *Grand Prix* stands out as a notable exception, as does *Winning*, starring real-life racer Paul Newman, released in 1969. Then there's *Le Mans, Days of Thunder,* and *Driven,* the recent Sylvester Stallone racing flick set in the world of CART. If a Hollywood producer had followed the 1994 Indy car season, she would have seen all the elements of a classic ensemble drama set out neatly before her. Roger Penske, the shrewd businessman and relentless competitor with a military school education, had put together an unusual three-car team for one purpose: a successful assault on the PPG Indy Car World Series. The team consisted of Al Unser Jr., the baby-faced scion of a famous American racing family; Emerson Fittipaldi, an ageing but suave Brazilian and a Formula One veteran with a taste for the good life and the smile of a shark; and Paul Tracy, a beefy Canadian kid who loved nothing better than to drive fast and breathe down the fireproof collars of some of the racing heroes he used to look up to. A quick pan down pit lane would have revealed the rest of the players. There was young Jacques Villeneuve, bespectacled, ponytailed, the obvious product of a cushy private school education on the continent. But the cold eyes of a fierce competitor gleamed behind those gold rims. Those eyes were focused first on the Indy car championship and then on the Formula One world championship, a feat that his late father never achieved. Then there was Michael Andretti. In the United States, you can't speak about racing without mentioning his family name. His skills and competitiveness took him to the McLaren Formula One team in 1993, following in his father's footsteps. But times had changed, while his attitude hadn't.

So he spent the year being kicked around by his car, his team, and the media. But he was back where he got his start, and he could taste the championship champagne already. A guy named Chip Ganassi ran Andretti's new team. Ganassi had had little success as a driver, but thanks to some wheeling and dealing he was building a team that he hoped would topple Penske's team. Add to the cast the prickly Brit Nigel Mansell and the rowdy Californian and former off-roader Robby Gordon and a blockbuster was on its way to theatres everywhere.

By the start of the 1994 season, Al Unser Jr. had signed on with Marlboro Team Penske to provide a three-pronged attack on the Indy car championship, something that had eluded the team since Danny Sullivan claimed the title in 1988. Unser had ended his long relationship with Rick Galles, who'd brought him into Indy car racing in 1983, inviting him to join the team for which his father, Al, and his uncle, Bobby, had also driven. With Fittipaldi, Tracy, and Unser now making up Team Penske, nobody doubted that it was poised for success. The results from 1993 were clear. Tracy and Newman-Haas's Mansell had five wins each that season. Fittipaldi had three wins, including the Indianapolis 500. Unser won once in 1993 with Galles. His career total now sat at 19 wins, which included the Indy car PPG Cup in 1990 and the Indianapolis 500 in 1991. The Team Penske drivers were to compete in new 1994 team-built cars, each powered by a new Mercedes Ilmor V8 engine, with full sponsorship from Marlboro. At 31, Unser was still at the peak of his skills. At 47, Fittipaldi still had the spark that had carried him through his F1 years. And, at 25, Tracy was just hitting his stride.

The season brought another Canadian into the fray —

albeit one who made his home in Monte Carlo. Jacques Villeneuve, son of the legendary F1 Ferrari driver and newly minted graduate of the Formula Atlantic series, was driving for the new Forsythe-Green team with sponsorship from Imperial Tobacco's Player's brand. Villeneuve was under the management of Barry Green and under the tutelage of race engineer Tony Cicale. His reputation and family name preceded Villeneuve, and, while he had a great deal of experience driving on road and street courses around the globe, he hadn't spent as much time on ovals and speedways as the rest of the crop of Indy drivers. His skills, however, would make him the equal of most of them.

Mackenzie Financial ended its sponsorship of Scott Goodyear, and he wound up driving with beer money from Budweiser on the Budweiser-King team led by former drag racer Kenny Bernstein.

Tracy didn't have a great start to 1994. The season began in March at Surfers' Paradise, a street circuit situated on Australia's Gold Coast. Michael Andretti made it known he was back with a vengeance as he took the checkered flag. Tracy finished 16th after experiencing electrical problems with his new car. It looked like it might be a long season.

The next stop, at the one-mile oval in Phoenix, saw Villeneuve take the pole with a time of 20.442 seconds until Tracy edged him off it with a time of 20.424 seconds. The race was marked by a spectacular multicar collision caused by Hiro Matsushita's Simon-Lola touching wheels with Teo Fabi's Hall-Reynard as the Italian tried to lap the Japanese. Gordon Kirby described the "wild-multi-car accident" in *Autosport* magazine:

The leaders were running directly behind this pair. And as Fabi and Matsushita's car spun into the retaining wall, Tracy found himself with nowhere to go. He was taken into the wall by Matsushita's car, which was then hit amidships by Villeneuve. The young Canadian rookie's Reynard t-boned Matsushita's car and was then in turn hit by [Dominic] Dobson. It was remarkable that Villeneuve escaped uninjured from his wrecked Reynard which ended up partway down the pit lane.

According to Timothy Collings in his book *The New Villeneuve*, observers of the accident said Villeneuve appeared not to heed the yellow caution flags that were flying as a result of the Matsushita-Fabi collision and appeared to ignore Mario Andretti, who was decelerating ahead of him. Villeneuve claimed that he hadn't seen the yellows. Tracy was also unhurt but was out of the race.

Following the melee at Phoenix, Tracy experienced an even scarier moment during qualifying for the Indy 500 in May. On May 13, during the last full day of practice, Tracy appeared to lose control as he exited turn four of the 2.5-mile oval. The car slid off the banking, across the pit road entrance, and onto the infield grass. It then went back across the track and slapped the outside wall, first with the rear and then with the front, before it spun back down to the inside, coming to rest against the infield wall. Tracy had to be extricated from his car by safety crews. Although they were on the scene quickly, it took them several minutes to get Tracy out of the damaged car. Suffering from a concussion, a bruised foot, and a sore neck, he spent the night in hospital in Indianapolis under observation. During the practice session at Indy, there was much speculation that Penske's new Mercedes engines were going to lock up the front three positions on the starting grid, but the new power plant seemed to overpower Tracy. After the incident, there was some concern over whether he'd be able to compete against Fittipaldi and Unser in qualifying. Tracy would have to be cleared by a neurosurgeon and then pass a physical by the speedway's medical director before being released and cleared to drive the following day. The powerful three-car team was the favourite going into preparations for the race.

The new Mercedes engine that Penske had unveiled was raising some eyebrows among followers of the sport. He had taken advantage of a loophole in the United States Auto Club rules that let him run a different engine in the Indy 500 from the engines he was using for the rest of the series. The stock-type push-rod engine had hurtled Fittipaldi's car to the 244–45 mph range along Indy's straightaways, the first time such speeds had been reached at the storied track. His practice lap speeds, reaching nearly 231 mph, had blown away the field. The move was a gamble for Penske, who was attempting to lock up the 500 with at least one, if not all three cars, leading the run to the checkered flag.

Penske would get his wish. At the end of the famous 500 miles, all three Penske cars, their controversial engines screaming, roared across the finish line with Unser in the lead, followed by Fittipaldi and Tracy. It was Paul's first finish at the 500.

On Detroit's Belle Isle in the Detroit River, Tracy qualified just behind Fittipaldi with a speed of 105.845 mph on the winding course. Mansell was on the grid behind Tracy. Unser had dominated the season so far by winning the four previous races, and Tracy had been overshadowed by his team's success. But following his qualifying run, he looked forward to the upcoming race as well as the ones at Cleveland, Toronto, and Road America — on two street courses and a road course respectively. He'd come up with a third at the Milwaukee Mile the week before. The previous year, he placed third at Portland and then went on to win the Cleveland, Toronto, and Elkhart Lake races. "I'll admit, for the most part, this season has been frustrating," he said in the Toronto *Sun*. "I have the same car as Al and Emerson, but not the same results. But you have to remember Al and Emerson are two of the best. Between them they have each won the Indy car series, four Indy 500 wins and 43 career wins. With this stretch coming up I hope to get myself back into contention." At the time, Tracy was 12th in the standings with just 16 points. In comparison, Unser was leading with 63 points. Detroit's Belle Isle had proven to be a good track for Tracy. In 1992, he led the race there for 19 laps, the first time in his career he'd led a race. In 1993, he led for 27 laps.

On race day in 1994, it looked like Unser might provide another lesson in domination, easily getting past Mansell on the second lap of the race. Then Tracy passed Mansell a few laps later. The Brit was the only true competition for the Penske squad at that race, but the passes by Unser and Tracy foreshadowed his luck. Mansell kept fighting until 12 laps from the end, when his race ended. Unser led for 49 laps and then made a pit stop ahead of the rest of the pack, which stopped a lap later when a yellow flag came out after Adrian Fernandez crashed. Unser held the lead after the caution, followed by Tracy, Fittipaldi, and Mansell. Fittipaldi had moved into third spot when Mansell was forced to slow down by Villeneuve as he exited the pit lane. Tracy moved into the lead on lap 55, but his passing Unser wasn't one of his most graceful manoeuvres. As he tried to get inside Little Al on a turn, their wheels touched, and Unser was punted across the track and into a tire barrier. By the time he got his car untangled, he was out of contention for the win and finished the race in 10th spot. Al took the incident in stride and, with a typical shrug after the race, said, "As far as the race is concerned, sometimes you eat the bear, and sometimes the bear eats you. Today the bear ate us." Tracy was left in the lead with a clear path to the checkered flag. Once he got there, he admitted the collision with Unser was his mistake. Fittipaldi finished second, and Robby Gordon rolled across the line in third. "It was a tough way to win," Tracy said after the race. "We had to make a move there. I made a mistake, and I'm going to have to apologize to Al. All I can do is offer my hand in apology. It was my mistake." Yet winning the race took the edge off any guilt he may have felt. (While he would never be as quick with a quip as Little Al, he was learning the Penske way of appearing humble and graceful before the TV cameras and tape recorders.) The win at Detroit was Tracy's sixth career win but his first since the 1993 finale at Laguna Seca the previous October. The win also marked the fifth straight victory for Team Penske and the first such streak in its 25 years of existence.

After Detroit, Tracy took a bit of time away from the track, at least the Indy car track, to return to his first love, karting. On the weekend following the Detroit race, he headed to Barrie, Ontario, where the downtown core of the city about an hour north of Toronto had been turned into a kart track for the weekend. Tracy was asked to drive around the circuit in a Mustang pace car, but he wanted to be closer to the street and instead took a spin around the .8 km course in a kart, in the process setting the fastest lap time of the weekend at 35.95 seconds. Organizers estimated that a total of 35,000 spectators attended the event, which got an unexpected boost from one of Canada's up-and-coming Indy car stars. While friends and associates point out that Tracy is often shy and uncomfortable in front of people he doesn't know, he still has a flair for the dramatic and enjoys making a public splash. Riding around in a pace car, while considered an honour by many, just isn't as much fun as driving a kart. Plus, nobody really sees who's waving out the window as the pace car speeds around the track. But the crowd will certainly notice the driver of a kart screeching through the streets.

Paul's panache has extended to Toronto's Molson Indy. Every year, on the Friday before the race, a private party for sponsors and teams takes place at a swanky downtown restaurant, usually Wayne Gretzky's. While members of the public can't get in — unless they work for a sponsor or know someone who knows someone — many fans gather outside and watch their favourite drivers make an entrance. And Tracy loves to make an entrance. Most years he's shown up astride a wildly painted Harley-Davidson wearing wraparound sunglasses and sporting spiky hair. He usually doesn't wear a helmet since he drives only about a block to the restaurant on a street that's closed to traffic. His fans love it, and it's guaranteed to get him into the next morning's papers. In 2000, Tracy, true to form, appeared in a photo in the Toronto *Sun* on a hog, its gas tank and fenders painted green, black, and purple, flanked by two red-coated members of the Royal Canadian Mounted Police.

When Tracy headed back south and rejoined the circuit in late June, the usual suspects had stamped their places on the starting grid once again. With a speed of 114.768 mph in his Newman-Haas Cosworth Lola, Nigel Mansell grabbed the provisional pole on Portland's road course, coming up just shy of Emerson Fittipaldi's track record of 115.730 mph set in 1992. Tracy was second by the end of Friday's session with a speed of 114.745, followed by Unser and Fittipaldi. Mansell, however, found his efforts scuppered once again by the Penske squad as Unser took the pole position away from him the following day, breaking Fittipaldi's speed record in the process with a run of 116.861 mph. Mansell was unable to break the Penske spell during this stretch of the 1994 season and now found himself surrounded on the starting grid by red-and-white cars. He started in second place for the 102-lap race, behind Unser, followed by Fittipaldi and Tracy. Jacques Villeneuve sat in fifth spot.

A fan favourite, Portland's road course is known for its Festival Curves at the end of the front straightaway, and it has been the scene of some of the series' best racing. In 1986, for example, Michael Andretti ran out of fuel as he headed toward the finish line and lost to his father, Mario (on Father's Day), by 0.07 seconds. British driver Mark Blundell's first career Indy car victory came at Portland when Blundell beat Gil de Ferran to the finish line by 0.0027 seconds, the closest finish in Indy car history, in 1997.

But this time there was no such drama. In fact, the race was reported with a ho-hum tone suggesting that even the media were getting bored with the success of Roger Penske's team. While some of the drivers described it as a tough race, it was really tough only for Mansell, who was involved in a battle for fourth place with the always scrappy Gordon. The Californian managed to pull ahead by a nose in a last-lap duel, dropping the Englishman to fifth place. Unser was first across the line, leading an all-Penske top three, with Fittipaldi in second and Tracy a distant third. Unser earned a $160,000 bonus for winning from the pole and told the *Associated Press* after the race that "my teammates kept me honest all the way through," yet he wasn't really challenged for the lead, controlling top spot for 96 laps, including the last 30.

Returning to Toronto to race has always held special appeal for Paul Tracy. Although he hasn't lived in the city in which he was born since beginning his Indy car career, he's still considered the hometown racing hero, as Jacques Villeneuve is when he drives in the Canadian Grand Prix or Greg Moore was when he competed in the Vancouver Molson Indy. When the Indy car circus rolled into Toronto in 1994, Tracy's team was at its peak. Unser had won five times, including the Indy 500. Penske cars had led all but two laps since the Indy 500 in May — 467 of 469. Mansell had led the other two laps, and Michael Andretti had the other win. In the eight races before the Molson Indy, the team had led 922 of 1,016 laps and 352 of the past 354. The team was doing just what Penske had intended: his drivers were dominating the field with almost military precision. But was it all about to come to an end?

Both Gordon and Mansell were ahead of the Penske cars following the first day of qualifying, and Tracy admitted that the other teams were beginning to make gains on the red-and-white cars, telling the *Vancouver Sun* "I think from here on it's going to be a battle." Gordon set a course record on the way to grabbing the provisional pole. He made his way around the temporary road circuit through the Canadian National Exhibition grounds with a time of 58.154 seconds at a speed of 110.191 mph. Fittipaldi had set the previous record of 58.560 seconds. Setting course records had nearly become a second job for the Brazilian. Gordon had never set a provisional pole before in Indy cars. As well as being an off-road racer, he drove a NASCAR stock car the month before for Carl Haas and his partner, Michael Kranefuss. Haas, half of the Newman-Haas partnership, was hoping to expand his racing business into stock cars. Following Gordon on the provisional grid was Mansell. "It's so nice to see Robby up here," Mansell said at a press conference after qualifying; then he turned to Unser: "Nothing personal." Unser, Fittipaldi, and Tracy qualified fourth, fifth, and sixth respectively. Unser still led the drivers' championship standings with 127 points. Tracy was 63 points behind in fifth place.

Tracy's prediction about the other teams was beginning to come true as race day dawned in Toronto. While Unser leapt into the lead as the green flag fell, his engine expired on the second lap, and so did his chances of gaining any additional points. Fittipaldi stayed in the hunt all afternoon but couldn't get past Bobby Rahal or race leader Michael Andretti. Meanwhile, Tracy was having some bad luck of his own. His front and rear wings were damaged during the first lap, and he was forced to head to the pits for extensive repairs. His race was far from over, though, and his performance could have inspired some of the circuit's veterans. He fought his way back from dead last and ended up in fifth place, dragging fellow Canadians Goodyear and Villeneuve into the top 10 behind him. It was Andretti who took the checkered flag, and Rahal finished second. It was Andretti's second win of the season, but it was the first race to truly upset the Penske juggernaut. Mansell failed to finish the Toronto race again. Rahal, the three-time series champion who'd had middling results since his last championship two years earlier after trying out various chassis and engines, seemed to be experiencing a renaissance. His Honda V8 engine seemed to be improving, but he knew it wasn't good enough yet to beat the Penske cars at their own game. "We were really fortunate when Al and Paul went out early," he told the *Vancouver Sun*. "That made it easier for us later in the race. I don't think we've met the Penske challenge yet, but we certainly have a good engine and chassis and that is helping to narrow the gap. Today's finish can only be a springboard for the rest of the season."

There were now seven races left. At Mid-Ohio, the Penske domination returned as Unser again led his team across the finish line. Tracy had to scramble back into contention after getting a stop-and-go penalty when he passed Robby Gordon under a yellow flag. Tracy, whose second win of the season had so far eluded him, had qualified behind Unser, and he led for most of the race and seemed to be well on his way to that victory after passing Little Al on the second lap and only giving up the lead when he pitted on lap 29. Fittipaldi took the lead at that point, but he pitted on the next lap and gave the lead back to Tracy. On lap 53, the race began to unravel for the leader. Teo Fabi's car had stalled in turn two. A tow truck trying to move it away was partially blocking the track. Tracy was forced to lock his car's brakes as he tried to avoid it. Gordon, who slid sideways, allowed Tracy to move past him on the inside. Gordon regained control of his car and pulled back onto the track in front of Unser. Tracy was assessed the penalty, which he immediately protested, saying there was nowhere else for him to go when Gordon slid wide around the turn. "I wasn't planning on passing him, but he locked up his brakes and almost slid off the track," Tracy said. "What am I supposed to do? He slipped wide." He tried to speak to CART officials, but they weren't interested in his defence. Tracy stayed on the track until lap 57, when he made a regular pit stop, and Unser assumed the lead. Little Al pitted a lap later, and Tracy took his penalty at the same time, putting Unser back in the lead, which he built up to seven seconds. Tracy, ever the underdog, began to fight his way back, but Unser eluded his grasp, and in the end Paul lost the race by 1.6 seconds. Unser held on to the championship lead with 153 points, and Tracy remained in third spot with 90 points.

The results were nearly the same a week later when the circuit arrived in Loudon, New Hampshire, for the Slick 50 200 on the one-mile oval. This time Fittipaldi led, only to lose that lead to Unser with five laps left when he ran low on fuel. Fittipaldi had built up a lead of over 20 seconds and was gambling on a yellow caution flag that would allow him to pit and refuel. His gamble didn't pay off, and he was forced to coast into the pits with an empty tank. By the time he reentered the race, Unser had sped by and won it by 89/100ths of a second ahead of Tracy. Fittipaldi still made it an all-Penske winners' circle by finishing third. It was the fourth time that season that the team finished 1–2–3.

With four races to go in the 1994 season, critics began complaining, and rumours began flying. Teams that had been soundly defeated by one or all of the Penske drivers started complaining that Penske had an unfair advantage over the rest of the field. Break up the team, they said. Don't allow Penske to have three drivers. He's got too much money, and the series is becoming nothing but a Formula One-style procession. Gordon, rarely at a loss for words, was probably tired of seeing a Marlboro car zoom past him and said that Penske was finding ways to bend the rules. The United States Auto Club, the sanctioning body for the Indy 500, sensed the bitterness and began talking about changing the rules. In August, it pulled what Penske called a "politically motivated" move and changed the rules for 1995. In an interview with the *Vancouver Sun*'s Mike Beamish, Penske bristled at accusations that he'd done something wrong. "Unfair advantage?" he said.

> *What they're really trying to say is we spend more on racing than other people. That's sour grapes. I can assure you there's many teams now and in the previous years that have had equal budgets or larger. At the end of the day there's no door that I knock on to get funds that isn't available to anyone else. The state government isn't providing my funding. It's out there to earn. Quite honestly, we're not running an illegal car. We never have. We're not going to.*

What was really happening was a fulfilment of Penske's goals. The team owner had set out to dominate the races of the 1994 season and win the championship. Those goals meant he needed faster cars and better drivers than any other team had. Tracy recalled the testing he did on the Mercedes Ilmor engine before it was to run at the Indy 500. The rules dictated that cars running in the 1994 race had to have a Buick stock block, cast iron engine that would produce 45 inches of turbo boost. He said Penske secretly built his stock block Mercedes engine, which met some of the Indy criteria but produced 55 inches of turbo boost. Tracy then secretly tested the engine at Nazareth and Michigan. When Penske brought it to the Brickyard and it began to blow away other cars, officials ordered its boost cut back to 50 inches.

At the same time, word began to circulate that Michael Andretti would make the move from Chip Ganassi Racing to the Newman-Haas team and that Paul Tracy would join him. While Tracy had one more year left on his five-year contract with Penske, the team owner was expected to release him, possibly with the right of first refusal to bring him back in 1996. It would be a big move for Tracy considering that all of his victories had come as a member of the Penske team, still considered the team to beat. According to people close to Penske, at the time the captain thought that Tracy had done what was expected of him. He'd driven hard and won some races. But, most importantly, he'd given the team valuable testing information that it probably wouldn't have got from Fittipaldi and Unser because, as veterans, they weren't as willing to do the grunt work. Plus, when Penske's business and military school background is factored in, it's easy to see that Tracy's job was to run interference for his fellow drivers and perhaps to push them harder. Unser and Fittipaldi were still capable race car drivers, but they may not have been as hungry for wins as the 25-year-old from Scarborough. Tracy was able to light fires under his two teammates.

When the teams moved on to the Road America track at Elkhart Lake in Wisconsin in mid-September, the season was nearing an end while the seat shuffling among drivers and teams, known as "Silly Season," was reaching its peak. Speculation surrounded Michael Andretti's future, and questions remained about Tracy's future, as they did for fellow Canadian Scott Goodyear. The season was to be Mario Andretti's last, and Nigel Mansell would say goodbye to the U.S. racing scene after the final race at Laguna Seca. Still another Canadian, Jacques Villeneuve, was securing his future. In his Team Green Ford-Reynard, Villeneuve cruised to his first victory after being chased by both Tracy and Unser. His win was the result of some great driving. Villeneuve had tested at Road America in August, and he'd learned the twists and turns of the four-mile, 14-turn course under the direction of his race engineer, Tony Cicale. On race day, they decided to go with less downforce to maximize speed on the straightaways and under braking. The tactic worked. Tracy had won the pole and seemed to be headed for his second victory of the season when Arie Luyendyk slid off the track on lap 32, struck a barrier, and wound up sideways across the track. It was the second full-course caution of the 50-lap race, and when it restarted on lap 36 Unser made a move to get past Tracy on the outside. Paul, distracted, didn't see Villeneuve make a daring move to the inside, and the young French Canadian passed them both. Tracy gave chase, but his engine gave out on lap 44, so Unser took up the fight but couldn't get around Villeneuve. Jacques maintained a half-second lead over the remaining Penske cars and won by about five car lengths, his car running out of fuel as he crossed the finish line. Road America had been good to the Villeneuve family. His uncle, Jacques Villeneuve, scored his only Indy car victory on the track in 1985. What was disappointment for Tracy was jubilation for Unser, who clinched the Indy car championship with two races to go. Unser didn't add to his three consecutive victories, but he did add the 1994 championship trophy to the one he picked up in 1990.

Tracy added to his victories and to Penske's record when he won the next race on the Penske-owned oval near Michael Andretti's backyard in Nazareth, Pennsylvania. Tracy knew the Nazareth track well, having driven thousands of laps there when he was testing for Penske in 1991. It was yet another case of Penske domination as Unser and then Fittipaldi followed Tracy across the finish line. Tracy beat Unser to the checkered flag by 8.459 seconds. Fittipaldi was another six seconds away but still found himself in second place in the championship standings going into the final race of the season. Villeneuve was seventh this time, and Goodyear was eighth. It was the seventh win of Tracy's career, and it moved Paul past Andretti into third place in the championship standings. At the press conference following the race, Unser was obviously happy that the only three drivers at the table all wore Marlboro-embla-zoned Penske driving suits. "We've been trying to shut everybody else out from the first day," he said. "It's not boring to us."

Had Tracy not won the race, he would have been excused for being distracted. His wife had given birth the previous Tuesday to the couple's second child, a boy, Conrad James, and Paul had begun to show some pressure cracks as he openly criticized his engine's performance to the media during the week. He stepped back from such criticism after the race. "It's all a credit to the team," he said, displaying some of the media diplomacy no doubt drilled into him by Penske. "Last week, I had a lot of anxiety because my wife was having a baby, and I said some things about the engine when I got out of the car that I shouldn't have. But everything's okay now."

While Tracy waited to hear whether Penske would release him from his contract or hang on to him for another year, the world of Formula One beckoned. In September, before the last race of the CART season, Tracy headed to the Estoril track in Portugal, where he met with members of the Benetton team, watched the Portuguese Grand Prix from the team's pits, and had a test drive in the Benetton-Ford. Rumours had circulated that Tracy was heading to Portugal to replace the team's top driver, Michael Schumacher, who'd been suspended for the race. They were untrue, but the chances of a test were very good. "The trip to Portugal gives me a chance to see an F1 race, watch the Benetton team up close, and, if things work out, perhaps have a test drive in an F1 car after the race at Estoril." Tracy would get his wish. But while in CART he was a star, to the Formula One world he was just another talented driver. F1 teams try to beat the competition to pick up any driver who might be a good competitor, and the Benetton team urged Tracy to sign a contract before he got into the car. The team wanted him for three years and pressured him to sign or the test wouldn't happen. Paul mentioned that

> It was basically a contract that said I was signed to Benetton, but there was no guarantee . . . that I was going to drive. I'd get paid a certain amount. The money was decent. It didn't say in the contract that I was going to race. It just said I was under contract, so they could run somebody else at any time. That season

I think they went through four or five second drivers in the car. Schumacher was the number one, and I think they had J.J. Lehto, . . . Jos Verstappen, and . . . Johnny Herbert. They went through like three or four drivers, so that was kind of the contract — basically, that if I didn't perform very well, they could just park me. . . .

Tracy wasn't sure what to do, so he called his father, who wasn't surprised that his son was confused, since in his eyes Paul had gone to Europe with "amateurs." Tony had expected to accompany his son on the trip, but Paul had opted to go with No Fear's Jeff Surwall and Dave Stevenson, who was now Tracy's business manager. Stevenson assumed that role when Tracy began living full time in the United States and needed someone to handle his taxes and look over his contracts. Paul says that he and his father didn't have a falling out but that the elder Tracy didn't trust anyone and thrived on politics and getting his son a better deal. But Paul wasn't always interested in getting a better deal. He was looking for security. "My dad's more of a wheeler-dealer type. He always likes to be playing games and negotiating and that kind of stuff, whereas I don't really like that too much. I'll take a little less money to have a more secure contract." It was Tony who'd set up the test. He and F1 team owner Eddie Jordan are longtime friends. The series' top executive, Bernie Ecclestone, had expressed an interest in seeing Tracy drive an F1 car, and Jordan had helped to arrange the test with Benetton. So, when Paul called his father to ask for advice, Tony made some calls. He was an old friend of Ecclestone, who helped to persuade Benetton to ease up on its contract demands.

While not breaking any lap records, Tracy ran the car around the track with a time equal to that of the team's second driver, J.J. Lehto, three seconds slower than lead driver Michael Schumacher. Had he been qualifying, he would have joined Lehto in 14th spot on the grid, in the seventh row.

Going from driving an Indy car to a Formula One car is much harder than it appears. Partly because Formula One cars drive only on road courses, they aren't as fast or as powerful as Indy cars, but they are fast in turns and are easier to slide around a track. Al Unser Jr. best described the differences to Bob Judd of *Road and Track* following a test with Williams in Spain in 1991: "A Formula 1 car is kind of like a quarter horse. It accelerates, brakes and turns real quick. But it runs out of breath around 165 mph. At 165, an Indy car is startin' to stretch its legs." Regardless of experience, no driver just steps from an Indy car and into an F1 car and qualifies on the pole.

Tracy enjoyed his taste of F1, but CART was calling him back. He had an oral agreement to join the Newman-Haas team and was likely going to sign the deal. With that team, he was guaranteed to race, and he was confident that the Lola Ford Cosworth car would be competitive. "I look back on it now — Benetton struggled in '95. The car wasn't very competitive against the Williams, and I had a pretty good season in '95. I won a couple of races. I look back on it, and I don't think I made a mistake. I think it would have been worse going to Formula One and struggling than doing what I did." Tracy's size may also have been a factor. At about six feet tall and 180 lbs., he's larger than most F1 drivers. In Formula One, cars are subjected to stringent rules about how much they can weigh, taking into account the combined weight of car and driver. Jacques Villeneuve is about five foot six and Tracy's fellow driver on the current CART circuit; Cristiano da Matta is five foot four and weighs 130 lbs. Both are ideal sizes for F1 cars. Tracy was also aware of the difficult time Andretti had when he competed in F1, and of course he wasn't eager to repeat that experience.

It had been his dream to drive for a Formula One team, but Paul knew the conditions weren't right with Benetton. He had the right amount of experience and aggression, a keen testing ability, and the car control needed to handle the finicky F1 cars, and fellow drivers, such as Scott Goodyear, thought that Tracy was the most logical choice to make the jump to F1 from among the current crop of Indy car drivers. "He just has so much natural ability and talent. I think one of the best things in his career was to get it harnessed a little bit by Rick Mears," said Goodyear. "My wish all along was that he would have had the opportunity to go and compete in Formula One. I think he would have been one of the top names that we all talk about today, like Senna and Schumacher and Montoya." If Tracy went on to Formula One, everyone knew that Villeneuve would likely be the next Canadian to go, based on his family name, European heritage, and of course, driving skill.

Back in the United States, the final race of the CART season was approaching. It was back at Laguna Seca, where Tracy won the year before. He was riding high. Although his racing future had yet to be decided, he was coming off a win in Nazareth, he had beaten Michael Andretti to third spot in the standings, his teammate had won the championship, and he was enthused that racing fans, not just Canadians, were watching his every move. Tracy showed fans he was still a driver to be reckoned with. He led all 84 laps around the winding, scenic road circuit and gained his eighth CART victory and his second straight win at Laguna Seca.

The great Mario Andretti didn't fare nearly as well. He damaged his car on the first lap and was classified 19th after his engine blew just a few laps from the end of the race. It was a sad way to end a racing career, but Andretti knew, probably more than anyone, the meaning of the phrase "that's racing." In his career, he'd won the Formula One world championship, the Indy 500, the Indy car championship, as well as the Daytona 500.

His son was now taking Nigel Mansell's spot on the Newman-Haas team for the 1995 season, and Tracy had decided to take Andretti's spot. Four days after the 1994 season ended, Tracy signed a three-year deal, worth U.S. $10 million, to drive for Newman-Haas, according to a report on TSN. Tracy's sponsor would be Budweiser, which was ending its association with the Kenny Bernstein team and its driver Scott Goodyear. Goodyear was reportedly Newman-Haas's second choice if Tracy failed to sign. Penske had in fact retained an option to bring Tracy back for the 1996 season. He wanted a proven driver ready if Fittipaldi decided to retire after the 1995 season.

As Mario Andretti watched Tracy take the checkered flag from the pits, he might have realized he was watching the end of an era. A Canadian won the race. One ex-F1 driver was leaving, and another was getting set to follow. The CART series was no longer a low-rent version of Formula One. It was now competing on the same footing as the world circuit and was attracting some of the best drivers and teams in the world. Tracy had shown he could compete against the best and come out a winner. During his time with Penske, he had broken away from the influence of his father, had been courted by a Formula One team, had married his high school sweetheart, and had had two children. He'd grown from the young man who said he'd drive for free and no longer needed the guidance of a former champion such as Rick Mears. Tracy still had more to do, though. More races to win and a championship to grab. He was now ready to join the son of one of the most famous racers in the world. But Paul Tracy was now nobody's son. He was his own man. His confidence had been given a boost and he carried that momentum into the 1995 season.

CHAPTER FOUR

Newman-Haas and the Andretti Rivalry

1995

In 1995, Paul Tracy had a new team, a new sponsor, and a new teammate, Michael Andretti. The two men with the equally aggressive driving styles would now be forced to work together as a team while fighting like hell with each other on the track to win the championship. "I took Nigel's spot, and then Dad retired, and Paul took his spot. Budweiser came on board. I think he [Penske] owned his contract, and he loaned him out to Carl [Haas] for a year," said Andretti. While there may have been a plan to pair the two drivers, Andretti suspects Penske was faced with three active drivers at the end of the 1994 season and may have believed he was better off with the two veterans for the next season. But he intended to hang on to his young charge for as long as possible, hoping to bring Tracy back after he'd spent some time with Andretti, expecting Fittipaldi to retire after 1995. It appears Penske was trying to get the best of both worlds. "I don't think Penske knew what he was going to do with Paul," Andretti said. Penske was in an enviable position when it came to drivers, though. Al Unser Jr. was still in his prime, Tracy could still be an asset to the team (and a season away couldn't hurt), and Fittipaldi, with his years of racing experience, still had some fire left. Tracy had a lot to look forward to in 1995. Even if things didn't work out with Newman-Haas, he had the chance to go back to the team where he'd had all of his Indy car success. But, if the partnership with Andretti worked out, he could flourish with the team and potentially benefit from Andretti's experience. That is, if they could get along.

After placing third in the championship in 1993, his first full season driving Indy cars, Tracy was looking for more money, and, compared with the salaries of Unser and Fittipaldi, he thought he deserved it — considering that, when he first signed on with Penske, he probably could have made as much money driving a New York City taxi. "My first full season, '93, I was third in the championship, I had five wins in the season. I tied Mansell for wins. He had five, I had five," he said. "I was making $50,000, and Emerson was making $3,000,000. My contract for Penske went $30,000, $50,000, $65,000, $100,000 for a four-year contract."

Tony Tracy went to Penske to try to renegotiate the deal before the 1995 season, but Penske wasn't interested in renegotiating. He wanted to develop a satellite team — a Penske car operated by a different team manager but owned by him. He was pushing for such a deal with either the Bettenhausen or the Hogan team. That idea didn't interest Tracy. He believed he'd put in his time and didn't want to be shunted off to a new, and possibly uncompetitive, team even if it was under the Penske umbrella.

I didn't want to do that because at that time I had finished third in the championship, and I'd beaten my teammates in the championship twice. Al won the championship in '94. I was third. The basic reason was there was a lot of flak about cigarette sponsorship in '94. We had three Marlboro cars, and there was a lot of TV exposure, media exposure, and the government was coming down hard on cigarette companies, so Marlboro felt they had to pull back and only do two cars instead of three. Al had a contract, and I guess I was the easiest one to kind of put someplace else, and I didn't really like that too much because I felt I'd earned my position on the team, having finished third in the championship twice, and by this time I'd won, you know, eight races, and I didn't feel I should be put into a small, underfinanced team as a satellite driver.

Both the Bettenhausen and the Hogan teams presided mainly over the back of the pack at that time, so the deal was even less appealing to Tracy. "Penske would have helped them financially, but it was still a team that was not as capable at the time as Penske racing," Paul said.

We argued over that quite a bit. I had an offer from Newman-Haas to go to Newman-Haas. I had a test with Formula One. I had an opportunity for Formula One. . . . We argued to the point where I wanted to go to Newman-Haas because they were offering me a lot of money over what I was getting paid, and it was an opportunity for me. Not really thought over, but Penske finally said okay. "I want an option to get you back in one year."

When the deal was signed, it was the best one Tracy could have hoped for. "If I had gone to the satellite team, I was going to make $125,000 that next year 'cause I'd be still under the same contract but on a smaller team, and when I went to Newman-Haas I made $1.5 [million]. It was a big difference."

While Penske held the option to bring Tracy back in 1996, no definite plans had been put in place. The other uncertain aspect of the Newman-Haas deal and the Tracy-Andretti partnership was the similar personalities of the drivers. Having two aggressive drivers on a team was, on the surface, an ideal situation. The challenge for the team was to make sure not all the attention was lavished on Andretti, making Tracy feel like the number two driver. It would also be a challenge to keep Tracy from returning to his old ways now that he was no longer under the watchful eye of Penske. This year, they'd also all be competing for the Indy 500 prize, and 1995 would prove to be the final year for Indy cars at the storied race following a dispute with track owner Tony George.

The 1995 season opened in Miami, and Tracy was joined once again on the circuit by Jacques Villeneuve, in his second Indy car season — he was proving to be a better all-round driver than his father and was driving for Team Green, which had become a rival to the best of the Indy teams. Fellow Canadian Scott Goodyear was also back. From 1990 to 1993, Mackenzie Financial sponsored Goodyear. He drove for Kenny Bernstein's King team in 1994 in a car sponsored by Budweiser and then transferred to a Honda team in 1995. "1994 was the last year of the contract for the Budweiser King team, and they were about ready to lose it. When I went there, we were trying to help turn it around because they had been with those guys for so long and never had any success," he said. "But the problem was really with the running of the team. I resigned from that team in May, and they lost the sponsorship in June of that year, in '94. The team was a mess. We won a race for them, won the first race for them in years, at our second Michigan win in '94 at the Marlboro 500. But trust me, it was more out of luck than anything else." Tracy was renewed by the change in teams but didn't show any change in his aggressive style. A new team and a new sponsor couldn't put a damper on his urge to go as fast as possible. At the Miami race, his driving became a disappointment to his team, his fans, and Budweiser. He crashed on the first lap of the race, continuing a trend that he'd begun in qualifying by spinning out several times, and he had to plead his case before critics, who questioned his aggressive driving style. Villeneuve won the race.

After making his early and ungracious exit in Miami, Tracy turned his attention halfway around the world to the race at the 2.8-mile Surfers Paradise on Australia's Gold Coast. In provisional qualifying the Friday before the race, Tracy sat third on the grid behind rookie Gil de Ferran. His teammate, Andretti, had the early pole for the street race, which he won the year before, when he drove a Reynard Ford for Chip Ganassi. Both Andretti and Tracy had a difficult time in qualifying. They were among the group of drivers held back during qualifying by frequent red flags. The drivers complained about a rule that penalized them if they caused delays by crashing during qualifying. They were penalized for up to four minutes in the pits. Such penalties disrupt the rhythm of qualifying, when drivers are trying a number of options on their cars to get the optimum speed, and both Tracy and Andretti spoke out against the rule. "Should you be penalized for that . . . trying too hard?" Andretti said to the Montreal *Gazette*. "It's frustrating for all of us, but safety comes first." Tracy was harsher with his criticism. "We are professional drivers. The consequences if I crash the car can be that I end up in the hospital for two months. It's not for somebody else to dictate how we drive in qualifying. There's enough penalty if you crash." Despite the rules, the Newman-Haas duo started the race near the front. While Tracy was seeing some results of his more conservative driving approach, he watched as his former teammates at Penske struggled during provisional qualifying. Fittipaldi and Unser ended the day in seventh and ninth place respectively.

Andretti led the early portion of the race, which began under a caution flag after Belgian Eric Bachelart stalled his car during the warm-up. Tracy did his best to stick to the leaders. Andretti ran into transmission problems with eight laps remaining in the race, and Tracy passed him as he slowed down on the track after losing second gear. Tracy sped on to the checkered flag. Bobby Rahal finished second, nearly seven seconds behind. Villeneuve had also left the race with a broken gearbox. "I knew he [Andretti] had a gearbox problem, but we ended up having quite a good drag race," said Tracy. "He was driving a great race and had it under control. It's bad luck." With his ninth win, Tracy was vindicated in the eyes of his critics. At this point in his career, he'd found a comfort zone on street tracks.

The next race, on the Phoenix oval, had all the ingredients of a street fight. Tracy and Villeneuve qualified in the second row — Villeneuve became the first driver in the field to clock a lap under 20 seconds during the Saturday practice session — and the rest of the 21 drivers were within a second of the time of pole sitter Bryan Herta. Fittipaldi sat next to Herta in the front row.

Tracy moved into the lead in the championship series standings with his fourth-place finish. Villeneuve finished fifth to move into second place in the standings with 30 points, two behind Tracy. Robby Gordon, who rivalled only Tracy with his aggression, won his first race in 41 Indy car starts. The Californian's radio broke down early in the race, so Gordon had to make a series of frantic hand gestures as he rocketed by the pits to let his crew know what changes he wanted on the next stop.

Tracy's championship lead didn't survive the trip to sunny Long Beach. Andretti qualified his Lola Ford in the front row with a speed of 109.006 mph. Tracy was next in line with a speed of 108.861 mph. Tracy made it until lap 16, when he clashed with Gil de Ferran as they both tried to enter turn three. Tracy was squeezed out, bumped over the curb, and was out of the race. His former teammate, Al Unser Jr., went on to win.

With an up-and-down season so far, Tracy was still talking about consistency or, in his case, the lack of it. He knew he had to finish regularly in the points if he was going to take a serious run at the championship. So far, he had two wins but had crashed at both Miami and Long Beach. He pointed to Scott Pruett, who'd had several solid but unspectacular finishes and was now leading the championship, as a driver with an ideal approach to racing. While he outwardly praised the team for its work preparing the car, Tracy was concerned that Andretti had been doing the bulk of the testing, and he continued to do so between Long Beach and the race on the oval at Nazareth. Tracy was apprehensive because he didn't have as much time in the car between races, and as a result the cars were being set up in a way that suited Andretti. Tracy was also worried that the team's focus was beginning to shift away from the two of them to just Andretti.

Avoiding Tracy's wreckage was just one of the challenges for Emerson Fittipaldi when he won the race at Nazareth. It was another DNF for Tracy, who crashed on the 30th lap, which allowed Villeneuve to move into second place in the standings.

The famed Brickyard was the next stop on the circuit. Almost as soon as the checkered flag fell on the race at Nazareth, the teams began to make preparations for the Indy 500. The race falls on the Memorial Day holiday in the United States, and drivers and teams traditionally take the entire month to get ready. For some drivers, such as Al Unser Jr., Rick Mears, Mario Andretti, and Emerson Fittipaldi, a win at the Brickyard is something they've already added to their résumés. For others, such as Michael Andretti, Scott Goodyear, and Paul Tracy, it's a dream yet to be realized. For still others, it's their one shot at racing success. Lyn St. James, the veteran female driver who can't get sponsorship to take part in the entire series, sees the Indy 500 as her chance to get noticed by a team that needs a full-time driver. Some drivers spend the rest of the year working at regular jobs just to pay for their chance to qualify and race in the 500, although they are fewer every year. The big Indy car teams such as Newman-Haas, Penske, and Forsythe-Green pour thousands of dollars and hours of time into the chance to claim the Borg-Warner trophy as their own.

In 1995, the early buzz during practice surrounded the Flying Dutchman, Arie Luyendyk of Team Menard, as he turned in the fastest lap in Indy 500 history at 234.106 mph. After setting such a blistering pace around the 1.5-mile oval, Luyendyk got out of his car and told the Associated Press, "I think there's more in it. If I could have run more today, I would have gone 235." Not to be outdone, Tracy cracked the 230 mph mark with a lap of 231.315. Menard set the pace during all seven days of practice before qualifying using an engine that the rest of the teams just couldn't keep up with. The Buick V6 was based on a push rod engine block, which was allowed 55 inches of turbo boost under United States Auto Club rules, the sanctioning body for the 500. Penske tried using a similar engine in 1994, but it was banned by the USAC because it decided that it was a purpose-built racing engine, not a converted stock engine. While Tracy and Andretti couldn't match the Menard times, they knew it would be tough for the Menard engine to stand up to 500 miles of punishment, especially if Scott Brayton and Luyendyk tried to hold off the rest of the field from the front row.

Two weeks before the race, Tracy qualified as high as third before adjustments to the car added too much aerodynamic drag and made it difficult to drive, dropping him down to seventh spot. He anticipated that the track conditions would worsen, which in turn would make his car looser to handle. But the adjustments to the wings made the car considerably slower. He pushed it as hard as he could and as close to the concrete walls as possible but still could only produce an average speed of 225.695 mph, well off the pace. He would fall farther through the pack to 16th spot as other drivers took to the track. Fellow Canadians Scott Goodyear and Jacques Villeneuve fared much better. Goodyear managed to land in third spot in Sunday qualifying after rain forced cars off the track the day before, further widening the gap. Villeneuve started in fifth spot after surviving a crash on Friday. Luyendyk and Brayton grabbed the top two spots. Tracy wasn't happy about starting from the middle of the pack, but at least he wouldn't have the Penske team to deal with. For the first time in 26 years, the Indy 500 field would be devoid of the red-and-white Marlboro-clad Penske cars. They had failed to qualify. "This is more than disappointment," said Emerson Fittipaldi to the Associated Press. "This is a shock."

A series of problems kept Penske out of Indy. Fittipaldi as well as former Indy winner and team adviser Rick Mears said the team was confident in preparations for the race but not overconfident. The Penske team did most of its testing before the month-long practice and qualifying marathon at the Brickyard, when the weather was cooler. Driving on the track during warmer temperatures proved to be a challenge for the Penske cars, which couldn't get up to speed. The Mercedes engine that powered Unser to a win in 1994 was now banned from the track, so Penske was without a dominating power-plant. Unser was driving with an injured shoulder, and Fittipaldi was occupied with his various business interests, which contributed to his poor performance. Tracy, who used to act as test driver when the other two men were too busy, was no longer providing the kind of information they may have needed. Greg Moore and Trans Am series driver Scott Sharp were signed on to do some testing, but neither had Tracy's experience. "We won races in '95," Roger Penske told *Road and Track* in February 2001. "They changed the rules twice to get us out of there. When we have an edge, people like to cut our legs off. But if anybody else has an edge, it's just business as usual." Tracy told the Associated Press that Penske just failed to prepare adequately. "Looking at it from my standpoint, I don't think they got all their homework done and were not maybe aware they had a problem when they got here." Despite the seriousness of Penske's problems, it was easy for Tracy to have a laugh from afar at his former employer's expense. As he watched Fittipaldi and Unser struggle to qualify, he remarked: "Al and Emerson must not be trying very hard — I'd have been in the fence a couple of times by now."

With Penske out of the Indy 500 for the first time in over two decades, some more history was being made on the starting grid. Three Canadians had a chance to win the race for the first time. Due partly to their qualifying performances and partly to their driving in other races during the season, Goodyear and Villeneuve were mentioned as potential winners. Goodyear had come close in 1992, losing to Unser in the closest finish in Indy history. Villeneuve had placed second in 1994 in his first attempt. Preparing for the 1995 Indianapolis 500, Goodyear was pleased that there were three Canadians in contention to win the race. As well, he was happy that some fans and media still remembered his first Indy car win in 1992 at the Michigan 500, a race that Tracy finished second.

I can recall from the front pages of the paper, "Canadians Finish One, Two," and that's never been accomplished before at such a big race. I think that helped people say, "Shit, you know, these guys are all right, they can compete at this level," which was everything I ever wanted, because I always knew that Canadians could do it if they were given a chance, but we never seemed to be able to get a chance by corporate

Canada to have support, which was really aggravating to me at that point in time. I learned to accept it. I learned to find ways around it, which was basically move out of Canada and have to find other ways to do it.

Tracy knew he would have to adjust his driving style to suit the unforgiving track. "This place is hard on people. It's tough to pass," he said to the Toronto *Sun*. "You can't attack the race track, and that's my style. You have to sit and wait. I think I have a good shot if I play the race like a waiting game."

On race day, playing that game was effective for the first part of the race, but electrical problems eventually prevented Tracy from working his way to the front of the pack. He completed 136 of 200 laps before heading out of the contest. He managed to avoid a frightening first-lap crash, which claimed five cars and seriously injured veteran 500 competitor Stan Fox. Tracy's wife, Tara, told Paul to be careful on the start because she'd had a premonition there was going to be a crash. With 11 rows of three cars starting at once, Tracy nonetheless threaded his way through them without damage and moved up to ninth place on the first lap. He went into the pits to have a punctured tire repaired and fell to 13th spot, but he managed to fight his way back up to sixth place before a failing sensor switched off his engine.

Even when it was all sorted out, the 1995 Indianapolis 500 was still a bizarre affair. Jacques Villeneuve won the race, the first Canadian to do so. He'd taken the win with a hard but clean drive that saw him overcome a two-lap deficit, during which time he never lost his cool. It also helped that his crew was especially alert that day. Two times he was able to stay on a lead lap when a yellow flag flew, aiding him in his efforts to unlap himself. That coolness allowed him to capitalize on one of Scott Goodyear's most famous mistakes. Goodyear passed the pace car while leading the race, earning him a black-flag penalty. The pace car appeared to be late coming onto the track and didn't come up to speed quickly enough, and Goodyear seemed unable to slow down in time to stay behind it. Villeneuve admitted after the race that he also had to brake hard to stay behind it. The win moved the French Canadian into first place in the championship standings.

Tracy was able to ease the disappointment of not winning the Indianapolis 500 by coolly taking the checkered flag at the Milwaukee Mile on June 4 — taking the win away from Al Unser Jr., who'd led most of the race, and ruining a Penske comeback after its Indy humiliation. Tracy had performed well on the famed oval in the past, and 1995 was no exception. With 22 laps left to go, he pounced when Unser was slowed down by a collection of cars trying to stay on the lead lap. "Al's car was loose, and he couldn't drive hard into the turns," Tracy said after the race. "He got boxed in up high by some slower cars, I stayed low, and I was able to get past him in traffic. After that, I knew I had enough to beat him." After his last pit stop, Tracy managed to open a lead of about five seconds over Unser, and he could have gone even faster, but he knew that "It doesn't matter how much you win by, as long as you win." With the win, Tracy joined Villeneuve as the series' second two-race winner. Villeneuve finished sixth, adding points to his place in the championship standings, which he was now leading with 65 points. Robby Gordon sat in second spot with 53 points, followed by Tracy, Bobby Rahal, and Scott Pruett, who all had 52 points. Unser had 51 points.

In July, Tracy was still talking about winning the

championship for Newman-Haas, believing he'd found the consistency that had eluded him while at Marlboro Team Penske. "I think I could have won the championship the last two years. We just didn't have the consistency you need. That's what I'm going to concentrate on in 1995," he told the Toronto *Sun*. At the same time, pit lane rumours persisted that Roger Penske would exercise his option and bring Tracy back in 1996 as the teams moved on to Elkhart Lake. Silly season had begun, and drivers were getting ready to join new teams for the next season. But before heading to Elkhart Lake's Road America and then on to Toronto, Tracy felt the urge to do a little karting, which he'd been doing ever since he started racing. This time he made the mistake of taking part in a kart race and broke his left ankle in a collision. Tracy was able to return to racing because, while on the track, he didn't need to use the clutch to shift gears; he needed it only when he pulled away from the pits. But that's when he felt the pain. To avoid the painful knocking of his foot against the inside of the cockpit, he was fitted with a carbon-fibre shield over his left driving shoe. With a steel plate and five screws in his foot and ankle, he still managed a second-place finish in Elkhart Lake, losing to Villeneuve.

The win in Wisconsin was his third victory of the season. Villeneuve and Tracy were the circuit's only multiple winners coming into the Toronto Molson Indy, and much of the media attention was focused on the Canadians racing on the Indy car circuit. According to the Montreal *Gazette*'s Pat Hickey, the Canadian Grand Prix, which runs on Circuit Gilles Villeneuve near Montreal and takes place before the Indy cars arrive in Toronto for the first of two races on Canadian soil, is popular with people around Montreal and the rest of the world, but most Canadians prefer Indy car racing. Up to 1995, the ratings for the Molson Indy were 44% to 150% higher than those for the Formula One race. Crucial to that success was the fact that three Canadians — Villeneuve, Tracy, and Goodyear — were competing in the Indy car series, while no Canadians were racing in Formula One. At the time, coverage of the race was competing with the British Grand Prix and a NASCAR race, but the usual rebroad-cast of the Grand Prix race after the late CBC news was bumped by a rerun of the Toronto Molson Indy.

In Toronto, Tracy was still hobbling around on crutches when he started in 10th spot. The Toronto course tended to be bumpier than most, and his Lola Ford wasn't handling well. With his foot banging around inside the car, Tracy tried to make the driving more comfortable by putting foam inside the left side of the compartment (known as a "tub") and on the side of his racing shoe. During the race, he ran as high as third. But his foot went to sleep, and after a collision with Mauricio Gugelmin he dropped back to 16th place and eventually finished in eighth place.

In Cleveland, Tracy tussled with André Ribeiro on the start, and both ended up leaving the race. Jacques Villeneuve won again, but it was Robby Gordon, a friend of Tracy's and no stranger to overly aggressive driving, who grabbed the spotlight. Gordon was accused of bumping cars and rough driving by both Villeneuve and Andretti. He earned a U.S. $10,000 fine for, among other things, swerving into Andretti at the end of the race and giving him the finger. Gordon maintained that it was he who'd been pushed around the track by Villeneuve and Andretti. Andretti, involved in several other racetrack incidents during the season, was placed on probation for a "cumulative record of incidents," in the words of an Indy car spokesperson.

As the season wore on, Tracy thought that his combination of hard work and luck wasn't going to pay off in a championship yet again. His struggles continued in the New England 200. He started 14th on the grid and was moving through the field rapidly, jumping into third spot after 43 laps. André Ribeiro and Michael Andretti were ahead of him. Then his car developed an oil leak, and 99 laps into the race he was black-flagged by race officials. He ignored the flag for two laps before pitting. When he did go into the pits, the engine was inspected and then ordered shut down by race officials. Tracy was understandably angry — he was still chasing some valuable points — but his subsequent outburst was seen as just another display of the now classic Paul Tracy Attitude. He got out of the car, made a couple of hand gestures, and then pushed his way past an Indy car official. The incident cost him a total of $12,000: $5,000 for making an "obscene gesture," another $5,000 for pushing an official, and $2,000 for ignoring the black flag for two laps. "It was a bogus call," Tracy told the Associated Press. "It's really disappointing. We had a problem with the car, and they called us in and wouldn't let us return. We could have fixed the problem, got back out, and scored some points, but they wouldn't let us. I don't think they should eliminate a guy who is trying to run for the championship."

So, with all that wreckage following him around, Tracy could be forgiven for throwing his hands up after the race in Vancouver. By the time the racers got to the second Canadian race, he'd lost the spark that had carried him through the first part of the season. He'd qualified between 8th and 15th spots throughout the season. What irked him, he said in an interview with the Toronto *Sun*'s Dan Proudfoot, was that, as he qualified poorly, Andretti found himself consistently much higher on the grid. And Tracy believed the reason for Andretti's success was that the team now regarded Tracy as second best and was concentrating on Andretti's Lola Ford Cosworth. That, Tracy contended, was because his relationship with team owner Carl Haas had deteriorated since he'd told him he would return to the Penske team for the 1996 season. Haas made a business decision and decided Andretti could still win the championship, and it was worth more to the team to invest time and money in the driver who was staying rather than the one who was leaving. "The cars are always set up the way Michael likes them," Paul said. "That's because he's done all the testing, while I've had one test session — at Laguna Seca, which gives me a better chance of starting with a car set up for myself. The car just won't handle here [in Vancouver] — it won't turn into the corners, and if you touch the throttle (to aid turning in) the thing just jumps out. I guess that's the way Michael likes the car. That suits his style because he likes chopping at the wheel and stabbing at the throttle, but it doesn't work for me."

Tracy started the race a disappointing 12th but finished it the highest of all the Canadians — in eighth place. Villeneuve started from the pole but ended the race in 12th place in his Reynard Cosworth, and Goodyear was in fourth spot on the grid but ended up in 14th place in his Tasman Honda Reynard. Villeneuve's problem at first was his tires, and then it was a broken gearbox. Goodyear spun while attempting to overtake Bobby Rahal on the 10th lap of the 100-lap event, and then Goodyear and Villeneuve bumped each other when the latter's gearbox broke, sending Goodyear into the pits to replace a tire. Tracy worked his way up to third place, but some erratic driving pushed him back through the field. Penske team driver Al Unser Jr. won the race.

Before the CART race at Monterey, some of Tracy's old records were being broken. Greg Moore was busy breaking Paul's Indy Lights record as he was getting ready to make the leap up to the next level. Tracy had nine wins in the first 12 of 14 Indy Lights events, and Moore scored 10 wins in a 12-race season. In his last race, he still won after becoming airborne in his Player's Indy Lights Lola after driving over a curb in the morning warm-up session.

Surprisingly, when the big cars ran on the Laguna Seca circuit, Tracy had one of his best drives of the season, chasing Gil de Ferran to the finish with Mauricio Gugelmin and Michael Andretti snapping at his rear wing. Villeneuve finished 11th and took the Indy car crown, becoming the youngest driver and the first Canadian to do so. His closest rival in the series battle, Unser, finished the race sixth. Unser would have had to finish first or second to be in the hunt for the championship, pending an appeal of his disqualification in Portland. As soon as the race was over, Tracy said he was looking forward to again wearing a Penske driving suit in 1996 and was heading into testing over the winter.

Tracy believes that he gave the Newman-Haas team his best shot but in the end was defeated in his efforts to take the championship by bad luck, some driving beyond his abilities, and a team that was geared, right from the start, toward Andretti. "When I signed for the team at Newman-Haas, Michael wasn't keen on it," Tracy said.

He actually basically told me up front that this is his team, and, you know, that's the way it is. And I said, well, I just thought I could come in and just do my thing, you know, and the team really was based around him and Mario. Mario had driven there most of his career in Indy cars. Michael had driven his whole career in Indy cars basically with Newman-Haas, so the team was really based around him, and I didn't think it was going to be that bad, and when I got there I didn't get a lot of testing. He got most of the testing.

Yeah, I had a good team. I had a good season. I didn't finish as well in the championship as I would have liked. I think I was fifth in the championship. I won two races. I had a good year, but it was just . . . it wasn't the right place for me. You know, I got along with my guys really well and still get along with all of the guys that I worked with, that worked at Newman-Haas. It just wasn't the right fit for me. The match wasn't very good as a team. It was kind of two separate teams.

Although disappointed with the season, Tracy still had several consistent months. He notched two wins for Newman-Haas, three second-place finishes, and one fourth-place finish. That was good enough for 115 points and sixth place in the championship.

Andretti says today that the relationship between him and Tracy was more harmonious than his former teammate remembers, and contrary to Tracy he doesn't believe the team was built around him. At the time of the interview, the two drivers were getting ready to be part of the same team once again. Andretti was joining Team Motorola as its only driver. The team was managed by Team Green but had Motorola as its main sponsor. The two legendary combatants were trying to take a mature attitude toward working together once again. "Actually, I personally didn't have any problem with Paul in '95; in fact, I think we were pretty good at exchanging information and things like that. We were compatible in a lot of ways," said Andretti. "That actually was a good year for us, and I'm hoping that we can continue to have that same sort of thing. . . ."

CHAPTER FIVE

The Return to Penske

1996-97

The Indy car championship had eluded Paul Tracy once again in 1995. He'd spent a year in a team and with a driver with whom he didn't always get along. But he'd continued to seek consistency in his driving, and while he'd won two races he hadn't come close to achieving the success of his high-watermark season of 1993. He'd gotten the best deal, however, by signing with the Newman-Haas team. He could have spent the year humbled at the back of the grid driving for a Roger Penske satellite team, forced to work like a chastised student, struggling to make amends for slights real or perceived by headmaster Penske.

For a young driver, though, Tracy had a lot to be thankful for. His forceful driving — coupled with the often forceful business acumen of his father — ensured that fans would speak his name and that prominent teams would notice his driving. Not every driver has the fairy-tale good fortune of starting a racing career with Penske's team. His name alone is almost synonymous with competition and success.

Yet by 1996, Tracy wanted and deserved more. He'd proven himself to be a competitor. He could drive up front with anyone on the circuit. He was heading back to Penske more seasoned than when he left, he no longer regarded himself as the young upstart, and he didn't want anyone to think of him like that either. Tracy was, in a sense, returning to Marlboro Team Penske on a high note. He left the team in 1994 after winning the pole and the race at Laguna Seca, and he'd be working with the same team and crew as when he left. He was also pleased that Penske had made room for him on the team by moving Emerson Fittipaldi to the satellite team, sponsored by Mobil One, with Marlboro taking a smaller sponsorship role. This apparently was meant as no outward slight toward the Brazilian. Instead, it provided him with a team that would work solely for him and gave Penske a chance to spread around his sponsorship money.

During his first qualifying session for the Marlboro Grand Prix in Miami in 1996, Tracy set the fastest lap in early practice on the 1.5-mile Homestead oval with a speed of 194.936 mph. He then turned his attention to driving the Penske Mercedes Ilmor on full fuel tanks to prepare for the race. Target Ganassi driver Jimmy Vasser was second fastest, and Canadians Greg Moore and Scott Goodyear — who was making his first foray into Indy-style cars since the Molson Vancouver Indy of 1994 — found themselves in seventh and 21st places respectively.

Tracy had a great start in the race, and at different times during it he pulled away from the rest of the field. The trouble was that none of the caution periods worked in his favour, and his Goodyear tires didn't perform well. He was able to get the jump on the field on the restarts, and then his gearbox selector failed as he came out of the pits on the 83rd lap of the 133-lap race. Vasser was then able to get around Gil de Ferran when he was boxed in by traffic and went on to take his first win. In addition to Tracy's early dominance, the race was marked by a daring high-speed pass by the rookie Moore, who jumped past the leader to unlap himself and went on to finish seventh. Tracy was disappointed with the loss but knew he had a long season ahead of him, and the Penske cars were beginning to show some promise.

Shortly after the season began, the animosity between Paul Tracy and Michael Andretti worsened. Tracy still had hard feelings from his year at Newman-Haas, and Andretti's rough driving earlier in the season had taken its toll on Tracy and other drivers. During the second race, in Australia, Tracy and Andretti came together, and Tracy was bumped off the track. Never one to back down from a fight and no stranger to a CART penalty, he thought Andretti should have been penalized, even though Andretti apologized to Tracy after the race. CART officials chose to take no action at that point. During the fourth race of the season, at Long Beach, Andretti hounded the back ends of the cars driven by Mauricio Gugelmin and Teo Fabi of the PacWest team. After the race, Andretti tried to explain to Gugelmin that the Brazilian had been in his blind spot as he'd attempted to pass Adrian Fernandez. During that conversation, things started to look like the end of a Saturday-night dirt-track race as PacWest staffers roughed up a Newman-Haas junior engineer who was with Andretti.

Because he thought CART officials hadn't heard him, Tracy decided to go public with his frustration and tried to have some fun at Andretti's expense before the Long Beach race. With the help of sports apparel company No Fear, one of his sponsors, Tracy had T-shirts made with "Michael Andretti's Driving School for the Blind" written on the front. On the back was a caricature of Andretti with a blindfold over his helmet visor; he was carrying a white cane surrounded by pieces of cars belonging to other drivers. Gugelmin, Vasser, and Robby Gordon all wore the shirts to a drivers' meeting. They'd all been victims of Andretti's jostling on the track.

When Andretti saw the shirts, he was angry and complained to chief steward Wally Dallenbach. "Yeah, I was quite surprised by that. To be honest with you, I don't know how that came about. I guess because I got together with him [Tracy] in Australia," said Andretti. "I think Paul left Newman-Haas feeling like I tried to steer the team my way and against him, which was not true in any way. If it did happen, it was only because I'd been there before. . . . I never did anything to do that. But I think he may have felt that I did, and I think he had some hard feelings, and I think that's where that [the T-shirts] started."

Tracy was angry at his former teammate, and the T-shirts were the result of pent-up frustration and a perceived lack of concern by CART officials. "It wasn't anything serious; we were just having some fun," said Tracy.

> He and I had had a lot of run-ins on the track, and most of them involved him shoving me off the track two or three times, and we'd had a few wheel-banging incidents, and he had gotten into other people.

Dallenbach called Tracy, Roger Penske, and team member Teddy Mayer to a meeting, telling them that the issue was best resolved by the officials and shouldn't be handled with an attempt at public humiliation. That, Tracy said, was partly his point, using the shirts to get the attention of the steward and prompt him to do something. Steve Horne, owner of Tasman Motorsports, also urged Dallenbach to penalize Andretti or at least warn him that his dangerous driving would not be tolerated. Tracy told the Toronto *Sun*'s Dan Proudfoot that he sent a letter to CART officials asking them to discipline Andretti, but their response was "Well, Tracy, you're no angel yourself."

By the end of that week, CART had bowed to the pressure and placed Andretti on probation for rough driving, but he was not being fined. "I am not a bull in a china shop," he said in a statement. "It's a competitive series, and the field is full of intensity as well as intelligence. Right now I want to put all of this behind me. I'm anxious to get back on track. Crew members or team members should never get involved, and officials should only become involved if the drivers come to an impasse." He then added that, "Until one of the PacWest crew members intervened after the Long Beach race, it was being handled the way it should, between two drivers. It would have ended in a handshake."

During the same period, Tracy had also developed an on-track rivalry with former off-road racer and sometime NASCAR driver Robby Gordon. Tracy and Gordon had been cut from the same cloth. Both were aggressive on the track and said exactly what was on their minds off the track. "We were both the same age, both came in at the same time, and we were competitive against each other. We get along well with each other, and we're pretty good friends off the track, but at the time we were pretty competitive with each other," Tracy said. "But . . . we never actually got into an accident with each other," unlike Tracy and Andretti.

Andretti put the joke back on his accusers as he handily won the series' next race in his hometown of Nazareth, Pennsylvania. During the race, both he and Tracy suffered bad pit stops, but Tracy's was by far the worst. Andretti stalled his car as he was leaving the pit following his first stop, but he recovered from the stall and didn't look back. Race leader Tracy scrubbed his car into the pit wall and injured three of his crew members. He came into the pit too fast, with blisters appearing on the left tires. He locked the brakes as he crossed the paint line — an often slick line that delineates the pit boundaries — and knocked down three crew members. Left-rear tire changer Matt Johnson was thrown into John Whiteman, who was holding the air jack. Matt Burns, the refueller, was also hurt. The crew waved Tracy out of the pit again rather than try to refuel the car and change tires in the melee. He ran over the air hose on his way out, and this cost him a stop-and-go penalty. He came in for the routine change five laps later and then served the penalty. "I felt so bad sitting there in the pit, looking at this guy [Johnson] on the ground, I lost all motivation," he said after the race, fighting back tears. "When he came on the radio later and said 'I want you to kick everyone's butt,' that got me motivated again." Tracy was motivated enough to pass Bobby Rahal for fifth place on the last lap. Feeling contrite, Tracy said, "We had the winning car, but my mistake cost us the win."

Normally, the month of May was spent preparing for the Indy 500; however, since Indy track boss Tony George had decided that most of the starting-grid spots would be taken up by drivers who regularly competed in that series, CART teams decided not to go. They staged their own race the same weekend at the Michigan International Speedway, a high-speed, D-shaped oval near Brooklyn. It was dubbed the "U.S. 500," and it was a gruelling endurance test that took its toll on many drivers. Tracy did his best to exorcise the demons that had been following him throughout the season and finished a respectable seventh, two laps behind winner Jimmy Vasser.

Tensions between Tracy and his Penske teammate rose in Detroit when Al Unser Jr. blamed Paul for being a poor teammate and taking him out of the race. On lap 47, when Tracy was fifth and Unser sixth, Paul narrowly missed hitting the wall in the tricky third turn and slowed down, allowing Unser to pull alongside him, believing that Paul would let him pass. But Tracy refused to give up the position, thinking that he could recover from his mistake, forcing Unser to lock his brakes and slide into a tire barrier. Tracy soldiered on and later tangled with Scott Pruett and finished 17th, three positions ahead of fellow Canadian Greg Moore.

In the next race, in Portland, there was still talk of the feud between the two Penske teammates. While few teams in CART have a definite number-one driver, drivers measure themselves most closely against their teammates, and few teammates in any kind of racing are close friends. In Formula One, there is a definite hierarchy in which the number-two driver is expected to help his teammate win races by not fighting for the lead and sometimes even by blocking other drivers from getting near the leader. Penske didn't have such a hierarchy. While they weren't overly friendly off the track, Tracy and Unser still knew they were part of a team and tried to act accordingly. Tracy, with his often erratic driving and poor results during 1996, was nonetheless an easy target for Unser to use to deflect the blame when he made a mistake. But Unser had also expressed his unhappiness with previous teammates when he was with Galles Racing before moving over to Penske.

In the Cleveland race, Tracy ran as high as third after starting eighth, but he was taken out of contention by a team mistake on the 21st lap. The crew kept him on the track while others pitted during the race's only caution period, and the mistake eventually dropped him down to 18th spot when he had to pit during a green situation. He still managed to fight his way to ninth place at the finish.

Tires had become a factor in the 1996 races. Jimmy Vasser had begun to dominate races driving a Reynard shod in Firestone tires and powered by a Honda engine. Tracy's Penske Mercedes Ilmor was running on Goodyear tires, and Paul had been pushing the car beyond the tires' capability in an effort to get on the podium more often. Tracy was still plagued by poorly performing tires and a lack of mechanical grip as he returned to Toronto for the Molson Indy. With just 49 points to his credit, he had to adjust his expectations from winning the championship to simply winning a race. As always, he was excited about the chance to race in Toronto, but because Unser, though winless himself, was still in championship contention Tracy was now focusing his attention on testing the team's 1997 car. But the Penske car just wasn't competitive, and Tracy had dropped to ninth place in the standings.

In Toronto, the *Sun*'s Dan Proudfoot reported that questions still surrounded Tracy and whether, based on his performance that year, he would be back with the Penske team in 1997. Tracy unequivocally said he would, and chief engineer Nigel Beresford backed up that answer. Beresford told Proudfoot he had returned to the Penske team from the Tyrrell Formula One team just to work with Tracy. "There are few guys anywhere in racing that you might work with who so apply themselves to being fast," he said.

> *Many are satisfied to be in the top five. With Tracy, he gives you everything plus 10 percent in order to be fastest. Whatever effort you put in, he'll double it. This makes everyone on the team very loyal to him — and frustrated when he puts himself in the position he has in some races.*
>
> *There have been days when we've given him a lousy car and he has carried it. He would never, ever, accuse us of giving him a crap car. So I would never fault him for trying too hard.*

Beresford added that Tracy still had the same attitude that Burke Harrison and Brian Stewart saw during his Indy Lights days. "His first comment after pitting will be 'What's my time? What's my position?' We try to keep a lid on it. Paul always wants to be fastest. It's probably not unfair to call it an obsession." His driving style, Beresford said, was simply to get to the front of the pack and stay there.

Getting to the front of the pack for the Molson Indy in Toronto was easier said than done. Tracy struggled with an uncompetitive car once again and dropped to 13th spot on the starting grid, his worst starting position in five Toronto races. This time, he was uncharacteristically calm about his results. "I guess I'm a little older, more mature," he told the Toronto *Sun*. "A couple of years ago, I would have probably thrown a temper tantrum. I used to get real ticked off when I wasn't in the top five."

The 1996 Molson Indy was a good race for no one, even winner Adrian Fernandez, whose first win was marred by the deaths of driver Jeff Krosnoff and volunteer track worker Gary Avrin. Krosnoff's car touched wheels with Stefan Johansson's car and flipped end over end down the Lakeshore straightaway, striking Avrin as he stood in a grassy area near the edge of the track. It was a subdued postrace for all of the drivers.

A chipped vertebra, a soft-tissue injury to his lower back, and bruised knees took the fun out of Tracy's early qualifying efforts on the high banks of the Michigan International Speedway. While Tracy was third fastest in Friday qualifying, on Saturday morning he spun his Penske Mercedes Ilmor and backed it into the wall at approximately 217 mph. He was treated at the hospital in Jackson, Michigan, before being flown back home to Phoenix. His first words to Penske publicist Susan Bradshaw after being treated at the hospital were "Was I still fastest?" While he was able to walk to the ambulance following the crash, Tracy would miss the Michigan race and the following race at the Mid-Ohio Sports Car Course. Oddly enough, reports suggested that he wasn't up to full speed in the Penske car when the crash occurred. It wasn't his first brush with the Michigan walls, but he'd done hundreds of laps on the track since breaking his leg there in his first start with the Penske team in 1992. At

Road America, still feeling the effects of the Michigan crash, Tracy slid into the gravel on the eighth lap and eventually finished 12th.

CART's contingent of aggressive drivers, Paul Tracy, Alex Zanardi, and Greg Moore, were told that Big Brother — also known as chief steward Wally Dallenbach — was still watching as they prepared for the street race in Vancouver. Tracy and Zanardi, along with André Ribeiro, were each fined U.S. $20,000 for taking "unjustifiable risks" during the previous race at Road America in Elkhart Lake, Wisconsin. As well, Tracy and Ribeiro were fined another U.S. $20,000 pending their performances in Vancouver and the final race of the season at Laguna Seca. "In the event of any rough driving infractions in these races, the suspended fine will be imposed, along with any additional penalties as determined by the stewards," CART champ car officials said in a statement. The drivers were individually informed of the stewards' actions. Moore, who crashed while trying to pass Ribeiro, and Gil de Ferran, who was shunted out of the race following contact with Zanardi, were told that their driving "had not been satisfactory" and that they were under observation by officials. Michael Andretti could be forgiven for snickering under his helmet. Rising to the opportunity to put his accusers in their place, Andretti won handily, holding off Jimmy Vasser, who desperately wanted to clinch the championship by finishing in the top six in Vancouver but was prevented from doing so by Bryan Herta. With Vasser shaking his fist at Herta, Andretti cruised to the checkered flag and back into the championship race. Zanardi was the early leader but dropped out of contention after striking the wall while attempting a pass on P.J. Jones. Vasser left the race with 142 points, and Andretti now had 128 points and Unser 125. Either one could snatch the championship away from Vasser heading back to California for the last race, but it would be no easy feat.

The sniping, rivalry, and warnings from Dallenbach to the drivers hid an important issue, at least in the eyes of Team Penske's Rick Mears. Mears said after the Vancouver race that many of the incidents during the season had happened because drivers were deliberately blocking one another. For example, Zanardi blamed Jones for braking too early heading into a turn in the Vancouver race, leaving the Italian both angry and out of contention for the championship. One reason Tracy was fined after the Elkhart Lake race was because he collided with Parker Johnstone, who blocked Tracy as he tried to pass on the last lap. "Our officials are working on it. The problems among the drivers have been building for a long time. Maybe the measures to put a stop to it weren't building at the same rate," Mears told the Toronto *Sun*. "Once drivers are warned, the minute they're observed doing it again they ought to be called into the pits immediately for a discussion on the matter. You wouldn't see any repetition after that."

Tracy was glad to see the end of the 1996 season. The championship went to a deserving Jimmy Vasser and had eluded the Canadian yet again. By the end of the season, Tracy's career had sunk into a valley compared to the peaks he'd reached with Penske before joining Andretti at Newman-Haas. Winning two races in the Budweiser car in 1995, Tracy reached the podium just once in 1996 and scored just 60 points toward the championship, his lowest since joining the team full time in 1992. "I was struggling, really struggling, with the car on the road courses. I had a bad season — just in general. The car wasn't very good. We struggled with it and struggled with it. We didn't have a very good year."

Part of his poor performance could be attributed to some personal changes. Out were the glasses and neatly combed hair. In were the contacts and spiky hair, which was already thinning and beginning to turn grey. Out also was the pudgy physique of a kid, and in was the build of a stronger, practiced, broad-shouldered athlete. And gone was his wife, Tara Cormier. Tracy blamed long hours behind the wheel testing and racing and the constant travel as the main factors in the break-up. The couple battled over the custody of their two children, who both live with their mother in Phoenix. Tracy says he sees them regularly.

Tracy met his second wife, Liisa Hunter, at a go-kart race in Phoenix, where she was watching her boyfriend at the time lose to Tracy. He began hanging around the office where she worked and where he stored his karts. "Paul would come in and sit in the office near my desk, but wouldn't say anything," she told the *Toronto Star* in October 1999. "He'd sit there and read these auto racing magazines. One day I asked him if he knew Japanese because he was reading a magazine that was all in Japanese. He said no, he was just looking at the pictures. I said 'that's good,' because he had the magazine upside down." It was still a while before Tracy asked her out on a date. "We were just friends," she said. "We'd go out on double dates but not with each other. However, we'd end up talking to each other and practically ignore our dates." They were married in 1997.

The world of auto racing is in a state of constant change. The drivers, the teams, the mechanics, the tracks, the cars.

Especially the cars. Throughout any season, team engineers and technicians are hard at work trying to coax the most minuscule speed increases out of their high-powered machines. When qualifying times are measured in 10ths of seconds, every adjustment is worthwhile. A season barely starts before a team begins thinking about the next one. So, while Tracy was having a difficult time winning races during the 1996 season, the focus of the Penske team shifted to allow him to use his skills as an excellent test driver to work on the 1997 car while Unser continued to battle away for the title. Roger Penske knew his chances of a championship were slim in 1996, but he wasn't about to wait for the 1997 season to come to him.

The team to beat in 1997 would be Target Chip Ganassi Racing, whose driver, Jimmy Vasser, won the championship in 1996 and celebrated his first race win. He was paired with the always feisty Alex Zanardi, who was sure to provide fans with at least one more tire-smoking doughnut in victory lane in 1997.

Penske, realizing that his team couldn't succeed in its current formation, shuffled personnel during the off-season, but he refused to switch from the underperforming Penske chassis to a more competitive Reynard chassis. Yet the choice of a Penske chassis with a Mercedes Ilmor engine and Goodyear tires would come back to haunt the team.

Off the track and in the boardrooms, the racing series was no longer known as Indy car. The split with the Indy Racing League and the ongoing dispute with Indianapolis Motor Speedway owner Tony George resulted in the series being prevented from using the words *Indy car* to describe itself. It now referred to itself as CART (Championship Auto

Racing Teams), the name of the sanctioning body of the series and the corporation that manages it. Indy car functioned as a recognizable brand name, and CART has yet to build a memorable brand around the current name. Even to the casual fan, NASCAR is instantly identified with stock car racing, but few people — especially the new fans the series wants to attract — know what CART is until someone mentions the series formerly known as Indy car.

Tracy was undergoing some changes of his own at the end of the 1996 season. Despite his underperforming car and spotty success, he felt secure in his four-year contract with Penske and was optimistic about a championship run in 1997. As the season got under way at the 1.5-mile Homestead oval in Florida, Tracy showed that he'd lost none of his drive to win as he chased Michael Andretti to the checkered flag for second place to start the season. Once again the Penske car proved to be unreliable in qualifying, but Tracy was able to wring some hidden power out of it when he started from the 16th spot on the grid. The sticking point was still the Goodyear tires. Both Tracy and Unser complained that the Goodyears still weren't as good as the Firestones that had helped Vasser to the title.

Tracy was nonetheless pleased with his standing at the Homestead race and offered an explanation for his poor performance during 1996. "Last year I would drive with such anger, and it was a distraction," Tracy told the Associated Press after the Homestead race. "But this time I was a lot more relaxed. Hey, this is the first time I've even finished the first race of the season in my [CART] career. Other than not winning, it was a great day."

By the end of the race in Long Beach, the anger and

distraction were back, this time with a dash of attitude. Fingers were being pointed angrily in Tracy's direction, and Paul was being blamed for running a driver off course, damaging a car, and puncturing someone else's tire. The manner in which Tracy starts a racing season — early success followed by promises of a new attitude and a more cautious approach to driving — was becoming a broken record. Greg Moore, Jimmy Vasser, and rookie Paul Jasper were all angry with Tracy. The mainstream media liked to consider the two as fast friends from the moment that Moore joined the series; however, while they shared a home country, they had little else in common. Moore was younger, with a cocky swagger and natural charm that made him a fan and media favourite. Tracy, cut from a darker cloth, was prone to bouts of sullenness when things weren't going his way. While often friendly when spoken to, he rarely cracked a smile and hid behind sunglasses. The one thing they did have in common was their aggression. Moore was starting his CART racing career with the Player's Forsythe team and enough talent to force some extra heroics out of his car. Like Tracy, Moore had no particular reverence for any other driver on the circuit. He was there to win.

In the opening laps of the Long Beach race, just after the first caution period ended, Tracy and Moore collided going into a turn, and Moore was sent spinning off course. By the time he got back onto the pavement, he was four laps off the pace. A malfunctioning fuel pump took him out of the race completely on the 46th lap. As expected, the drivers later had different versions of what had happened. "I braked normally, and Paul did a dive-bomb move, locked up [his wheels under braking], and hit me," said Moore during a radio

A youthful Paul Tracy gets comfortable in Ron Fellows's Formula 1600 Hawk MK-21 at the Shannonville racetrack in September 1982. (Photo courtesy Lynda Fellows)

Paul Tracy is congratulated by team owner Carl Haas (left) and his father Tony after he won the Indy car race at Surfers Paradise in Australia, March 19, 1995. (AP Photo)

Tracy hits the wall in a fiery crash during practice for the Marlboro 500 at Michigan International Speedway on July 27, 1996. (AP Photo)

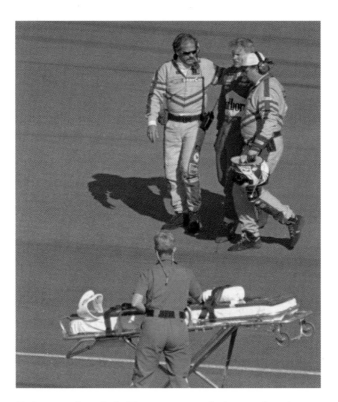

Safety workers help Tracy to an ambulance after the crash. He was airlifted to a hospital in Jackson, Mich., where he was reported to be suffering from a fractured vertebra. (AP Photo)

Paul Tracy's Marlboro Team Penske vent man John Whiteman (centre) and left rear wheel changer Matt Jonsson (second from right) are run into by Tracy in a botched pit stop during the Bosch Spark Plug Grand Prix at Nazareth Speedway on April 28, 1996. Tracy was in the lead at the time of the incident. He locked his brakes as he entered the pit and slid into the wall, sending the two crew members flying. (AP Photo)

Paul Tracy goes airborne after colliding with Christian Fittipaldi at the Toyota Grand Prix of Long Beach on April 5, 1998. (AP Photo)

The late Greg Moore and Tracy chat over a pile of tires at the Toronto Molson Indy on July 16, 1999. (CP Photo)

Paul Tracy gets a hug from Greg Moore's mother Donna after qualifying for the Vancouver Molson Indy on Sept. 2, 2000. Tracy started from second on the grid and went on to take an emotional win. (CP Photo)

Tracy shares the podium with Greg Moore (left) and Gil de Ferran.
(Ramesh Bayney photo)

Al Unser Jr. (right) briefs teammate Paul Tracy on track conditions as Roger Penske listens in before Tracy's final qualifying effort for the Cleveland Grand Prix, July 12, 1997. Tracy started 10th, Unser started 18th. (AP Photo)

Paul Tracy jokingly massages Al Unser Jr. on Nov. 1, 1997, during a photo session for visiting champ car drivers in Japan, in advance of the inaugural race at Twin Ring Motegi in Japan. Christian Fittipaldi stands next to Tracy and Richie Hearn is sitting next to Unser. Tracy was getting ready to begin his first season with Team Kool Green. (AP Photo)

Tracy offers congratulations to Michael Andretti after Andretti won the
Marlboro Grand Prix of Miami at Homestead on March 2, 1997. Tracy finished
in second place. (AP Photo)

Former Target Chip Ganassi driver Juan Montoya greets Paul Tracy before their practice runs at the Molson Indy in Toronto, July 16, 2000. (CP Photo)

Juan Montoya gets hung up by Tracy and P.J. Jones on the victory podium after Montoya won the race at Nazareth Speedway on May 2, 1999. Jones finished second and Tracy third. (AP Photo)

Tracy leads the victory celebrations after his 'last-to-first' win at Road America on August 20, 2000. Adrian Fernandez (left) and Kenny Brack joined Tracy in the spray. (Ramesh Bayney photo)

Team Kool Green teammates Dario Franchitti and Paul Tracy smile for the camera.
(Ramesh Bayney photo)

Hanging out trackside with friend and competitor Jimmy Vasser.
(Ramesh Bayney photo)

The Team Kool Green pit crew takes a look at Tracy's number 26 car.
(Ramesh Bayney photo)

Tracy confers with team owner Barry Green in the pits.
(Ramesh Bayney photo)

Sporting green hair, Paul Tracy waits to qualify for the Marlboro 500 on October 28, 2000, at the California Speedway in Fontana, Calif. (AP Photo)

Tracy plays on Lake Ontario in front of the Toronto skyline on July 17, 1997. (CP Photo)

After a practice round for the Marlboro 500 at the California Speedway in Fontana, Calif., Tracy takes a call on his cell phone in the pits on Oct. 30, 1998. (AP Photo)

Sylvester Stallone chats with Tracy at the premiere of Stallone's film *Driven* at Mann's Chinese Theater in Hollywood, April 16, 2000.

After doing donuts and attracting some police attention, Tracy checks out his signature in rubber at the Canadian National Exhibition grounds in Toronto. Tracy was making a promotional appearance for the Molson Indy on June 18, 2001. (CP Photo)

interview. "Paul did something stupid — again." Tracy said he'd got a clear run on Moore and had held the line going into the corner. "I was on the inside and he moved over right as I got beside him," he said to the Toronto *Sun*. "I locked up and we hit wheels and it kind of knocked him off." Tracy managed to stay in the race to finish seventh but was also hit by Jasper as Tracy came out of the pits. He struggled for the rest of the race, ran as high as fourth, but then spun out, allowing Al Unser Jr. and Parker Johnstone by him. To compound problems, Vasser complained that Tracy hit him at the start of the race, causing a punctured tire. Tracy countered by saying he was actually the one who was hit as he and the rest of the field tried to manoeuvre around a putt-putting Roberto Moreno.

Tracy's name was coming up often following such incidents. Some occurred when Paul was racing for position, but others came as a result of his own machismo, however misplaced. Witness his run-in with Alex Zanardi as the two raced in Australia. Zanardi moved over on Tracy, who didn't give way. He was just doing what his father had taught him to do — make other drivers fight every lap of the race for the victory. Tracy later admitted that the move, which knocked him out of the race and forced him to sacrifice valuable championship points, was more about rattling sabres than it was about good racing. "It's a principle sort of thing with me. He's the kind of driver who will try to intimidate you, and, if you let him get away with it once, it will happen all season long." For all his talk about maturity and adopting a new outlook, Tracy still wasn't going to let another driver push him around on the track.

Tracy answered his critics going into the next race on the

Nazareth oval, one of three tracks owned by Roger Penske. Not only did he win the pole, but he also set a record for the fastest lap ever on a one-mile track with an average speed of 191.174 mph and a time of 18.831 seconds, beating his 1996 record of 18.874 seconds. Michael Andretti was next in line, followed by rookie Canadian Patrick Carpentier. Tracy thought he had the car to win the race, praising it as a "great short-oval car" (and tacitly admitting that it wasn't as great on superspeedways or street courses). And win the race he did, ending a 27-race dry spell for him and providing the Penske team with a welcome downpour after a long and incredibly difficult drought.

Not that the win was easy — Tracy had Andretti to contend with for most of the day. Andretti's Swift Ford Cosworth was much better than Tracy's Penske Mercedes in traffic, and Andretti passed Tracy on the 35th lap only to have a tire deflate, which forced him to pit and handed the lead back to Tracy. Andretti dropped a lap off the pace, but in his typically fearless style he roared back to pass Al Unser Jr. for second place on the 177th lap of the 225-lap race. Andretti was first helped and then hindered by the unusual number of caution flags — 76 laps were run under yellow flags — which allowed him to get close but never close enough to overtake Tracy. He hounded Tracy as much as he could until Juan Fangio's burning car brought out the last caution flag three laps from the end of the race. Unser rolled home in third spot, and Penske made an unusual appearance in victory lane to greet his driver, who promptly planted a big kiss on the staid businessman's cheek in celebration.

Tracy's doubts about his car were now quickly becoming distant memories. His trip to Brazil for the Rio 400 resulted in another win when Paul picked his way through a series of crashes to take the lead when Bobby Rahal pitted with two laps to go after running out of fuel. Tracy himself had just enough fuel to take the car home and gambled that he had more than Rahal after the three-time series champion pitted to fill up earlier in the race than the Canadian. To those watching or driving in the race, including Rahal, the Rio 400 appeared to belong to the veteran. "He was so fast on the straightaway that, barring traffic or a bad mistake on his part, I didn't think I would have been able to overtake him," Tracy told the Associated Press. "I had to push him to make him run out of fuel." Tracy's sneaky strategy worked. "I'm numb," said Rahal. "My fuel gauge said I had more fuel, but it coughed coming out of the corner, and I just ran out. I led all the laps but the one that counted."

Heading into the Gateway track near St. Louis, Tracy found himself in an unusual position. He was leading the PPG Cup point standings, and he was now the unofficial number-one driver on the Penske team. Unser had held that title, but Tracy's two consecutive wins and strong qualifying sessions meant that it was now his to hold. While quick to point out that Unser could just as easily have taken the lead were it not for some bad luck, Tracy also relished the role of being a top performer working for one of the most demanding bosses in racing. After all, it had its perks. The cars were set up identically, but the driver who was on a hot streak got the new parts first.

Tracy put himself next to Raul Boesel on the front row for the Motorola 300 at Gateway International Raceway, happy with the performance of his Penske Mercedes Ilmor. With an average speed of 187.739 mph, he was happier still that he'd got ahead of teammate Al Unser Jr. and fellow Canadian Greg Moore.

From the moment the green flag dropped, the race became a classic Paul Tracy drive. He dropped from second at the start to 19th and a lap behind when he pitted under a green flag. It turned out to be an inspired move by the crew to call him in at that time. He went into the pits on the same lap as race leader Boesel after all the other drivers on the lead lap pitted under a yellow flag. Tracy, using all of the track instead of just the line the more cautious racers had drawn around the centre of the track, eventually set his sights on Patrick Carpentier, who'd now picked up the lead with two laps left. Heading toward what he thought would be the first victory of his young CART career, the French Canadian had a more pressing matter on his mind: he was running out of fuel. Not far behind him, but busy dicing wheel to wheel with Unser, Zanardi, and de Ferran, was Tracy. His dash around the track drew the crowd of 48,500 to its feet as Carpentier watched the red-and-white Marlboro car grow bigger in his mirrors. Carpentier's fuel situation was getting worse when his team owner, Tony Bettenhausen, came on the radio and told Patrick to slow down or he'd never make it to the end. "I was full-out in fifth gear trying to pull out a longer lead," Carpentier told the Toronto *Sun*. "Finally I gave in and shifted into sixth, then as soon as Tony told me 'good job,' I went back to fifth. My hope was that Paul wouldn't be able to get by Gil and Alex to get at me. Then I looked in my mirrors and said 'he's coming, Tony, I can see him,' and he said 'I can see him, too.'" Carpentier knew he was beat and let Tracy pass without a battle, content to take second place in just his third CART race. "This rates as one of the most exciting races I've ever had," said Tracy. "Certainly the best since Louden [New Hampshire, in 1993], when I was the one being run down by Nigel Mansell, and he got me."

Tracy had just won the 99th race for Marlboro Team Penske and had given both himself and the team a taste of redemption. With cars and drivers as closely matched as they are on the CART circuit, it's very difficult for any team or any driver to dominate. Not that Tracy was dominating the series after winning three straight races, but he was leading the points standings. More importantly, from a professional perspective, in his fifth year of full-time racing, he was finally living up to the potential that many racing observers believed he always had. His father, Roger Penske, and even his racing nemesis Michael Andretti knew that he could be fast and successful on the track, but they also knew that he had to put his attitude and his desire to simply be fast on hold or he'd be doomed to a career with flashes of brilliance but little sustained success. Andretti had become adept at exploiting Tracy's weaknesses and would sometimes lie in wait for the Canadian to make a mistake, thinking of him as one of his closest rivals. Tracy was no stranger to winning races, but most drivers and fans thought he'd show moments of brilliance only to flatten his car against a wall or shake his fist at a fellow driver. Now he was winning races with one hand on the steering wheel and with the other shaking a fist at his fellow drivers.

Perhaps the wins made Tracy realize that he was more than just a driver on a racetrack. He appeared to realize, and not a moment too soon considering his dreadful 1996 season, that he was part of one of the best teams in racing and that, if he wanted to win the championship, he couldn't do it alone. He had to drive smarter and think of the larger goal of taking home the trophy at the end of the season. He hoped that it was Penske's goal also and that the team owner intended to provide the best car for him to take the CART championship.

In 1990, Al Unser Jr. scored four consecutive wins, when the series was called Indy car, on his way to winning his first championship title. As Tracy's teammate in 1997, he had to watch as the Canadian, who'd pushed himself into the role of the Penske team's number-one driver, took a run at that record at the famed Milwaukee Mile in West Allis, Wisconsin. Tracy was up for the challenge, especially on the track where he won in 1995 and finished third in 1996. What appealed to him about the Milwaukee track was that, with its low-banked turns, he could easily run side by side with almost any other CART driver, and he was looking forward to a closely fought race. Coming into it, he was overjoyed with his recent success, calling his three wins in a row a career "milestone." Before the seventh race of the season, Tracy was leading the drivers' standings with 86 points, and his closest rival, the hard-charging Zanardi, who'd won the race at Long Beach, now had 67 points.

Excessive speed was an issue once again during qualifying. In the Saturday attempts, Tracy qualified third fastest and was among the pack of 22 drivers who smashed the 165.752 mph track record set by Raul Boesel in 1994. Tracy went a whopping 180.595 mph but was beaten to the early pole by Patrick Carpentier, who set a speed of 182.144 mph in his Goodyear-shod Reynard Mercedes. Mauricio Gugelmin came between Tracy and Carpentier with a speed of 182.073 mph also driving a Reynard Mercedes but shod with Firestones. One reason for the jump in speed was the repaving done in the off-season (making the Milwaukee Mile, strangely enough, now 1.032 miles long), giving it a smoother surface. Tracy knew the better surface would lead to higher race speeds, and as a result cornering would be trickier and driving in traffic more difficult than the previous year.

Tracy's feud with Zanardi dragged on into Milwaukee, where the two exchanged words following Saturday practice. Zanardi believed Tracy had deliberately got in his way as revenge for a close call earlier in the session. The confrontation ended with Tracy saying that Zanardi had threatened to kill him. Zanardi's response after the race was "I need my car to try and win races and not to get in other people's way or to kill people."

Despite the clash with Zanardi, Tracy managed to better his Saturday lap record and knock Carpentier off the pole with a speed of 184.286 mph and a time of 20.106 seconds. He would start with a clear view of the track and a clear picture of himself winning his fourth straight race. Gugelmin started alongside Tracy, with Carpentier and Boesel in the second row and Parker Johnstone and Greg Moore in the third.

Tying Unser's record of four consecutive wins in a season wasn't in the cards for Tracy. The Penske Mercedes returned to its old tricks, and he struggled with it the entire afternoon. He still managed to turn the fastest lap but was outshone by Moore, who at 22 years, one month, and 10 days became the youngest driver in CART history to win a race. He led for 104 straight laps, never fell below his starting position of fifth, and was able to beat Tracy twice on restarts. When Tracy and the others on the lead lap pitted on lap 135, Moore's crew opted to keep Greg out, and he led the pack to the checkered flag.

Zanardi and Tracy were still squabbling after the race. Tracy accused the Italian of blocking him about halfway through the race when Zanardi had fallen well off the pace. "It was very, very difficult to get by him," Tracy told the Toronto *Sun.* "I don't know what he was thinking. He's two laps down and I'm racing for the lead." With a sixth-place finish, Tracy held on to the series lead with 94 points, and Andretti moved ahead of Zanardi with 70 points after finishing second.

In Detroit for the next race, Tracy, along with several other drivers, had a bizarre qualifying session in the Motor City. Greg Moore fishtailed his way around the track trying to increase his speed. Scott Pruett crashed during the first qualifying session as did Mauricio Gugelmin, who was lucky to avoid serious injury when a wheel that he thought was heading directly for his head instead bounced away and landed in Lake Tacoma, a large pond on Belle Isle. A track worker eventually used scuba gear to find it.

Tracy also became involved in another feud, this time with Moore, whom Tracy accused of using unfair tactics to slow him down during qualifying and ruining one of his fast laps. Moore had run his fast lap, and Tracy was held up as he tried to run his. Tracy angrily said that Moore should have moved out of the way while other drivers were trying to qualify; Moore said that he tried to let Tracy past but that it was difficult on a tight road course such as Belle Isle, and he maintained that he had every right to be out there because he was working on his race setup. Gugelmin's crash, while frightening for the Brazilian, also caused a headache for Tracy. He was in the midst of completing his fast lap when the session was red-flagged because wreckage blocked the track. He would have been third fastest had he been able to complete the run. So the winner of three of the past four races was scheduled to start the Detroit race in 12th spot.

But he didn't start at all. It turned out that all the flying around the track and the high g-loads on his neck had left Paul with badly strained neck muscles. That injury was coupled with an upper respiratory ailment. During the warm-up before the race, Tracy experienced dizziness and blurred vision and pulled the car back into the pits. So, mere hours before the race, he flew home to Phoenix, where he underwent a magnetic resonance imaging (MRI) scan after being checked out by CART doctors at the Detroit track. CART's doctors determined the dizziness was caused only by heavy lateral g-loads during cornering. Tracy was disappointed, of course, to give up championship points but expected to be out only until the next race in Portland.

Moore won the race, his second win in a row. His total of 85 points moved him into third place, behind Andretti. Tracy still held the championship lead with 94 points.

Following the MRI, which came up negative, Tracy's condition was diagnosed as benign paroxysmal positional vertigo after a visit to the Mayo Clinic in Rochester, Minnesota. Shortly after the Detroit race, Tracy was supposed to try driving his car again, but tests done at the Mayo Clinic were able to bring on the dizziness that he experienced behind the wheel. Doctors at the clinic said the vertigo could be the result of a chest infection, and Tracy had developed a cold before the Detroit race. To overcome the problem, he had to wear a neck brace and keep his head perfectly stable for a few days, even having to sleep upright. But he was eager to rid himself of some of that discomfort and score some additional points during the race in Portland.

Rainy weather caused that race to end at the two-hour time limit, after the racers had completed 78 of 98 laps. Mark Blundell in his Reynard Mercedes beat Gil de Ferran in his Reynard Honda by 27/1,000ths of a second — the closest finish in CART history, beating the previous record of 43/1,000ths of a second set when Al Unser Jr. beat Scott Goodyear to the finish line at the 1992 Indianapolis 500. Tracy fought a valiant battle and finished seventh, moving his points total to 100. None of his daring was dimmed by the time away, but his judgement may have been impaired. He was the first driver to switch to slick tires as the rain began to clear. It turned out to be too soon when he slid off the track.

But it wasn't just Tracy's judgement that led to the off-course excursion. The Penske car was also returning to its ill-performing ways, lacking grip on the course's low-speed corners. His crew tried to remedy the problem by adding more down force to the car in testing sessions between the races at Portland and Cleveland. That only slowed the car further. Still, Tracy was optimistic that the team had found the right setup as they headed to the wide straightaways of Burke Lakefront Airport in Cleveland. Now in the second half of the CART season, his lead in the championship was threatened, and he needed the best car on the track if he was to put some distance between himself and Andretti and Moore, not to mention Zanardi.

The main problem with the Penske Mercedes was its aerodynamics, said Tracy.

The underwing wasn't very good on the car. You had to run the car really, really stiff and low, and on the ovals that's okay because the tracks are smooth, so you can run the car low to the ground. But when you go to street courses and road courses, they're bumpy and rough, and there are manhole covers, and you've got to get the car off the ground to clear some of this stuff, and the suspension needs to be soft. On the street courses, you've got to run soft because the corners are tight, and the stiffer you run the car the less grip you have in slow corners. In a 30 mph corner, you're running really stiff springs, and there's no grip, but that's the way we had to run the car, because if you raised the car off the ground and ran soft springs the underwing didn't work very well.

So it wasn't any good, and they were not willing to make changes. I said, "Let's switch cars to a Reynard." And they said, "Well, we're working on next year's car, we'll just wait until next year." I said, "I might not have next year." Then, at the end of the year, the last three or four races, they bought a Reynard and started testing. It was way better, but they bought it to do evaluations with.

Zanardi won in Cleveland and celebrated by spinning six doughnuts after crossing the finish line. Neither Andretti nor Moore finished the race, and Tracy fought from 17th place to finish seventh again. The win gave Zanardi another 20 points, and Tracy moved up to 106 points, with Moore at 95.

Until this point in the series, which was heading to Toronto, Tracy had managed to make an underperforming car into a championship contender. He'd duelled for the championship before, but in 1997 he was showing more consistency than in the past, despite missing a race because of his illness. He gathered points in seven straight races and finished steadily in the top 12 despite some poor qualifying results. The only time he finished lower than seventh was when he tangled with Zanardi. And Tracy and Andretti agreed that not only finishing races but also placing well were going to be crucial to the championship as the teams headed to the two 500-mile speedway races left on the schedule following the Molson Indy in Toronto. "The two keys are Michigan and Fontana, running well and finishing," Tracy told the Toronto *Sun*. "That's because of the high possibility of mechanical failure, when 40 points are available." Andretti added, "First finish all the races, but those two are the hardest to finish."

Leading the CART series coming into the Molson Indy was something new for Tracy, and it didn't go unnoticed by his teammates. Former CART champ and current adviser to Marlboro Penske Racing, Rick Mears told the *Sun* that Tracy had finally matured to the point where he was comfortable competing and not winning every race and that he'd become smarter when it came to winning races. Mears believed Tracy would always be in the spotlight because he was naturally aggressive, but he'd also draw attention when he began to calm down. Paul was learning to make aggressive moves when appropriate, and Mears believed that such judgement would be the key to his long-term success. A perfect example of the new attitude, Mears said, came when Paul admitted to his crew over the radio at Homestead that they didn't have the car to beat Andretti that day. As well, Tracy's chief mechanic, Clive Powell, was impressed that Tracy drove hard and well even though he was angry following a penalty that dropped him to 17th spot from third spot in Cleveland.

Tracy knew that his biggest competition in Toronto would come from Greg Moore and Michael Andretti. Andretti was making the Toronto track his second home after several wins there. Moore was hungry for another win. Neither won the pole — that went to Dario Franchitti — but Moore outqualified Tracy and landed ninth on the grid. A disappointed Tracy was down in 13th spot, again because of a poorly performing car. Frustrated, he said that he and Unser had tried to get the best out of the car, but it appeared to be designed incorrectly. "It's never the same from lap to lap," he said after qualifying. "It's like sitting on top of a crocodile. You never know which way it's going to go." He was only able to keep up during a race, he added, because race speeds aren't as high as qualifying speeds. What worked on ovals didn't appear to work on street courses.

Tracy finished 10th in the race and wasn't happy about it. Mark Blundell won his second race of the season, and Alex Zanardi finished second. Tracy was fortunate to hang on to the points lead with 109, but Zanardi was creeping forward and ended his day with 106. Moore notched a DNF, and Andretti didn't add a lot of points — those were the only bright spots of the day for Tracy. He wasn't happy with his car, and he wasn't holding back. "Everybody says 'good job' when you finish 10th, but I'd rather stay home than finish 10th," he told the *Sun*. Oddly enough, his team didn't back him up this time. Dan Luginbuhl, Penske's second in command, said that there was nothing wrong with the car and that it would be fine for the next race, in Michigan. Tracy wasn't convinced, insisting that the car needed to be much better if he was going to win the championship. He hoped that improvements could be made to the car before the race at Elkhart Lake in August.

Looking back, Tracy sees the Toronto race in 1997 as the "beginning of the end" of his time with Penske.

> *I drove my balls off like crazy and qualified at the back. I outqualified Al every weekend by half a second or more, so he was no better off than I was, and we were both qualifying at the back of the field every weekend on the road courses. I'd won three races to start the season off on the ovals and was leading the championship, and I basically knew that this was the beginning of the end of me trying to win the championship, because we were going into the road course swing of the season.*
>
> *I was racing in Toronto — the biggest race of the year for me — and I drove my heart out the whole race, and I ended up finishing 10th, and at the time I'd never driven as hard as I drove that day to end up 10th. I got out of the car, and I was just pissed about it, and I exploded on TV and said the car was basically no good and we need to do something pretty drastic, and that upset Penske. . . . That was kind of the beginning of the end between the two of us.*

At the next race, at Michigan International Speedway, owned by Roger Penske, drivers were concerned about crashing. Speeds were approaching 240 mph, and the concrete walls that rimmed the track were unforgiving. Emerson Fittipaldi had his career-ending crash there in 1996, as did Danny Sullivan in 1993. Some drivers wanted to remove the track from the schedule altogether, but they knew that fans were always treated to a spectacle there. There had been some discussion about shock-absorbing walls, but they are very expensive and hadn't been tested extensively anywhere.

The race was just as tough on cars as it was on drivers. Greg Moore's car gave out after just 19 laps. Bobby Rahal led for 25 laps, and Scott Pruett led for 32, but both ended up crashing in turn two. Dario Franchitti and Michael Andretti both dropped out with transmission failure, and Raul Boesel and Jimmy Vasser also suffered from broken transmissions. Tracy, still not happy with his car, finished fourth. Its telemetry broke down during the race, and the radio went dead, cutting off most communication to the pits. To make matters worse, Tracy's helmet was stolen from the Penske transporter before the race. While the result wasn't as bad as it could have been, Zanardi now assumed the championship lead with 127 points to Tracy's 121.

Tracy's poor luck continued in Mid-Ohio, where during qualifying his Goodyear tires came apart, as they did on cars driven by Al Unser Jr., Gil de Ferran, and Christian Fittipaldi. The problem was later corrected after a fault was found in a certain batch of tires but not before an unhappy Tracy qualified in 15th spot on the grid. He was hoping for a top-10 or top-12 finish but had to settle for no points after dropping out of the race following a collision he couldn't avoid. Zanardi took the win and added to his points. He now had 148 points, and just a maximum of 22 points was left up for grabs in the season. Andretti said he was pretty much out of the running, and Tracy knew he needed luck and a good car if he was going to seriously challenge Zanardi. He wasn't hopeful he'd have either.

As the teams headed to Road America, Tracy wasn't the only one upset over the performance of his car. Unser was also frustrated and had gone without a win all season. He hadn't finished 7 of the 13 races to that point, six because of mechanical failure. He also thought that fans assumed it was his fault that the car wasn't performing well because, after all, Penske owned the team, and Marlboro was one of the most generous sponsors, so how could he not have the best car in the field? Tracy's race at Road America lasted less than a lap after Gualter Salles's car spun in front of Paul, sending him into the infield and flipping him upside down.

At Vancouver, Tracy continued to exercise his right to free speech about the Penske car, saying that he'd be a force to be reckoned with if he was driving a Reynard. "I believe I'd win the championship if we had Reynards and our package was otherwise unchanged," Tracy said. "Certainly, we'd be more competitive." Penske spokespeople said that Reynard had become more competitive because, with more than 20 cars on the track, it was able to improve the cars as the season progressed, something Marlboro Team Penske couldn't do with its two cars. By the time the teams reached Vancouver, Penske had all but given up on the 1997 car and was working on the 1998 car, scheduled to begin testing in November. Vancouver was still another washout for Tracy. He went out on the first lap, Mauricio Gugelmin went on to take the win, and Zanardi continued on a tear.

Tracy didn't fare much better in the Toyota Grand Prix of Monterey. Although he had one of his best qualifying efforts of the season, starting from 12th spot, a blown engine ended his day and didn't give him any more points.

Going into the final race at Fontana's California Speedway, Alex Zanardi had clinched the 1997 championship. As speeds soared into the 240 mph range during qualifying, Tracy and Unser believed their cars had a great chance of winning the race given their performance on ovals. Zanardi crashed in qualifying, and Patrick Carpentier suffered a concussion during another qualifying crash. Tracy didn't stay in the race long enough to see whether the Penske car could make the 500-mile trip. He crashed when his car went off the racing line and into the marbles on the 12th lap. Mark Blundell went on to grab his third win of the season. Tracy had failed to finish a race between the U.S. 500 and the final race of the season, and he finished fourth overall.

On October 9, Tracy's career with Penske came to a sudden stop. His manager, Dave Stevenson, called Paul at home to say that Penske had arranged a meeting with him and a new sponsor and that Tracy was expected to attend it. Paul flew to San Diego for the meeting, met a Penske team representative at a hotel, and was fired. "This is what I didn't like about what happened," Tracy said.

> I had two years on my contract left, and I got a call from my manager, and he said, "Hey, Penske's going to be in San Diego. He wants you to fly over, and you're going to go to lunch with some potential sponsors." So I fly over there, and we show up at the hotel and go up to his room, and it's Penske's attorney and a representative from the team, and they basically told me in three minutes that I was fired and being let go of my contract, and that was it.

Tracy had considered that Penske wouldn't take kindly to his car being criticized, but he'd been looking ahead to testing next season's car when he was fired. He'd thought the situation had been smoothed over. So he did what every driver does when left without a ride. He started working the phones.

CHAPTER SIX

Swimming in the Kool Green

1998-99

Paul Tracy didn't want to be looking for a team for the 1998 season. But that's what he and his manager were doing. While plenty of teams would have been interested in signing him, most had secured their 1998 lineups by early summer. It was now late fall. "The first call that I made was to [Gerald] Forsythe at the Player's team, and he was committed already to Greg [Moore] and [Patrick] Carpentier, so there was nothing he could do," Tracy said. "I made four or five phone calls to people, and everyone was committed. There were no rides. Then I talked to Barry [Green]. They had talked about running two cars. . . ." Green told him that the team wanted to sign another driver, but they couldn't come to terms, so they decided just to stay with Dario Franchitti. But Green mentioned that Brown & Williamson, the maker of the Kool cigarette brand, might want to add Tracy to the lineup. Green told Tracy that he'd get back to him. Eventually, they came to terms. Tracy signed to a one-year deal worth U.S. $1.5 million, half of what he'd been earning at Penske, but the contract included incentives such as performance bonuses. The 1998 season opened with Tracy taking his first spins in the Team Kool Green car, a team that would have a more significant effect on his career than the Penske team.

As manager of Forsythe-Green Racing, Green was instrumental in squiring Jacques Villeneuve to his Indianapolis 500 win as well as his CART championship. By signing both Tracy and Franchitti, Green immediately positioned the team as one of the leaders among CART competitors, ready to tackle top teams such as Penske and Newman-Haas. Green has been called a "hands-on" team owner, and he was ready for what many believed would be a trying time for the Australian as he attempted to push Tracy toward the same success he'd enjoyed with Villeneuve. Green had a reputation of being a good man to work for, and while he believed in winning he didn't believe in the militaristic regime that powered the Penske team.

Franchitti, a Scotsman with an Italian father, had spent 1997 with Hogan Racing and been runner up for rookie of the year. He was a smooth and fast driver who'd been schooled in the European racing minor leagues of touring cars and Formula Three. He'd shown promise with Hogan and was looking for a seat in a faster car, finding it with Team Green. He'd also made it clear that one day he wanted to compete in Formula One.

His new teammate, Tracy, had shown that he was a force to be reckoned with on the track. Driving for Marlboro Team Penske, one of the richest and most powerful teams on the circuit, had given him access to some of the best equipment

— most of the time — and some much-needed testing time on tough racetracks such as Nazareth. But he'd also shown a penchant for aggressive driving and trying to make up the difference himself when the car wasn't performing at its peak, often ending up in a crash.

The man who'd occupy his seat at Penske for the 1998 season was Brazilian André Ribeiro. Ribeiro, 31, had finished in 14th spot in the 1997 championship and had spent his first three seasons in CART with Tasman Motorsports Group, run by Steve Horne. He had three CART wins to his credit.

No Fear's Jim Hancock remembers how despondent Tracy was when Penske fired him. "He was totally unprepared for it," said Hancock. But it didn't take Paul as long as he expected to find another ride. During the 1997 season, Hancock knew Paul was in trouble. While he'd progressed as a team ambassador since his early days on the team, he'd slipped back into his old habits and become difficult to deal with, as illustrated by his public criticism of the car and the team. So Hancock was asked to step in and act as an unofficial adviser to Tracy. His job was to get the driver back on track. To get him focused on racing and winning. "I was called by Roger Penske to a number of races to calm Paul down," said Hancock.

He'd get out of the car and say it was a piece of crap. In the motorhome, we'd talk, and I'd say "You can't say that. Look whose name is on the front of that car. Say it's loose into the turn or something like that — but you're making personal statements, and he's going to take it that way." I told him "If I had 10 equally matched cars, I wouldn't pick you to drive one of them.

If I had the 10 cars and the engineer and the team manager, then maybe."

Hancock tried to stress to Tracy that racing was not just about driving and winning. In most ways, it was like any other business. Penske certainly considered it such and was not willing to work with people who didn't want to work for him or weren't willing to act as a part of the company. Hancock also knew that, whether Paul admitted it or not, he was beginning to feel stifled by the atmosphere at Penske. He was being told what to do and how to appear, and he didn't receive as much coaching as he needed or wanted. Yet, despite Hancock's intervention, Tracy continued to be difficult to work with, and eventually Penske had enough.

But Hancock agrees that Tracy and Team Kool Green are a much better fit than Tracy and Penske or even Tracy and Newman-Haas. "It's better for him on a number of levels; they're more respectful of his emotional and psychological being," he says. Tracy agrees that Team Kool Green has been better for him. What he appreciates most is that he doesn't feel like he's working for a giant corporation.

> *When I started on the team, it was very small, and it was a bunch of guys that had worked together for a long time. It was more of a fraternity almost. There's really not a lot of bureaucracy, voting, and engineering. If they want to do something, they just go and do it, whereas with Penske there was Penske Cars and Penske Racing. There was, like, 180 employees total. When I went to Team Green, there was only 40, a lot smaller . . . group. And they were committed to Reynard and*

Honda, and that was the package I wanted to be with. It's just totally different. The way things are run is totally different. They don't sit down and have board meetings and decide what you're going to do and have a vote on it. It works better for me.

By 1998, Barry Green had had a distinguished career in auto racing and was respected within the sport. While he'd had success running Indy cars, he was really just getting started. Like many other team managers, he got his start as a driver in karts, Formula Fords, and Formula Three cars. He worked as a Formula One mechanic in the early 1970s with Team Surtees and was an owner-driver on the F3 circuit in 1978 and 1979. He moved up to become the chief mechanic for film star Paul Newman's Newman Racing Can-Am team, which finished second in 1981 with Teo Fabi driving and third in 1983 with Danny Sullivan at the wheel. The team also earned five wins and six poles. From there, Green moved up to the big leagues and became the crew chief for Forsythe Racing, a team run by Gerald Forsythe, in 1983. (That was the year that Fabi, the diminutive Italian and Indy car rookie, racing against drivers such as A.J. Foyt and Mario Andretti, stunned the American racing world by winning six poles — including that of the Indianapolis 500 — and taking the checkered flag four times. He went on to be named rookie of the year.) Green went on to become the crew chief at Kraco Racing, working with well-known drivers such as Michael Andretti and Bobby Rahal. From 1990 to 1992, Green managed Galles-Kraco Racing and started to have some big-league success. Al Unser Jr. won the 1990 CART championship with the team, while teammate Bobby Rahal placed fourth in the standings; the team earned 11 wins that year. In 1992, Unser won the Indy 500, and teammate Danny Sullivan took the Long Beach Grand Prix. The following year, Green approached Forsythe again to form the Forsythe-Green Formula Atlantic team, with sponsorship from Imperial Tobacco's Players brand and with Canadians Jacques Villeneuve and Claude Bourbonnais handling the driving. Villeneuve grabbed rookie-of-the-year honours, and Bourbonnais finished second in the points. Both drivers' performances were good enough for the entire team to take the step up to CART racing in 1994. Forsythe told *On Track* magazine in May 1994 that Green had handpicked his team — hiring Tony Cicale, whom he described as "the best race engineer in the business" (he'd worked with Mario Andretti) — to coach Villeneuve and prepare him to compete against the veterans of champ car racing. It was in 1994 that Villeneuve was named CART rookie of the year and won his first race, at the Road America track. In 1995, he won the Indy 500 — after recovering from a two-lap deficit — and took the Indy car championship. In 1996, Green formed Team Green and ran a Ford Reynard car for Brazilian Raul Boesel under sponsorship from Brahma Sports. In 1997, he formed Team Kool Green and began an association with Honda and Firestone. He hired Parker Johnstone (currently an ESPN CART race commentator) to drive the Honda Reynard, and together they managed five top-five finishes.

The 1998 season with Team Kool Green would prove to be a difficult one for Tracy. After his expulsion from the Penske team, he'd hoped to find a team he could stay with for a while and in turn develop a more mature approach to racing. Those hopes would remain unfulfilled. What appeared to be the lowest point of the season came when Tracy became involved in an altercation with Green at the race in Houston. After starting from the second row, he was following the race-leading Franchitti and pushed the Scotsman from behind, causing a collision and taking himself out of the race. That led to a finger-pointing and shouting match between Tracy and Green, and the photo that appeared on sports pages the next day showed Tracy holding Green by the shirt front as crew members reached out to restrain him. But the season would become worse still. After crashing in the final race of the season, in Fontana, California (with $1 million at the finish line for the winner), Tracy found out that he'd start the next season under suspension as a result of a collision with Michael Andretti in Australia. As David Phillips wrote in *Racer* magazine in December 1999, it was "a none-too-subtle omen that the sins of the past were to be visited upon him in the final year of the millennium."

By the fourth race of the 1998 season, Tracy had yet to see the checkered flag flying for him despite some solid results in qualifying. At the Nazareth oval, he's consistently turned laps over 190 mph, and in 1998 he did so again, but it wasn't enough to win the race. Part of his lack of success so far was plain bad luck. He was running second in Rio when Gil de Ferran ran into him. A similar accident happened in Long Beach. As Tracy prepared for the race on the Gateway oval, near St. Louis, he tried to explain the situation to Rick Matsumoto of the *Toronto Star*:

> *I feel I'm driving as well as I ever have been. Overall, we've had a lot of disappointments in terms of bad*

luck. The performance of the car's been getting better every weekend. We've qualified better, we've been racing better and we've been running in the top group. In two of the last three races, we've gone out of the race with guys running into us. And that's just bad luck. So I don't think the results speak for how well the car has done. It's just been rotten luck.

That kind of luck would eventually swallow the 1998 season, landing Tracy in 13th spot in the championship standings. It became the season that he'd rather forget.

Despite the incident in Houston, Green signed Tracy to another three years with the team and held on to the Kool sponsorship. Tracy agreed to a deal that extended into 2001, while Franchitti signed on until 2000. Brown and Williamson announced shortly before the signing that it would extend its sponsorship of the team for another three years; it was reportedly worth U.S. $50 million. That money would go toward running Team Green in CART as well as the Team Green Dayton Indy Lights program.

Although 1998 was a terrible year for Tracy, he knew he could draw on the resources of Team Green. Those resources soon included the very experienced Tony Cicale, who joined the team as an engineering consultant after Tracy's engineer, John Dick, left in April 1999. Right from the start, it was clear that Cicale's job would not be that of a typical race engineer. Over the years, he'd developed the skills to figure out not only what makes a race car tick but also what makes a driver tick. He was adept at working on a driver's attitude and confidence level, at getting a driver thinking effectively and performing better. And that's what his job was to be with Tracy.

After working with Jacques Villeneuve in both his Formula Atlantic and Indy car days, Cicale decided to retire. But when Green needed someone to straighten out Tracy's head, he called the veteran race engineer and urged him to come out of retirement. A quiet, bespectacled man, Cicale doesn't look like someone who works with fast cars and macho drivers for a living. An avid sailor and windsurfer, the Connecticut-born Cicale lives in Florida, preferring to grow his own vegetables and catch his own fish. He doesn't shop at a grocery store.

Almost as soon as he came aboard, Cicale could sense Tracy's frustration. As he told *Racer* magazine in December 1999, the first thing he decided to work on was the driver's expectations. He sensed they were too high. While the desire to win is hardwired into a race driver's DNA, Tracy had been trying to win every race, Cicale thought, even when he hadn't had the car to do it. "So I tried to get him to focus on not even thinking about winning a race or getting on the podium, but simply on making no mistakes. . . . Try not to focus on winning the event but, if you can, simply focus on making sure all your decisions are right. Then, ultimately, you'll win." The next area Cicale worked on was getting Tracy to realize that the car he was driving in 1999 was a lot different than the cars he drove for Penske from 1991 to 1997 and the car he drove for Newman-Haas in 1995. If Paul was expecting the same kind of performance or setup in the car, he wasn't going to find it. Cicale stressed that the team's job was to make the best car possible and that Tracy's job was to drive that car as well as possible. "The third thing is just being honest with him," Cicale told *Racer*,

*when he made mistakes to look at the mistakes and say,
"OK, why did we do it that way? What mistakes did I
make in setting up the car? How should I have dealt
with you differently? And, why did you do this?"
Ultimately, he had to accept responsibility for his
mistakes, and I think he's starting to do that. Where in
the beginning of the year he would say, "The car was
lousy," or "The guy ran into me," now he's saying "If I
would have done this differently, then that wouldn't
have happened." That's a real positive because, before
you can change . . . [people, they] have to believe there's
a problem. And I think for many years Paul believed
that it was either bad luck or a problem caused by
someone else, and it wasn't his responsibility.*

The 1999 season opened later for Tracy than it did for all
the other CART drivers, and Tracy, serving CART's first-ever
suspension, watched from the pits as current Indy Racing
League (and former F1 driver) Raul Boesel sat in the cockpit of the number 26 car for the season opener at
Homestead, Florida. But the Canadian was ready to jump
back in the car for the season's second race, at Motegi,
Japan. By then, he was talking again about winning the
championship, and he continued to voice his opinion that
CART had different rules for different drivers and that this
was part of the reason he had to sit out the Homestead race.
But since he was beginning to display a new driving attitude, CART officials told him that as far as they were
concerned he was starting the year with a blank page. Tracy
told journalists in a conference call before the Japan race
that he was just as aggressive as he'd always been, but the key

to his success in 1999 would be to properly channel that aggression. He also shrugged off suggestions that he was too aggressive, knowing that some fans still loved to see him mix it up on the track with other drivers. "It's a double-edged sword," he said. "You're a hero if you pull off an aggressive pass and make it work. If it doesn't come off, you're an idiot. You're not going to win races by sitting idle and waiting for people to fall off the track. You've got to be aggressive to win races. You've got to take chances. If you don't, then you're a 10th-place runner, and you won't be around long."

Tracy was showing a bit of rust when he started 10th and finished 11th in Japan, collided with another car while leaving the pits about halfway through the race in Long Beach, and then redeemed himself with a third-place finish at Nazareth in May. It was his first visit to the podium since he won at Gateway in 1997. He went on to finish 15th in Brazil and was classified 19th at Gateway, but he went out of the race after colliding with his teammate, Dario Franchitti, on lap 148 of the 236-lap race. The two were battling for second place at the time.

Then came the moment Tracy had been waiting for. He took the checkered flag in the Miller Lite 225 on the Milwaukee Mile. Following the 14th win of his career, which put him in eighth place in the championship standings, Tracy said he was lucky to have crossed the finish line at all, carrying about only two litres of fuel in his tank. "We've had a lot of bad luck go our way and a lot of misfortune," he said. "Now that we've got this win, it kind of erases some of the bad things, and it has lifted a weight off of everybody's shoulders." Countrymen Greg Moore and Patrick Carpentier finished the race second and fifth respectively. The Milwaukee win was followed by a fifth-place finish in Portland and a fourth-place finish in Cleveland, and Tracy was running as high as fourth at Road America when his rear wing broke. He ended the race in 11th spot.

Yet Tracy was on a streak, driving the way he'd intended at the start of the season — consistently and cleanly. He arrived in Toronto still in eighth place in the championship but doing all he could to improve his position. This year, itching for another win to add to his 1993 victory in front of the hometown crowd, Tracy instead dutifully followed his teammate across the finish line, settling for second place. Franchitti was locked in a battle for the championship with Juan Montoya and needed the win to gain an edge on the Colombian. A less spectacular season for Tracy meant he was subject to team orders and had to support his teammate's quest for the championship trophy. Still, the race had a great conclusion for the nearly 70,000 fans present.

Franchitti led the entire race, and 20 laps from the end it restarted following a caution period. He moved on, driving quickly but not overly hard, not willing to sacrifice an almost certain win by being too aggressive. The second Team Kool Green car was on the move, and the hometown fans were expecting a battle between their hero and his teammate, whom some diehards would grudgingly acknowledge as their second favourite driver because he was on the same team as Tracy. But the dash to the finish — the battle in which Tracy would likely drive over curbs and cut corners as much as possible to win in front of the hometown crowd — never happened. The Kool Green cars finished one-two in Toronto and then took a victory lap side by side. The fans didn't see the hometown boy take a checkered flag, but they did see him stand on the podium in second place with his car intact and some valuable points to his credit.

In fact, the end of the race was decided before it even began. In 1998, Tracy, frustrated by his poor season, collided with Franchitti in Houston and took himself out of the race, and the incident led to the shoving match between Tracy and Green in the team's pits. Then, during the 1999 season, the two teammates wound up out of the race at Gateway after colliding with each other, although in that incident it was more difficult to assign blame. Green then sat them down and told them that, for the rest of the 1999 season, whoever was in the lead was to win the race and that the other teammate was not to try to overtake him and risk knocking them both out of competition. Tracy told the *Globe and Mail* the message was simple: "This is a team. I get paid the big bucks to be part of a team and race like a teammate." He knew that, if the situation arose again, he would be asked to follow Franchitti home.

Such rules are common in Formula One, in which there is a definite hierarchy among drivers. But in CART such rules are rare. Drivers are hired as equals and race against their teammates as they do any other driver on the track. Plus each has his own pit crew. Drivers want to win, and sometimes sponsors want to win even more so. Team owners are aware of these pressures, and while they want to see healthy competition they also want to see their drivers finish the race. It's not an easy job to run a racing team, and it's certainly not an easy job keeping two guys like Tracy and Franchitti from racing flat out and occasionally taking each other out.

At the halfway point of the 1999 champ car season, Green was looking at a possible championship if Franchitti continued to drive well. His main rival, Montoya, failed to finish the Toronto Molson Indy, the second DNF in a row for him, and now the Scotsman was just seven points behind him.

And Tracy's season was going well. Paul placed third in the Michigan 500, placed second at Belle Isle, and finished second again at Mid-Ohio. He was now in fourth place in the rankings heading onto the new oval track at Chicago. Tracy was doing his best to maintain the balance between his desire for consistency and his desire to win. In Chicago, he managed to do that until he crossed paths with his archrival, Michael Andretti.

You'd be hard pressed to find two drivers on the CART circuit with more aggressive driving styles. Andretti is six years older than Tracy and has more experience winning races. He also carries one of the greatest names in the history of auto racing and demands respect on the track. On many occasions, he gets it. All other drivers know that, when they saw the black number-six car fill up their mirrors, they'd better move over and give up their positions on the track or get ready for a fight. Even if Andretti qualifies poorly or has some mechanical problem with his car, he's always a factor in a race. Few other drivers — Tracy among them — can make that claim. So when they meet on the track, fans are treated to a battle or at least some close, if not always respectful, racing. Their rivalry is similar to one of the rules of physics: irresistible force meets immovable object. But not every meeting on the track between the two has resulted in one of them crashing, and their battles give fans some of the best racing of the season. For instance, on their way to third- and fourth-place finishes at the U.S. 500 in Michigan three races before the meet in Chicago, Tracy applauded Andretti's skills in saving him from potential disaster. Tracy and Andretti were fighting for position on the two-mile oval at about 230 mph. "Michael and I, I don't think you could have put a piece of paper between us in the corners we were so close trying to get side drafts off each other," Tracy said then. He pulled out of the draft to pass Andretti as they were heading down the front straightaway and found Max Papis directly in front of him coasting along at about 30 mph after running out of fuel. "And I have to thank Michael because he moved over and gave me room to get in between him and Max. There could have been a massive pileup, I would have hit Max at about 230 mph, and that wouldn't have been a good thing. But Michael ran a good, fair race."

Still, the bad blood between the former teammates continued. After all, an altercation between them in Australia had led to Tracy's suspension from the season opener. Sometimes it was hard to remember that they'd been members of the same team the way they treated each other on the track. In Chicago, Tracy tried to grab the fast line on the track, and Andretti refused to give way. They collided, and both were knocked out of the race. Andretti accused Tracy of having a "death wish." Tracy had taken the blame for many such incidents involving other drivers, but this time who was at fault wasn't clear. Andretti could have given way, but Tracy could have too. Even officials who examined the incident weren't able to place the blame on either driver, preferring instead to concentrate on the rivalry that had grown between the two drivers. "Wally [Dallenbach, CART chief steward] talked to both drivers," CART spokesperson

Mike Zizzo said after the crash. "He told them he wants to meet with them together, the Thursday or Friday of the Molson Indy Vancouver, so they can express their views on the thing and hash it out. At this time, after viewing the tapes, Wally is taking no other action than that."

While the officials were appeased for the moment, Tracy and Andretti left Chicago angry at each other, each blaming the other for what had happened. But thanks to the clear thinking of Dallenbach and Tony Cicale, Tracy picked up the phone and called Andretti hoping to settle their differences once and for all. "Wally encouraged me to take the initiative and call Michael and try to clear the air," Tracy said. "My first reaction was 'Why should I call him? Let him call me.'" Dallenbach, like Cicale, tried to get Tracy to think in terms of the events that led up to the accident and whether or not it was avoidable, not the fact that both drivers are equally stubborn. Looking at the big picture of the fight for the CART championship, Dallenbach also pointed out that both drivers had cost themselves some valuable points and lost some sizeable prize money. Heeding the advice of both men, Tracy called Andretti. Michael's first words were "You should have moved over." Tracy said to *Racer* in December 1999,

> *I told him I didn't call to argue who was right and who was wrong. I said "what's done is done. It's water under the bridge. All we can do is go on from here." I said "hey, we've had a lot of crap going over the years. This is what I'm going to do. I'm going to give you racing room. I don't expect any from you; I don't expect any from anybody. You do what you want to do. I'm sorry about what's happened over the years; it won't happen again."*

Tracy said the call was productive, at least for him, and lasted about 40 minutes. Andretti said the call was much shorter, and his outlook was much less positive following the conversation compared with Tracy's. "I told him that if he'd given me half a lane more we could have finished one-two," he told the *Toronto Star*. "But look what we've done; we've taken ourselves out of the whole championship. We're done." Andretti, serious and intense, is used to getting his way when it comes to his team and his driving. While he has apologized to other drivers when his mistakes have cost them track position or taken them out of a race, clearly he believed that the crash at Chicago was Tracy's fault, and he wasn't willing to budge, other than to admit that they'd effectively taken each other out of the running for the championship and that in the interests of safety they should be careful when taking each other into corners.

There were five races remaining in the 1999 season, and Tracy was still in fourth place in the championship with 122 points, two points behind Andretti, 50 points behind series leader Montoya, and 46 points behind teammate Franchitti.

Then the bubble burst again for Tracy. After his initial qualifying run in Vancouver in preparation for the Molson Indy on September 5, CART stewards disqualified his car. Each car goes through a technical inspection following qualifying, and Tracy's was lacking the mandatory two inches of clearance between the ground and the undertray. The disqualification initially placed Paul at the back of the grid, but he was able to recover in the remaining qualifying session to start the race from the third row. His race didn't go as well when he had trouble avoiding the walls around the street circuit. Andretti fell behind in the early going, and Tracy challenged Montoya for the lead, which he grabbed briefly until he spun, stalled the car, and then got back in the race in third place. Later he lost control at the chicane and struck a tire wall. That occurred just a few moments after Franchitti skidded into a different wall. "When I got around Juan, I spun and bumped the wall," Tracy told the *Globe and Mail*. "I'm pretty sure that bent the toe-link and the car was getting increasingly worse with oversteer. Finally I gave it another brush against the wall. That bent it even more. The car was really poor in handling and I was just trying to stay on the track. In the last chicane, it broke. When I got out of the car, the right rear toe-link was snapped in half."

Following the Vancouver Molson Indy, Tracy finished fourth in Monterey and then enjoyed a dominating win at the Texaco-Havoline Grand Prix of Houston. It was a payback for the lousy time he had at that track the year before. Tracy got off to a great start to take his 15th career victory, finishing just over 13 seconds ahead of Franchitti, who'd struggled back from 18th spot. And Tracy did it with just one fuel stop. Team orders remained in effect; however, short of stopping on the track and waiting for Franchitti to catch up to him, there wasn't much Tracy could do to help his teammate win the race. Certainly, Franchitti would have loved the win and the extra points as insurance in his fight against Montoya, but the day belonged to Tracy, and his main rival for the championship crashed on the 13th of 100 laps, allowing Franchitti to close the gap somewhat. It was the third one-two finish for the team in 1999. The win moved Tracy into third spot in the standings with 155 points and two races remaining. "I hate to say that any place owed me one, but . . . [i]t's better to have the gold boot [the race winner's trophy] in my hand than in my butt. I got it right this year," Tracy said following the race. "I think I've matured as a racer. I really feel a strong bond with this team, and that's what's key. It's showing in the whole team's performance. I just can't say enough about the job they've done for me." It was the team's fuel strategy that helped to make the difference, and Tracy acknowledged that the race couldn't have been won without the work of his pit crew. "I was fine over the last few laps. We could make the fuel mileage pretty easily," he said. "I was making 2.3 plus [miles to the gallon], and I only needed 2.1. I just can't say enough about the job the Team Kool Green crew did with the car. Tony Cicale gave me a great car, and Firestone gave us awesome tires. We put a lot of laps on them, and they held up. We showed everyone that Paul Tracy is a road racer and not just an oval specialist."

Returning to the scene of his 1998 indiscretion, Tracy arrived in Australia with the championship still within his grasp — and so did his teammate. And it was Franchitti who showed that he wanted to steal the championship away from Montoya by winning with a margin of 2.609 seconds over Max Papis in his Ford Reynard. Montoya started sixth but managed to get as high as second behind Franchitti before crashing on lap 49 in turn nine of the street course. "It's nice to win in Australia," Franchitti said. "Barry said to me, 'You've got to win in Australia, mate.' We finally did it for him. It's great because his entire family is here. He can hold his head up high tonight when we have a huge party!" Tracy started fourth and moved up to third on the start behind Scott Pruett. His tangles with the CART lawmakers continued when he was assessed a drive-through penalty for passing

Bryan Herta before the start-finish line. Tracy served the penalty on lap 13 and dropped to 10th place. He drove hard to the end of the race, experiencing turbo boost problems all the way, and finished seventh. He remained stalled in third place in the championship rankings, collecting seven points and bringing his total to 161 points, 10 more than Michael Andretti. "We got screwed on the start," said Tracy.

In the race, we lost something in the electronics or the boost right after the first stop. I was really slow coming onto the straightaways. We struggled and just couldn't keep up on the straights. As soon as I went to full throttle, it would stumble and fall. But the car was superior in the corners; I could catch right up under braking. Then the field would pull six or seven car lengths ahead of me on the straightaway. That's how Tony [Kanaan] and other guys passed me today. I think we might have finished on the podium quite easily even with the boost problems we had. At the end of the day, we were seventh and scored some points. We'll take it.

Team owner Barry Green said he was "disappointed" with the steward's decision to bring Tracy in for a drive-through penalty when it appeared that Paul had simply been trying to avoid another car. "Maybe they've got a better seat than I do. But it looked like it was evasive action by Paul. I don't understand. You can't stay in the line and get hit from the rear if he thinks the car in front of him is slowing. And that's what I saw, but it's the chief steward's call. At least they took some time to review it, and that was their call. I'm very disappointed."

Coming into the last race of the season, Team Kool Green was looking at possible first- and second-place finishes for its drivers — both in the Marlboro 500 at California Speedway in Fontana and in the championship. U.S. $1 million would go to the race winner, and the same amount would be handed to the CART champion. Tracy was capping off a difficult season in which his newfound maturity had been put to the test, but he'd been able to put together a string of consistent finishes and two wins. He'd shown he deserved a spot on a winning team and was able to give a good return on the investment made in him by Green and Cicale. Franchitti had three wins and had shown that the inconsistency of his pre-Kool Green past was an anomaly. But neither driver would have wanted to predict what lay before him. By the end of October 31, 1999, one had held the CART championship in his grasp only to watch it slip away, and both had lost a friend.

Tracy started the race in 19th spot and ended it in 18th spot, sidelined by an electrical problem on the 141st lap. He would rise no higher than third place in the championship, but it was a career best. Franchitti started eighth and finished 10th after a pit miscue caused him to lose too much time on the track, and he was left chasing Adrian Fernandez and eventual champion Juan Montoya, who finished fourth. Franchitti and Montoya were tied with 212 points, but the latter's seven wins compared with the former's three wins gave Montoya the title.

But the championship, the million dollars, and the celebrations were all marred by the death of one of the most popular drivers on the circuit. On the 10th lap of his last race for the Player's Forsythe team, Greg Moore's car left the track at about 240 mph while exiting turn two, skipped through the infield grass and over a gravel trap, and slammed into a concrete wall, disintegrating on impact. Moore was airlifted to Loma Linda University Medical Center, but Dr. Jeff Grange, medical director of the California Speedway, pronounced him dead at 1:21 p.m. Dr. Steve Olvey, CART director of medical affairs, said Greg had sustained massive head and internal injuries. At the time of his crash, he was in the middle of a particularly aggressive drive.

Moore started the race from the last spot on the grid after he broke a finger and cut his hand the day before when he was struck by a pickup while driving his scooter in the track's paddock area. Although his hand was in a cast and fitted with a special brace, he was cleared by CART doctors to drive after taking six laps before the race without difficulty. While many have speculated that his injuries may have contributed to his crash — he also bruised his hip — no one will ever know for sure. "He was extremely excited about racing, very confident, felt that the hand would give him no difficulty," said Olvey. "We feel very strongly that the hand was not related to the cause of the accident."

Race winner Adrian Fernandez was behind Moore when he went out of control. The racing had become particularly intense, and Fernandez, at that point in 20th spot, decided to ease back until the race settled down. "He was in a bunch of cars battling and I believe someone in front of him slowed," Fernandez told the Toronto *Sun*'s Dan Proudfoot. "Touching the brake would be all it would take, especially with him close behind another car so it took his air away [reducing the downforce essential to maintaining traction]. I don't specu-late there was any mechanical problem that caused it. A bump on the track? No, I don't think so. Just, it's very, very easy to lose control when you lose your air." Player's Forsythe vice-president Neil Micklewright said there'd been no indication from Moore that there was any problem with the car, and until the crash it had appeared to be performing well.

Moore's death shocked Canada and shattered his friends, family, team members, and fellow drivers. The race continued, the Player's Forsythe team pulled Moore's teammate out of the race, and a distraught Patrick Carpentier was consoled in the pits. CART CEO Andrew Craig said there was never any thought of stopping the race, although flags at the track were lowered to half-mast. Commentators for ESPN were criticized for appearing to concern themselves more with the race than with the fact that a driver had just been killed. Only pit reporter Gary Gerould showed any emotion publicly when his voice broke as he tried to speak to Juan Montoya about Moore's death following the race, but then he returned quickly to the issue of fuel consumption when he addressed Target team owner Chip Ganassi. Ganassi said he was "speechless" and didn't want to talk about the race itself, despite the fact that one of his drivers, Montoya, had just won the championship.

In his brief career, Moore had become a favourite among fans, the media, and drivers themselves, who were won over by his charm, charisma, and sheer driving talent. He told Roger Penske when he signed with the team for the 2000 season that he was going to give him his 100th win. Moore had become the glue that held drivers together. With a few exceptions, most of the current crop of CART drivers are in their 20s or 30s. Circuit veterans such as Paul Tracy, Michael Andretti, and Roberto Moreno came into CART when many of the top drivers — Emerson Fittipaldi, Mario Andretti, and

Nigel Mansell — were several years older, had families, had won other championships, and were either finishing their careers in CART or continuing to race in a series that had more of the speed and most of the glamour of Formula One but less of the politics. When Moore came along in 1996, he quickly established himself as a pure racer who was able to squeeze the most out of his car and show that he could easily run with the veterans. He was also an ideal representative for the sport — handsome, approachable, well spoken, with just a touch of cockiness. In the days following his death, hundreds of fans lined up at the Canadian Motorsport Hall of Fame to sign memorial books that were then sent to the Moore family.

The last Canadian to be killed racing was Gilles Villeneuve, who died at the age of 30 following a crash while practising for the Belgian Grand Prix. Moore was the second driver in the CART FedEx Series to die in 1999. In September, Uruguayan rookie Gonzalo Rodriguez, 27, a Team Penske driver, was killed during a practice at the Laguna Seca Raceway in Monterey. Rodriguez was the first driver killed in the CART series since Jeff Krosnoff died in a crash during the Toronto Molson Indy. Track worker Gary Avrin was also killed in that 1996 accident. A track worker was also killed during the Vancouver Molson Indy in 1990.

Moore had become close with many drivers on the CART series, but he'd become closest to Dario Franchitti. The two hung around, travelled, and celebrated together. A clearly shaken Franchitti obviously had no thoughts for the race or the championship at the end of the Marlboro 500. "Today I lost one of the best friends I ever had in Greg Moore," he said. "In the last couple of years, ever since I've known him, we shared a lot of good times together. He was the guy I competed the hardest with on the track, and he was the guy that I had the most fun with away from the track. The guy was going to be a champion, many, many times over. He was my friend. With what's happened, nothing else matters."

Franchitti was joined in his grief by the rest of the drivers, including Tracy, who'd also become close to Moore in the past couple of seasons. "Today was a disappointing day for everybody. The loss of Greg is a hard thing to try and stomach," he said.

> But I've talked to a lot of drivers now, and we all just remember Greg on the grid today. He was sitting there in his car with a gimp hand, smiling and ready for the race, ready to go out there and try to win it. His spirit was that way. He wouldn't give up a chance to get in the car, even if his leg was hanging off. That's how I want to remember him — not seeing the accident but remembering all of the good times that we had. He was a guy who always had a smile on his face. He was always upbeat and always in a good mood. He had a great spirit, and I hope that continues on in this sport.

Following the race, Tracy spent a sleepless night talking on the phone to his father in Toronto and trying to come to terms with the loss of a friend.

Max Papis's team owner, Bobby Rahal, told his driver by radio of Moore's death after he crossed the finish line in second place.

> He [Moore] is up there in the sky, and these are the

messages that God sends to us. I'm so sad. There are no words. . . . There is nothing. Greg was a special person in and out of the track. I came across the finish line, and I thought I'd won, then Bob came on the radio and said, 'I have very bad news to tell you.' I had no idea . . . no idea. We are not here for this. . . . We are not here for this.

"We lost a championship today, but more importantly everyone in our community lost a great friend in Greg Moore," said Barry Green. "It's a sad day for motor racing. . . ."

Adrian Fernandez saw Moore's car leave the track and went on to lead the last 10 laps of the race in his Patrick Racing Ford Reynard to take the checkered flag and the U.S. $1 million prize. "It's so hard, because Greg was such a good friend of ours," he said. "We've been racing for a while, and we shared so many moments, inside and outside the track. I can't express how sad I feel. The win doesn't mean anything. My heart goes out to his dad; I'm sure he's hurting. We should all remember his family in our thoughts. We will remember him as a great friend, a great gentleman, and a fantastic race car driver."

Juan Montoya, CART's youngest champion (at age 24 years, one month, and 11 days), topping 1995 champion Jacques Villeneuve (who was 24 years, four months, and one day old) — fitting for a sport that measures qualifying times in tenths of a second to be as precise with ages — was also saddened by Moore's death. "First, I want to say I'm really sad about what happened to Greg. I think he was a great guy, and I'm really sad for his family and friends. I think he was a great guy to be around."

But it was Montoya's boss, the tough, shrewd Chip Ganassi, owner of Target Chip Ganassi Racing, who spoke the most eloquently about Moore's death and who perfectly voiced its effect on all 15 CART teams and 25 drivers.

We certainly don't want our light to shine at the dimming of others. . . . I've known Greg for five or six years. I think everybody who's ever driven one of these cars can tell you that maybe he's not burdened with these things anymore. Our sport seems so small and insignificant in times like this. Maybe this is a good time for everybody to take a step back. Everybody in this sport needs each other. Maybe it's time for us all to be back together.

CHAPTER SEVEN

Helmet Carriers

Fans, Showbiz, and Marketing Paul Tracy

Even the most casual sports observer will tell you that fans can make or break a game. Whether it's the college students who paint themselves in Toronto Maple Leafs colours and dance in unison in the upper reaches of the city's Air Canada Centre; the World Cup soccer fanatics who drape their cars in their home country's flag and drive through city streets honking horns, blasting their national anthem on the stereo and cheering frantically out the window; or even the five year olds who wear their junior team jerseys and helmets just to watch *Hockey Night in Canada* on Saturday night with Mom and Dad, fans have the power to build an athlete up and just as easily tear him or her down. Without them, there'd be no compelling reason for a racing team to turn that first wheel or a baseball team to toss that first pitch, and there'd be no convincing reason to spend millions on advertising and marketing and producing hats, T-shirts, and posters.

Racing fans are like most other fans. They memorize biographies and achievements of their favourite teams and drivers, and they absorb technical details such as a race car's wing angles and tire and gearbox performance the way an avid baseball fan memorizes batting averages, a team's home and away records, and a player's home runs. Some follow entire circuits and attend all races, while others are loyal to certain teams. The loyalty of some fans doesn't even have to be based on a team's success. Take the Minardi fan club of Montreal: members are avid fans of the Italian Formula One Minardi team, which has never won a race. All other teams have overshadowed it, especially its Italian counterpart, Ferrari. Still, the club hosts its annual dinner during the Grand Prix of Canada festivities, and in 2000 its members were thrilled that drivers Gaston Mazzacane and Marc Gene responded to their invitations and attended the dinner. F1 drivers mingling with ordinary fans is almost unheard of. But the Minardi drivers wished to express their gratitude to the fans for such devotion. For the members of the club, being a Minardi fan is about more than simply rooting for the under-dog. It's about supporting a team that has had many tough seasons but is still in the game. A team that usually garners attention only when one of its cars collides with a Ferrari or McLaren or one of its drivers tries to prevent Michael Schumacher or David Coulthard from passing. In short, it's about competition and heart, not just winning, being the most important parts of the sport.

CART began with a series of races on oval tracks and speedways contested only in the United States, and its fans, while not as wild as some of their beer-and-barbecue NASCAR brethren, were mainly white men who enjoyed watching fast cars chase each other around a circle. Now that champ car racing has become an international series that includes races on temporary street circuits and road courses in nine countries, as well as on ovals and super-speedways, the fans have changed and reflect its more multicultural style. Open-wheeled champ cars are closer in style to Formula One cars, and some F1 fans are also CART fans. What they get in return for following the CART series is drivers whom they can identify with, who race on tracks that they're familiar with, and whose faces and names are easily recognizable. As well, at most CART races, fans get ample opportunities to meet their favourite drivers up close. Tickets can include access to the paddock area, the pits during race preparation and qualifying, and, for the lucky and well connected, the corporate tents where drivers and team members mingle with their sponsors. A driver such as Helio Castroneves enjoys meeting fans and stops to shake hands and sign autographs before whizzing off to his team trailer on his motor scooter.

Paul Tracy has his share of fans and detractors among those who follow CART. When he first entered the circuit, he had few fans in the United States but was closely followed in Europe and received regular coverage by Canadian media. Now, though, his fans are less concerned that he's from Canada and more concerned that, after 10 years on the circuit, he hasn't won a championship yet is second only to Michael Andretti in his number of wins. What they all agree on is that Tracy's driving style attracted them to him and will keep them interested in his career. Some of his fans enjoy the fact that Paul appears to be a "regular" guy (though one with millions of dollars in his pockets and access to some of the world's fastest cars). They point to his size, his lack of a classic athletic physique, and his penchant for displaying flashes of temper along with a well-timed jab at a driver who has wronged him. While it's always an unfair perception that fans have of their heroes, racing fans like Tracy because they think he's a classic rebel. They like to see him win, but they're disappointed when he wins by driving safely and consistently, which is really what it takes to win races. Fans, especially his Canadian ones, know that when Tracy's on the track something is bound to happen. That something, they hope, will be a wallop given to an opponent as he tries to pass going into a 60 mph turn or a late-braking manoeuvre at the end of a 240 mph straightaway, a move that always makes TV audiences and grandstand fans hold their breath.

Tracy's fans don't hold their breath when it comes to their opinions of their favourite driver. Most drivers have fan clubs and accompanying web sites set up either by the fans themselves or by their team's public relations department, but Tracy's treatment on the web is different. Paul has several fan web pages devoted to him, but his "official" fan club site is still under construction. The official Team Kool Green site contains several photos of Tracy and teammate Dario Franchitti, but laws restricting tobacco advertising in various countries around the globe make it closed to all but qualified members who apply for access.

One of the best fan sites geared to CART racing is SeventhGear.com, developed and maintained by CART fans around the world, many of whom contribute photos and articles gleaned from attending races, listening in on press conferences, and picking up pit lane rumours. Former CART driver and current ESPN commentator Parker Johnstone is a member of the SeventhGear forums. Ask the members about Tracy and you'll get a variety of responses. Some fans revel in his hard-charging driving style. Others love that he speaks his mind about fellow drivers and seems to have no pretensions about his own abilities. Still others just enjoy the fact that, when he's on the track, often anything can happen. Silva, of Atlanta, a member of the SeventhGear forums, best sums up fan opinions of Tracy: "He is my favourite CART driver, he has no fear. He puts the car in places other drivers wouldn't consider. Often he crashes as a result, but you can never say he isn't fast. He goes balls out every lap. Although it isn't the way to win a championship, on some level I just think that it is the way a race car was intended to be driven." Other fans admit that Tracy isn't among their favourite drivers, but they acknowledge that he could be a CART champion and that his approach to racing has mellowed during the past few seasons. "He can win races, period, as long as he keeps all four of his wheels on the car," writes Bruce Anderson of Indianapolis. "His propensity for attempting ill-advised passes has waned a bit too in the last two seasons. I think he could be another top-five finisher in the points in '01. I don't particularly like him, but he is good."

While many racing fans claim to watch the sport because they love to see highly skilled men drive cars at the edges of their abilities, others want to see action — crashes, spins, smoking tires. Throughout his CART career, Tracy has provided more than his share of each, and fans are grateful that he has. Not for them the strategy of calculating fuel mileage or a driver working his way slowly but surely through the pack, taking satisfaction in a third- or fifth-place finish. Take the fan who calls himself "PT is God" (he's actually Jason

Buck of Danville, Illinois): "Tracy is one of the toughest drivers out there, he hangs it out every race, every lap. As a fan I want to see action, not [Adrian] Fernandez counting his fuel mileage. I watched Tracy at Elkhart Lake when he came from the back. Now that was exciting racing. Tracy's my man for action because I love action on the track even if the consequences are not so good." Other fans have echoed those sentiments about Tracy's 2000-season run at Road America in Elkhart Lake, one of the most spectacular drives to the front in the history of CART. Diehard Tracy fans knew that he was capable of such a drive: a fast, hard-charging run from the back of the pack, cleanly picking off opponent after opponent, driving hard but not so hard as to put himself off the track. "Sitting in Canada Corner [at Road America] this year and watching Paul pick 'em off there each lap was one of the most impressive drives I've witnessed," writes Steve Cox of Indianapolis. "Paul just flat gases it and is one of my favourites. A real race driver wads one up once in awhile. He pushes the button to win and is not happy with a 'good run' even if he's starting towards the back. How does a driver know where the edge is if he doesn't cross it once in awhile?" Cali, of Pico Rivera, California, believes Tracy's image enhances the sport and gives CART a touch of edginess. In fact, CART, Honda (his team's engine manufacturer), and ESPN often use his image in television and print promos when they want to emphasize the danger and excitement of the sport. As Cali puts it, "His balls to the wall, all out aggressive driving style is what we fans like to see. I think his bad boy image and the publicity he receives brings a lot of needed attention to our CART series. Every sport needs some sort of bad boy or 'Dennis Rodman' because it appeals to a certain part of us." And as

Billy Lodin told the Toronto *Sun* in July 2000, on the eve of the Molson Indy in Toronto, "Tracy is the most feared driver on the track, and he will just fly by everyone on the track on Sunday. I just don't want to see Michael Andretti win."

In 1994, when Tracy was no longer popular with the management at Newman-Haas, he was still popular with his fans, in particular with an apparent group of thieves who may also have been fans. Tracy's image and the words "Face your fears. Live your dreams" appeared on a series of 10-foot by 20-foot posters for sports apparel company No Fear. The posters were placed near sports venues across Canada, and three of the posters were subsequently stolen.

Unlike some sports leagues that have waited until their teams were failing before letting fans get close to the players (witness the Toronto Argonauts, the Vancouver Grizzlies, or the Montreal Expos), CART has long been in favour of putting its athletes close to the fans. At any race, fans can ask their favourite driver for an autograph when he's not working with his team, or they can attend one of the team's autograph sessions. Tracy will sign pretty much anything on his way to or from his car and be happy doing it. "I'm fine with it," he said.

> *I don't have any problems with that. I mean, I don't mind giving autographs. Some people are weird about it. Dario gets weird about it, but for me it's just a part of the job. He doesn't like giving out his autograph a lot because he thinks his autograph is worth money, so he can be weird about it. Sometimes I tell him "Hey, fuckin' relax, it's only an autograph," but he has a little bit of a Formula One mentality sometimes.*

You'd think that a sport in which men, and it is almost entirely men, drive flashy cars at breakneck speeds, with engines screaming at eardrum-shattering volumes, would naturally attract a following. For the most part, it has. Formula One has a worldwide legion of dedicated followers. Stock car racing, or NASCAR, in which drivers compete primarily in the United States on oval tracks and super-speedways, saw its fan base rise dramatically throughout the 1990s. But CART is trying its best to increase its number of fans. In its favour, it has some of the best drivers in the world — Americans, Canadians, Brazilians, Swedes, Germans, French, and Italians — thrown into the series mix. It also boasts one of the highest levels of competition among all premier racing series. In 2000 alone, there were 11 different winners. The year before, there were 10. The racing is close on virtually all the tracks, which include ovals, such as at Nazareth, Pennsylvania, and at Twin Ring in Motegi, Japan; high-banked superspeedways such as in Michigan and Fontana; street courses such as in Toronto and Long Beach; and road courses such as at Road America and Laguna Seca. As well, CART has the fastest cars in open-wheeled racing. With their aerodynamics and high-horsepower engines, they're able to reach speeds of well over 200 mph. Formula One cars aren't built to sustain such high speeds.

But CART found by the end of the 1990s that it was no longer the only open-wheeled game in town. In 1996, Tony George, the owner of the Indianapolis Motor Speedway, became embroiled in a dispute with Championship Auto Racing Teams over rules surrounding the Indy 500. CART teams pulled out of the storied race because of that dispute, anticipating that the event would suffer as a result. George went ahead with the 500 anyway, bringing in drivers and teams under the United States Auto Club rules. The race still drew huge TV audiences, and George went on to form a separate open-wheeled racing series that runs only on oval tracks, the Indy Racing League.

That move left CART in a tight spot. Outwardly, executives insisted that the best drivers and cars were still in its series. To a certain extent, they were right. But they didn't have the crown jewel of American racing, the Indy 500, on their schedule. As well, while CART teams continued to use "Indy" to describe their cars, George, who owned the rights to the trademark from his ownership of the speedway, eventually prevented them from doing so. That CART is now just one of two open-wheeled racing series and is not allowed to use a very recognizable name to describe its cars has made marketing difficult. Since 1996, the series has tried using CART or the slightly more hip "champ car" to describe itself and is still working to build a recognizable brand for itself.

CART's CEO is working to accelerate that process. Joseph Heitzler says that getting the marketing right is one of the most important challenges facing the series and the corporation that is Championship Auto Racing Teams. Heitzler took over the CEO's position after interim CEO Bobby Rahal left to run the Jaguar Formula One team in 2000. Rahal maintains his stake in his CART team, owned by him and partner David Letterman.

One item on Heitzler's marketing agenda is dealing with the ban on sponsorship by tobacco companies set to take effect in Canada in 2004. It has concerned board members, and Heitzler doesn't want to alienate any tobacco companies that want to remain involved in racing. Executives of some tobacco companies believe that they can fight the ban and win, and Heitzler tends to agree with them. "I'm not convinced it's actually going to happen," he said. He praised cigarette companies for their long history of involvement in motorsports, and he's hoping the issue can be resolved so that they don't have to pull out altogether. If the ban stands, CART will likely treat it in the same fashion as it is treated in some European countries. Race cars that would normally be emblazoned with the tobacco brand name will maintain the brand's colours but use the driver's name, or an appropriately catchy and mildly cheeky phrase, in its place. For example, the yellow-and-black Jordan Honda cars normally emblazoned with Benson & Hedges instead use "Buzzin' Hornets." Jacques Villeneuve's Lucky Strike car uses "Look Alike" in its place.

Heitzler spent the end of the 2000 season and the early part of the 2001 season working on a marketing plan for the series, which he hoped to have in place before the middle of the 2001 season. He first adopted more of a team approach inside the sanctioning body's corporate offices. Employees are now referred to as "business associates," and a research firm was hired to speak to all stakeholders in the racing business, from sponsors to team owners to CART business associates to drivers. Heitzler is using what he calls a SWOT approach, whereby all stakeholders identify the "strengths, weaknesses, opportunities, and threats" facing CART.

In addition to the diverse cultural and national backgrounds of its drivers, CART has the fastest cars of any popular racing series. Its goal has been to get those drivers and their cars before the public and to get more fans to go to races, such as at the oval tracks in Michigan and Nazareth, venues where attendance has been in decline. CART has already added races in Japan, Brazil, and Australia and in 2001 went to Germany, England, and Mexico for the first time, offering a competitive alternative to F1.

Threats to CART, at home anyway, come mainly from NASCAR. The stock car racing series that started with a bunch of Deep South moonshine runners has evolved into a marketing juggernaut that now attracts such non-automotive companies as Kellogg, UPS, Tide, and Anheuser-Busch as well as extremely loyal fans. According to a NASCAR survey done by Edgar, Dunn and Company, and reported by *Time* magazine, attendance has doubled at races since 1990, and, in 2000, 6.5 million fans attended Winston Cup races, each spending about U.S. $65 a ticket. The survey also shed some light on the "average" NASCAR fan: 40% of fans are women, 64% have attended college, 70% have Internet access, 41% earn more than U.S. $50,000 a year, and the fans spend an average of U.S. $287 per year on NASCAR merchandise. The series was expected to be the fastest-growing earner during the next five years. In 1999, the series earned U.S. $1.398 million and is expected to take in revenues of U.S. $3.423 million by 2006.

According to CART statistics, the majority of its fans are college educated, with an average age of 37. In fact, 24% of its fans fall into that age group, while 78% are male and 22% female. They're likely to have graduated from college, and 29% have a postgraduate degree. They have an above-average household income of U.S. $55,000, and on average they watch seven races on television during the season. Thirty-six percent are likely to attend at least one CART event per season.

In 1998, 2,524,160 people attended the 20 racing events, an increase from 2,371,907 in 1997.

Heitzler wants to increase those fan numbers as he tries to learn from both NASCAR's successes and its failures. Each stakeholder involved in his SWOT program will appoint a person to work on sponsorship in the areas of television and promotion and will work with drivers, sponsors, and track promoters to develop other opportunities. Phase 1, as Heitzler calls it, began with a supplement in USA Today that appeared on March 8, before the first race of the 2001 season in Mexico. The six-page supplement included sections by engine manufacturers, features on drivers, a TV schedule, sponsorship information, and a report on the HANS (head and neck support) device that became mandatory for use by CART on oval tracks during the 2001 season. The device also became prominent in the aftermath of the death of NASCAR star Dale Earnhardt when many observers of the sport speculated that it could have prevented his death. Heitzler also believes that CART is in a position to benefit from the work that both NASCAR and Formula One have done. "In any business, there are benchmarks set by business leaders, like Starbucks or Coca Cola, and there have been benchmarks set by NASCAR. I'm amazed at the extreme amount of camaraderie between NASCAR and CART and Formula One."

Heitzler said he's had surprisingly little resistance to his plans from team owners and sponsors. Shortly after starting his job, he gained respect from drivers for listening to their concerns and by pointing out to them that they are crucial to the ongoing success of the series. Some critics have pointed out that CART hasn't done enough to help young American racers move through the ranks and has relied on the interest of European and Latin American drivers in the series. CART does want to include foreign countries in its marketing plan, and Heitzler doesn't want to downplay the contributions of foreign drivers and their sponsors. A generally tacit belief has been that U.S. fans in particular won't relate to drivers such as Helio Castroneves and Gil de Ferran the way they relate to NASCAR's Jeff Gordon, Tony Stewart, or the late Dale Earnhardt — possibly because their names don't easily roll off the tongues of casual racing fans. Heitzler thinks that attitude misses the salient fact that all CART drivers are athletes in the truest sense and have something to offer fans. That, coupled with the fact that they drive some of the world's most sophisticated, fast, and expensive cars, is where CART executives should take their marketing cues. "Any fan wants to watch athletes at their very best," he said. "The skills we get from the athletes are far superior to how their last name is pronounced, and it goes against what CART has to offer. We're going from a domestic environment to a global environment, and what we need to worry about is how to get the drivers and teams to all the locations around the world."

Heitzler says that the drivers, along with the technologies they use, will be essential in creating more entertainment options for the series. Tracy instantly jumps to Heitzler's mind as the kind of driver whom the series wants to highlight and who is essential to attracting and keeping fans. Especially during the 1998, 1999, and 2000 series, Tracy emerged as a sort of spokesperson for the sport, and he's becoming well known among members of the racing media as the source of a good quote. Add to that feature his penchant for changing hair colours and his love of wildly painted Harley-Davidsons. Along with Helio Castroneves — who has made a habit of climbing atop a fence and waving to the crowd when he won a race — and the doughnut-spinning Alex Zanardi and there's already the beginning of a solid cast of characters. Against guys like these, the often stoic Michael Andretti becomes a character himself. "Paul and I have had several conversations, and I let him know I appreciate his zest for the sport and his enjoyment of it, and I don't want to curtail any of that," said Heitzler. "I'm not going to prevent anybody from doing doughnuts after they win or prevent them from jumping on fences." About eight or nine years ago, Heitzler added, when the extreme sports scene started to gain prominence, sports marketing executives were slow to notice the business opportunities in high-adrenaline activities such as sky surfing and street luge. Before marketers acknowledged these sports, they were enormously popular with a select group of fans, and Heitzler thinks the same thing can happen with CART. It already has the high-adrenaline activity and the diverse characters; it just needs to be channelled properly.

In 2001, CART opened a Los Angeles office as part of its effort to woo the entertainment community, and Heitzler is working to get the entertainment media to cover its events, such as Sneak Preview and the announcement of the CART all-star team. So far, the annual gala event has included drivers, teams, and media but hasn't been open to the public, which Heitzler wants to do. In 2001, the gala was held in Anaheim, California, as part of the Sneak Preview events. Anaheim is about an hour from the epicentre of the entertainment business in Los Angeles, and Sneak Preview was the replacement for 2000's spring training, at which members of the media had access to drivers as they tested their cars on the Homestead track in Florida. Sneak Preview consisted of a few days of press conferences and media interviews, but no cars were on the track at California Speedway in Fontana. While well attended, some reporters griped that there would probably be as many interview opportunities as the season went on and that without cars on the track the event was pretty boring.

Before the beginning of the 2002 season, CART will open the all-star team event to the public and hopefully get valuable coverage on entertainment television shows and the mainstream media, coverage that will build up the series and driver profiles. Heitzler also wants the sport to appeal to younger fans — much like the Extreme Games have — and hopes to work out a deal with MTV to get CART in the faces of a younger generation by getting some coverage of the races and Sneak Preview from the youth-oriented music channel.

In late 1999, CART received a gift from Hollywood. Sylvester Stallone wanted to make a movie based on the Formula One circuit. When he couldn't get the necessary cooperation from the circuit's top executive, Bernie Ecclestone, he turned to CART instead. It quickly welcomed the idea. *Driven*, released in April 2001, features the same clichéd plot line that powers most of Stallone's films, but it uses actual footage of CART races, and many drivers appear as themselves in the film, both interacting with the stars and working in the background. From a marketing perspective, CART was more than happy to get its name — and the names of its sponsors — out to a potentially vast audience. For example, Stallone wears Mauricio Gugelmin's Nextel driving suit in the movie. Cars bearing the Nextel and Motorola names and logos appear prominently in the film. "The beautiful thing is that not only will the film serve as essentially a two hour commercial for sponsors that choose to get involved, but they'll get a lasting return," CART's vice-president of broadcasting, Keith Allo, told *Champ Car* magazine in April 2000. "This isn't like a commercial, something that's on for a time and then goes away. This will endure in perpetuity — it will never go away. Twenty years from now, this movie will still pop up in reruns on television. It's very powerful." CART was also wise to be involved in the movie's Hollywood première. Paul Tracy, Kenny Brack, Cristiano da Matta, and Mauricio Gugelmin drove their cars down Hollywood Boulevard, and Tracy performed a couple of doughnuts on the street to thrill the crowd. He then got out of his car and tossed his driving gloves to the fans.

Part of solving the marketing puzzle for Heitzler has been getting the CART board and team owners and other stakeholders to change their attitudes somewhat and admit that they didn't have all the answers about how to appeal to a wider audience and that they won't get them if they don't take active roles in the future of the series. Former senior vice-president of marketing at CART, Pat Leahy, told *Champ Car* magazine in April 2000 that the company had spent enough time fighting with IRL owner Tony George over a resolution to the CART-IRL split, time that it could have used to market itself. It looks as though IRL will remain a viable racing series, and CART has resigned itself to competing irregularly in the Indy 500, so now's the time to concentrate on its own business. Leahy wanted the sport to appeal to more women and the Latin American market. He also hoped that CART fans would help to spread the word about how great the sport is and attract more followers.

After CART unveiled its latest and longest schedule during

Sneak Preview, it made much of the fact that it was looking forward to racing in Brazil, home country to many CART drivers, for its second race of the 2001 season. Then the deal fell apart. In February 2001, CART announced that the arrangement with Rio de Janeiro was being overturned by the city's new mayor, who'd been elected on a platform of promising to halt any sporting and cultural events organized by the previous administration, which the new civic government believed to have been corrupt. Eventually, the race was cancelled, much to the dismay of CART, Brazilian fans and drivers, and race promoter Emerson Fittipaldi. Another badly needed marketing opportunity in a very important market was lost. "It was a very painful exercise," Heitzler said. "We pleaded the importance of it with the mayor of Rio, from both a nationalistic and financial perspective, everything that we could."

Despite that lost opportunity, Heitzler was extremely pleased to find that CART drivers are the most intelligent and business-savvy group of professional athletes he has ever worked with. In addition to their skills behind the wheel, the drivers, Heitzler said, are well versed in the technical aspects of their cars as well as the sponsorship and business aspects of their jobs. Brazilian Mauricio Gugelmin, head of the CART drivers' association, went into his first meeting with Heitzler armed with an 18-page executive summary of a report to present to him. Heitzler had never seen such a report from a professional athlete, and he was pleasantly surprised.

Zak Brown is a race car driver who also runs Just Marketing, an Indianapolis firm that pairs businesses with racing teams and drivers on the various circuits. Most of his business involves making sure that there are good fits between drivers and corporations. "We look for teams and drivers that have synergies, that can be from what nationality they are, to who the other sponsors are on the car, to are they a clean-cut Dario Franchitti or are they a little more rough, wild-boy Paul Tracy, and match up the personalities of the companies with the team and driver that have similar personalities," he said. He's worked with Volkswagen, Brown & Williamson, WWF, and Porsche — generally, the "who's who of blue-chip companies" that want to see their names on the sides of race cars — from companies valued at $500 million to ones worth "several billion." Tracy, Brown says, can be a hot commodity for a marketer because he has some personality. "He's got a bit of a mouth on him, and that's good," he said. "So you line him up with a company that's got a bit of a mouth on them. If you're a very buttoned-up, conservative company, you stay away from Paul Tracy and get on Bryan Herta's car." The Kool brand, Tracy's current sponsor, is an ideal brand to associate with Paul because it's aiming at a young and hip demographic.

If Brown were handling Tracy's marketing, he'd pair the driver with Canadian companies or those that have links to Canada. "In America, it's not a big deal for companies to sponsor an American, but Canadians are very nationalistic, very similar to how the Europeans and Brazilians go about it," he said. "The Brazilians are given a lot of Brazilian support, so the first thing I would do is see if there was any type of Canadian connection; that would be a good start." As well, he'd promote Tracy's youthful image. "He's probably more of a Tommy Hilfiger than a Polo — a younger crowd, hipper. Polo's a bit understated. And Paul Tracy's not understated."

Tracy has become used to being sponsored by a tobacco company. With the exception of the season he spent with

Newman-Haas, when he drove a Budweiser-sponsored car, his main sponsors have been tobacco brands. While Paul was with Team Penske, it was Philip Morris's Marlboro brand, and throughout his time with Team Green his sponsor has been Brown & Williamson's Kool brand. Other than the endorsements he's done for No Fear and personal appearances to promote races, Tracy really hasn't done any promotional or marketing work for himself. Any possibility of appearing prominently in the movie *Driven* was negated by his connection to tobacco, he said. "In terms of personal endorsements and TV commercials and all that kind of stuff, I've never had anything like that because of tobacco sponsorship," he said. "But I can't complain, on the other hand, because tobacco companies have the most amount of money to spend because that's the arena they can advertise in, and I've gotten paid very well, so I can't complain either way." That doesn't mean that Tracy would turn down any promotional opportunities, but he doesn't seek them out. "A lot of people aren't interested because of the association with tobacco companies," he said. "Toy companies and things that are geared towards kids, [so] it's tough. It's a tough sell, and I don't really pursue it all that much either. You know, I don't have any agency or anything or people that I work with that go out and try to find that stuff. If it comes to me, fine. But I don't actively pursue it."

CHAPTER EIGHT

A Kool Future

Karts, Racing Friends, and the 2000 Season and Beyond

As Paul Tracy and the rest of the CART drivers, engineers, team managers, media, and PR people prepared for the 2001 season, there were a few pieces of unfinished business. CART traditionally staged its spring-training event at the Homestead track in Florida. A love-in of several days between CART, its sponsors, and the media, spring training featured drivers and team owners available for press conferences and interviews, sponsor parties, some testing by teams on the track, and in 2000 the announcement of the first-ever CART all-star team. Unlike hockey and baseball all-stars, CART all-stars do little other than picking up trophies. They don't race together. They don't appear in ads together. They simply accept their awards with accompanying applause from the audience, pose for photos, and then leave. The audience is left to down the free drinks, sample the free hors d'oeuvres, listen to the entertainment, and then go home. CART CEO Joe Heitzler has plans to improve the event.

In 2001, with poor attendance bumping the Homestead race from the 2001 schedule, the event was moved across the country to California Speedway near the small town of Fontana, and spring training became the CART Sneak Preview. Gone were the cars speeding along the track, partly because of Dario Franchitti's spectacular crash at Homestead in 2000. Franchitti suffered brain contusions and a cracked pelvis. The accident set him back at the start of the season, and he never fully recovered. CART realized the PR problems that arose when a driver crashed in front of the representatives of major media outlets. Franchitti smacking into the Homestead concrete made most of the highlight reels that night. So, in 2001, Sneak Preview featured a tour of the Honda, Toyota, and Cosworth engine shops, the announcement of the all-star team, and two days of press conferences and interviews. The cars were on display next to the transporters, which are combination rolling offices and garages, but champ cars look strange when they're not moving at 200 mph. They lay on the pavement, silent in the sun, fibreglass sharks itching to strike.

Engine builders guard their secrets jealously, and it was a small miracle that CART officials managed to get Honda, Toyota, and Cosworth to open their doors to, of all groups, the media. But the shops were ready. As the half-empty bus rolled down the freeway north of Los Angeles toward the newly amalgamated town of Santa Clarita and the home of Honda Performance Development (HPD), Alex Zanardi and Tony Kanaan, together with their team boss, Mo Nunn, held court in the back. With his two CART championships with Target Chip Ganassi Racing, his pithy answers to reporters' questions, and his famous on-track doughnuts that followed almost every win, Zanardi was still a favourite among fans and reporters, even though he was returning from a disastrous foray into Formula One in which he sat out the 2000 season. Zanardi and Kanaan are both Honda drivers and were along for the ride to help journalists warm up to the engine manufacturer. There was really no reason for HPD to worry, other than the fact that both Toyota and Cosworth were also opening their doors to the media. Honda was firmly entrenched in the racing world, with Honda-powered cars winning five consecutive CART championships, and a new closed-course speed record was set in 2000 by a Penske car running a Honda engine. As well, Honda was expected to make waves in Formula One in 2001 by building engines for both the British American Racing team and Team Jordan. Honda supplies nine CART drivers with engines, including Tracy and Franchitti. It also wields considerable influence. The company was responsible for putting Michael Andretti in a Honda-powered car for the 2001 season after he left the Newman-Haas team and its Ford-powered Lola cars.

The media were greeted by professorial HPD General Manager Robert Clarke, along with President Tom Elliott, at the Honda shop, and they were treated to a dazzling array of doughnuts, fruit, coffee, pop, and pastries. The room also featured a collection of driver and car memorabilia. Helmets of most of the Honda drivers, including Tracy, Zanardi, and Scott Goodyear, were encased alongside trophies, Indy 500 rings, and racing pins, which HPD gave to the media following the tour. Clarke explained the Honda history and philosophy ("We're not a production company that does racing on the side. We're a racing company that builds production cars.") and outlined the company's racing history. In 1949, Soichiro Honda began his career as an auto tycoon by strapping an engine to a bicycle and calling his motorcycle the "Dream." An avid racer, at the age of 22 Honda modified a Curtis-Wright V8 aircraft engine to power a Ford chassis. He then used his contraption to set a Japanese speed record of 75 mph. Before the media were herded through the shops where the engines are actually built, tested, raced, torn apart, and rebuilt, they were treated to HPD's engine hall of fame, of sorts. Arrayed along a partition in the company's lunchroom are examples of all its champ car engines from its debut to the present.

But away from all the high-tech machinery in glass cases is a machine of a different sort. An internal competition resulted in the construction of Honda's very own margarita machine. Made from engine parts, it can actually produce margaritas thanks to a built-in blender and an electronic system containing each of its drivers' "profiles." Tom Elliott said the winning formula was provided by the Jimmy Vasser profile because the cool Californian "was the most familiar with the margarita." Quipped Robert Clarke, "Yeah, the Paul Tracy one is a bit erratic."

A trip through the engine shop drives home the Japanese heritage of Honda Performance Development. The place is as far away from your neighbourhood garage as a 17 year old's bedroom is to a suite at the Waldorf-Astoria. The white walls and floors are spotless. The workstations are spotless. Not one person who works inside those walls can be described as a grease monkey. In fact, there's no grease. Computers and sensitive measuring devices have replaced grease and the rubber mallet. Each workstation is loaded with identical tools in identical drawers. The walls surrounding the main engine area are home to black-and-white reproductions of print ads that ran following every Honda champ car win. Tracy is featured in several, as are Franchitti and the ubiquitous Zanardi, who dominated the champ car scene in 1997 and 1998. On the walls are banners that read "Performance + quality = success."

After the engine shop tours came the announcement of the CART all-star team. The announcement, or the "CART All-Star Extravaganza," as it was officially called, was held at the Sun Theatre in Anaheim, the heart of suburban California. Just inside the white walls rimmed with palm trees that surround the theatre, adjacent to the ticket booth, is a faux water tower reminiscent of the movie back lots of the 1940s and 1950s. On the night of the all-star event, spotlights lit the sky, race cars were wheeled into the courtyard, and drivers and teams had a chance to revel in their success and look forward to the 2001 season. CART drivers, a select group of media, fans, and Sylvester Stallone and musician Lenny Kravitz voted for and decided on the all-star team. A racing enthusiast, Stallone filmed *Driven* at several CART venues during the 2000 season, and Kravitz was a friend of the late Greg Moore and is also a racing fan.

The parallels between racing and music didn't stop there. Many of the drivers attending the gala took it as an opportunity to show off their personal styles, and the closest parallel to those styles could be found in rock and roll. Leather was the fabric du jour, with most drivers wearing at least a leather jacket. Tracy took that look a step further and added leather pants to his jacket and T-shirt. It would have been easy to confuse some of the drivers for members of the band the Goo Goo Dolls, who took to the stage after the awards. Alex Tagliani sported bronze hair and a hairline beard that ran along the edge of his jaw and upper lip, while teammate Patrick Carpentier sported spiked hair high-lighted by a tuft of black hair on his chin. Max Papis arrived with an entourage consisting of several men and two or three blonde women draped in Italian clothes and encrusted with gold. (During the awards presentation, Papis did his best to heckle whichever driver took the stage.) The only real contrasts among the drivers were the casually dressed Christian Fittipaldi; Mauricio Gugelmin, looking every inch the veteran with his suit and T-shirt, casting an amused eye at the drivers carousing next to him as he chatted on his phone; and Cristiano da Matta, who — small in stature and youthful in appearance, usually carrying a backpack and dressed in jeans and a T-shirt — looks like he's at the races because he wants to hang out with the older kids and their cool cars. Yet on the track he's as fast and as fierce as any veteran, and in 2001 he was ready to take Michael Andretti's spot on the Newman-Haas team and show just how fast he can be. Nearly each driver carried a cell phone. Tracy drove his own customized, banana yellow Acura NSX to the event and, arriving alone, headed straight to the cluster of drivers near the entrance, high-fiving and nudging each as he greeted them as if they were all old college buddies.

Before the all-star team members were announced, CART CEO Joe Heitzler addressed the crowd at Sun Theatre. A sharp, personable man, Heitzler, 56, introduced his wife and young son before speaking about racing, reminding members of the audience that they should remember their families because they bear the brunt of long seasons that constantly take drivers and crew members away from home.

At press conferences in the days that followed, Heitzler admitted to being somewhat overwhelmed by the breadth and depth of the job he'd officially taken over less than a month before, but his efforts to meet with the drivers in sessions that were closed to the press were greeted with enthusiasm by most of them. They believed that finally someone in charge was as concerned with slipping attendance at some races and the marketing of drivers as they were.

As each driver was called to accept his trophy for being named to the all-star team, a brief video of highlights was shown, accompanied by music of the driver's choice. First up was Adrian Fernandez, who accepted his award and offered the briefest of speeches. Paul Tracy came next, but not before his flag-waving image from Vancouver, his fist pumping in victory, his car running over curbs and spinning doughnuts, appeared on the screen, accompanied by Blur's "Song 2," which has been used in several commercials, including a popular Labatt Blue ad that featured racing shopping carts. Tracy strode onto the stage and accepted his trophy once the small chorus of "whoo-hooo" from the audience had died down. "Wow, two years in a row," he said. "Doesn't seem that long ago that everybody thought I was a dickhead. Thanks." The audience roared. Fellow drivers grinned and shook their heads. Tracy grinned, shrugged, and took his seat on the stage. When Gil de Ferran came onto the stage to accept the Mario Andretti trophy for winning the championship, the professorial Brazilian thanked his fellow competitors and quipped, "Actually, we still all hold the same opinion of Paul." Michael Andretti and Juan Montoya rounded out the all-stars — Montoya was already in Europe preparing for the 2001 season with the Williams Formula One team. The drivers posed together with their trophies and then dispersed as the party began.

Clearly, Tracy enjoyed being the brat in a room full of I-want-to-thank-my-sponsor drivers. He'd become familiar with controversy during his career, but he'd grown to the point where he was actually comfortable causing it. With the funky clothes, the newly dyed red hair (following in the footsteps of Jacques Villeneuve), and the cool, retro-style sunglasses, Paul was clearly a long way from his roots. Every race car driver, every professional athlete, for that matter, loves to be in the spotlight. It's what athletes live for, and it's how they make their money. And in the tightly knit world of auto racing, that spotlight can become pretty crowded. So, when you're a quiet, pudgy kid from Scarborough, Ontario, what do you do to get noticed your first time on the race track competing against drivers you've watched for years and idolized? You keep your head up, put your foot down, and drive like hell. After a few years of that, when you've crashed a few cars, broken some bones, and made and lost some friends, you realize that they're not going to stop saying things about you. About being wild. About being out of control. About being the guy who loves to go faster than anyone else even when you're in way over your head. Because you're not blessed with the gift of gab. Because you can't get up in front of a pack of reporters and fire off a witty riposte describing how you and that other guy both wanted the same turn at the same time and how neither one of you was willing to give way. So you think to yourself that you like the attention that comes with being the guy who stands out in the crowd and who isn't the typical family-loving, corn-fed, good old boy who'd rather thank God than spin a couple of doughnuts to celebrate a win. In fact, you've never thanked God in your life. First you watch the hair go grey. Then you crop it very short. Then you dye it blond. Then you grab a pair of those wrap-around rock star sunglasses and grow some biker sideburns. You tell them how you like Metallica and Jane's Addiction. You indulge your passion for growling Harleys painted in wild colours. Soon you are that bad boy. You've lived up to that hype. Now all you have to do is drive.

When the curtain opened on the 2000 CART season, much was being said about the "new" Paul Tracy. He was chosen as the most improved driver of 1999 because he managed to keep his aggressiveness in check and crashed less often. He also notched two wins, and the green-and-white, number-26 car was seen near the front of the pack more often than not. As well, Tracy was becoming more comfortable dealing with the media, more outwardly appreciative of his fans, and more of a spokesperson for his sport. When reporters needed a good quote, Tracy was there to oblige them. His wife, Liisa, was partly responsible for the change, as were the members of Team Green, who taught Tracy how to race hard yet gain points in the championship standings. "It's interesting how his personality has evolved over the years," said friend and former competitor Scott Maxwell. "Now, in the last two or three years especially, his persona on television and in front of the media is, I think, fantastic. He's become a personality and a really strong spokesperson." When Tracy was driving for Penske, Maxwell said, he looked as though he was concerned more with trying to live up to the Penske image than with being himself.

Going into 2000, CART's teams and drivers tried to distance themselves from the troubles of 1999 as much as possible, having witnessed the deaths of Uruguayan rookie Gonzalo Rodriguez at the Grand Prix of Monterey and Canadian Greg Moore at the final race at California Speedway. Racing can be a harsh business, and those outside the sport sometimes question how drivers can continue to risk their lives after yet another young driver has lost his. As the first race drew near, the inevitable questions about how drivers would deal with a new season without Moore began to surface. Two weeks before the start of the season, Paul Tracy and Barry Green took part in an on-line chat on the ESPN.com web site and discussed the upcoming season. Tracy was asked how Moore's death affected his preparations for the new season. "It's obviously been a tough off-season I think for everyone who was a close friend of Greg's. But I think the reality that he's not here will set in at the first race, which will probably be difficult for some, but we'll just have to see." Tracy also discussed, albeit briefly, his future, his competition, his relationship with Michael Andretti, and Formula One. He admitted he'd been considering racing in cars with roofs and fenders for a change, with either NASCAR or a sports car endurance series. He said he didn't know "of any Canadians who have been top-flight NASCAR drivers. I think it would be something to be the first." While Tracy was right (at the time there weren't any top Canadian NASCAR drivers), his countryman Ron Fellows has gained a reputation as a road-racing ace and drives infrequently on the NASCAR circuit, and he actually sold a Formula Ford car to Tracy's father in the mid-1980s. That Tracy was commenting on his future was yet another indication of his increasing maturity. He has admitted that he doesn't plan to stay in racing forever, thus prompting comments about his future.

CART was also struggling under the weight of its own problems and was counting on some millennial good luck to get it without incident through the season. Besides the unresolved rift with the Indy Racing League (IRL), it had gone through two seasons in which tragedy struck. As well as the deaths of Moore and Rodriguez, in 1998 three spectators were killed at the Michigan 500. The race on the high-speed oval was one of the most competitive ever, with the lead changing 62 times before Moore eventually took the checkered flag. Obviously, because of the tragedy, CART was unable to promote what had been one of its best races after losing access to the Indy 500. The series was still one of the most competitive in the world with its ovals and road and street courses. In 1999, there were 10 different winners and 12 different pole sitters. Formula One was about as exciting as a suburban traffic jam in comparison, with just seven different winners and five pole sitters. CART clearly has the competitive advantage over IRL, in which some of the drivers are open-wheeled or NASCAR refugees, some, such as Scott Goodyear, are talented drivers dealing with sponsorship woes from companies that want to enter racing but can't afford CART, and some buy into Tony George's notion that the best racing is still oval racing. But CART was losing ground when it came to effectively marketing both the series and the drivers, and it was having difficulty carving its own niche between NASCAR and F1. So, as CART entered the 2000 season, it was hoping to solve its internal problems and was counting on its teams and drivers to put on such a good show that it would be able to erase the past and secure the future.

For Tracy, the talk of a championship finish had already begun as the cars began to roll off the transporters at the

Homestead track in Miami for the first race of the season. With two wins in 1999 and a third-place finish in the championship, Tracy had managed to rebound from the dismal 1998 season. That he'd finished third behind his teammate, Dario Franchitti, helped the team's profile and taught Tracy another lesson in teamwork and patience. He managed to step into the spotlight during the season, but when his teammate needed to gain a foothold on the championship Tracy was willing to put his own interests second. In the end, Franchitti lost out to Juan Montoya; although they were tied in points at the end of the season, Montoya had the most wins. Still, the Franchitti-Tracy driving combination was one of the best in CART. The consistency of his team and the coaching of Tony Cicale also buoyed Tracy. So, as the racers prepared to run under the Florida sun, fans and observers of the sport were expecting a lot from all of the drivers, and Tracy was expecting a lot from himself.

The best evidence of a newly mature Tracy came when the green flag fell at the season-opening, 150-lap race at Homestead. His qualifying on the oval hadn't gone as well as he'd hoped, leaving him in 17th spot — Franchitti was even farther back in 22nd spot — with Gil de Ferran on the pole in his Penske Honda Reynard and defending champion Juan Montoya alongside in his Target Chip Ganassi Toyota. Tracy's position enforced discipline, and Paul had to either make a fearless dash to the front or work his way up slowly but consistently. He chose the latter method, and in the end it was the best choice, because the race quickly turned into an attrition-filled event.

On lap 21, Montoya was the first to leave the race with engine problems, and Adrian Fernandez took the lead until he was forced to retire because of an oil leak. That left CART rookie and former IRL competitor Kenny Brack at the front. He became the first rookie to lead a CART race in his debut since Nigel Mansell did it in 1993 in Australia. Brack held the lead for six laps until he was ousted by a hard-charging Alex Tagliani, who was following the example of the young Paul Tracy and doing his best to get noticed in his first-ever CART race. He managed to hold on to the lead for two laps until Mark Blundell passed him in his Pacwest Mercedes. Then Gil de Ferran took over, powering his Marlboro Honda Reynard to the front, where he remained for 41 laps. While in the pits, he was caught looking by a caution period when Mauricio Gugelmin's car ran out of fuel on the track. He came out in sixth place, where he'd stay for the rest of the race. Tagliani and then Tony Kanaan took the lead, but both were penalized for infractions committed during the caution period — Kanaan for entering a closed pit lane and Tagliani for a blend line violation (driving below the line that separates the track from the pit lane entrance). Both were relegated to the back of the field, where they lost any chance of winning the race.

Then it was Tracy's turn. With Max Papis snapping at his rear wing, Tracy was having one of his best drives, working his way through the field into the lead, which he hung on to for 32 laps. Roberto Moreno was hard on the heels of Papis, looking for any opening to take the lead. As Tracy and Papis came upon some slower cars on lap 141, Papis swooped past Tracy with Moreno in tow, and a few laps later he crossed the start-finish line to capture his first CART victory.

Tracy did what Cicale's training had shown him he could do — he worked his way up from the back of the pack, stayed away from major incidents, used his head and not his heart, and performed some smart driving. His car didn't perform as well as he would have liked, but this time he didn't try to make up the difference by driving too hard and putting himself into the wall. He finished third, stood on the podium, and was pleased that Papis had taken his first win in his second season on the circuit. "I'd like to say congratulations to Max," Paul said after the race.

> He's had a lot happen to him, and it's good to see him smiling again. I didn't have a great car all weekend. I had a push condition in the middle of the turns, and I was loose coming off, but we got good points coming out of here. It would have been better if there wasn't traffic, but this is racing. I was trying to dictate the pace and not catch a bunch of traffic, but we just had to take what we could get. To get third is a huge achievement for us. My guys gave me great stops. I can't say enough about the job they do. They take a lot of credit for what we do. Obviously, there were a few problems with the Fords, and that allowed us to have a good finish. From our team's perspective, this weekend was a big success.

Tracy had begun the season in good form, and he reiterated that his focus was on the championship at the end of the season and that he'd maintain that focus race by race. "Obviously we want to win," Tracy told the Associated Press on April 7 as he prepared for the Bosch Grand Prix on the oval at Nazareth, Pennsylvania. "If we can win we are going to try to win, but the focus is really just to keep gathering points all year and being consistent." He'd received 14 points for the third-place finish at Miami, and he'd already won twice at Nazareth, partly because of the testing miles he'd logged there while driving for Roger Penske. Because of Franchitti's preseason testing crash, Tracy had handled most of the testing and was now more familiar than his teammate with the 2000 car. "Paul stepped into the breach and did a great job in the testing," said Barry Green. "He handled the situation last year with that lost race [when he was suspended from the first race of the 1999 season] about as well as it could be handled, and he has shown a lot of maturity and strength in the last year." Green added that he had faith in the Canadian to be near the top of the standings by the end of the season. "I don't see why we couldn't win. There's incredible competition out there these days, but Paul is right there with the best." Tracy added that he knew he'd been too aggressive in the past and explained that he was now able to consider when to be aggressive and when to back off. "Obviously, it's a game of calculated risks," he said. "There are times when you have to take risks, but do you do it now or later? . . . Things happen real fast on the racetrack, but experience helps you calculate the risks and make the right decisions." The opportunity to make a pass doesn't occur often, he noted, and "Sometimes if you go to make a move and then you say, 'Well, maybe I shouldn't do that,' then it is almost too late. That's when an accident happens."

Thanks to a freak snowstorm, there was no racing at Nazareth on April 9. The race was postponed to May 27. The teams then made their way to another of Tracy's favourite tracks, at Long Beach, where Paul had won his first victory in 1993 with Penske. And on April 16, 2000, he won there again. The bump in the schedule that resulted from the Nazareth snowstorm didn't seem to affect Tracy, but his team struggled to find the right set-up for the car, and in the end he qualified 17th, the same place he'd started from in Miami. Tracy was furious with the results after Saturday qualifying, and that night Team Green engineer Steve Challis, who'd worked with Greg Moore on the Player's team, suggested using a set-up that he'd used on Moore's car. He dug into his notebook and came out with a set-up that led to Tracy's "best-ever ride," according to Barry Green. Changes to the suspension and mechanical set-up made the car more competitive for the 82-lap race on the temporary circuit.

But the race was still no cakewalk for Tracy. He kept his cool despite touching wheels with Michael Andretti as they left the pits early in the race. "His guy waved him out right in front of me," Tracy told the Associated Press. "It got me up in the air and, luckily, we hit pretty square and it didn't bend anything. After that we hooked up with Michael and came up through the field." Two yellow flags late in the race allowed second-place finisher Helio Castroneves and Jimmy Vasser to catch up to Paul. "I wasn't really looking at them too much, but I knew that Helio had to be concentrating on keeping Jimmy behind him and not really pushing forward," the *Toronto Star* reported him as saying. "I had an open track ahead of me so I just concentrated on being smooth and getting quicker and quicker on each lap without making any mistakes." With the 16th win of his career, it was the second farthest back a driver has won from on a road or street course in CART history. That finish was exceeded by Al Unser Jr. when he won from 19th place on the starting grid in 1986 on the former downtown Miami course.

Again displaying his newfound maturity, Tracy summed

up his race: "Being a lot less patient in the past, I would put my nose in where it shouldn't be and get it chopped off. This time I wasn't being overaggressive and we stuck to our plan," he said to the Associated Press. In addition to Tracy's use of Moore's set-up, Greg's memory was invoked by the second-place finisher. A weeping Castroneves, never one to hide his emotions, said, "I tell you, I couldn't control my emotions. We need to remember someone very special, Greg Moore." Castroneves had taken the place on the Penske team that would have gone to Moore for the 2000 season. "I know Greg would be happy," Castroneves said after his second-place finish at Long Beach. "I wish he was here to share this with me."

Tracy was now the leader of the championship standings after just two races, with 34 points, ahead of Vasser with 26 points and Max Papis and Roberto Moreno, who were tied for third with 20 points.

The season was still in its infancy, but already the racing pundits were talking about Tracy's newfound driving consistency. Paul refused to be drawn into predictions from those who pointed out, in the tradition of great sports trivia, that the past few winners of the Long Beach Grand Prix had gone on to win the FedEx Championship series. He admitted he liked the "role reversal," as he said to reporters before the next race on the near-rectangular track in Rio de Janeiro. Franchitti, Andretti, and even the almost unstoppable Montoya had struggled during the first races of the season, and Tracy was glad to put a points buffer between himself and them. He was again preaching consistency as the road to the championship, saying that it would be difficult for his opponents to make up lost ground if he continued to finish on the podium or at least in the top five.

With good results behind him, Tracy concentrated on qualifying in Rio. He was back in 11th spot during early qualifying rounds but improved to third place in the second session. His team's "right formula" again paid off. The crew didn't panic after the early session and helped Paul to gain valuable positions on the track through their work in the pits. The rookie Alex Tagliani, in just his third CART race, managed to secure pole position. As at Long Beach, Tracy had an advantage going into Rio after winning the race there for Team Penske in 1997.

The race itself saw Tagliani take the early lead and hold it for 35 laps. Tracy then took over, but Tagliani eventually returned to the front after a round of pit stops. Tracy remained in the hunt, but so did Jimmy Vasser and Adrian Fernandez, who started 16th. On lap 100, Tagliani had a spectacular spin that sent everyone behind him heading for cover. As he spun, the French Canadian made a bold attempt to correct the spin by stomping on the throttle and trying to get his car pointed in the right direction. But that manoeuvre only created a massive cloud of white tire smoke, which forced everyone behind him to hold his breath and hope he could make it through. "I saw Tagliani spinning in front of me and then coming back down [the track]," said Vasser after he raced to a second-place finish. "Then I think he lit them up and tried to do a doughnut or something. I lost him in the smoke, and I thought he was still rolling down. So I decided to go for the outside. It was basically a 50-50 chance. It was more luck than anything." Tracy ended up with a respectable third-place finish, and another visit to the podium, but not before he too was caught up in Tagliani's fireworks. "Jimmy and I went through the smoke, and I actually hit Alex's car. I clipped the wing, but the car was okay, and I was able to make it through." Tagliani's spin allowed Fernandez to jump into the lead and keep it. Tracy kept the championship lead with a 48–42 score over his closest rival, Vasser. A disheartened and embarrassed Tagliani went out of the race shortly after his spin.

Tracy's consistency remained intact following the next race at Twin Ring Motegi in Japan. Paul finished sixth after starting 20th and held on to the points lead after Andretti stepped up to take the win. Once again, Tracy worked his way through the pack. His eight points gave him a lead of 14 points over Vasser and Moreno.

Before Tracy and Team Green made the return visit to Nazareth, they went to Milwaukee for some test sessions, where Paul returned to his old form. He'd just turned a lap of 22.004 seconds — almost a 10th of a second faster than Franchitti. "I downshifted coming into turn three and the car just turned left," said Tracy to the *Toronto Star*. "I was pretty much a passenger after that." He escaped unhurt.

During the Nazareth race, Tracy qualified fourth but went through another fight, including sliding sideways to avoid hitting a spinning Michel Jourdain Jr. He also fought with CART officials. Paul was given a penalty that sent him to the back of the field only to be given a drive-through penalty during a later caution period for passing back-marker Luiz Garcia in his Mercedes-Benz Reynard from the Arciero Project Racing Group. An angry Tracy thought that Garcia had no business being on the track. "On the restart . . . [Garcia is] idling down the backstretch and everyone else is gone," said Tracy to the *Toronto Star*. "I pulled up alongside him and told him to go. He sits there and they give me a drive-through and it cost us a lap." While the original race at Nazareth was snowed out, the positions on the grid were determined before the snow fell. Garcia didn't qualify then but was allowed to race during the rescheduled event, and this didn't sit well with Tracy, who has often said that CART officials use different sets of rules for different drivers. "We had a car that was capable of winning," he said following the race.

> When I was behind Montoya, I was just pacing myself. I figured that we could get ahead of him on pit stops. The crew kicked butt in the pits again. But Montoya was being superaggressive on restarts, and I just let him have it. On the first couple of stops, we beat him off pit lane. It wasn't going to be an issue until the end of the race. I'm extremely disappointed with how everything turned out, but lapped cars cost us our race.

Tracy's teammate, Franchitti, had another dismal outing and spun out of the race on the start. Nazareth foretold the penalty-plagued season to come.

The day really belonged to the Penske team. Gil de Ferran notched the 100th victory for Penske, providing sweet relief for the man and the team after losing Greg Moore — who'd promised Penske he'd secure win 100 — and rookie Gonzalo Rodriguez in 1999. The team had also parted ways with Al Unser Jr., who'd given it two of his Indy 500 victories, had finally dropped the Penske and sometime Lola chassis in favour of the Reynard version, and had switched from the temperamental Mercedes engine to the powerful Honda one. Penske himself, the serious man called The Captain, was jubilant in victory, spraying champagne all over his crew and thanking his 30,000 employees who work in his various business ventures around the country. It was appropriate too that the win came at Nazareth, on the Penske team's home track. Tracy unwittingly had a role in the Penske celebrations. He'd provided the previous win for the team, its 99th, at Gateway on May 24, 1997. On this day in Nazareth, Tracy gave another small boost to the Penske team by scoring only three points and helping to tighten the championship race.

The champ cars next went to Milwaukee, where Tracy won the race in 1999. It was one of his more dramatic victories as he nudged his car across the finish line, keeping an eye on his fuel pressure light. For that race, the cars had been equipped with smaller wings that allowed them to stay on the track longer and conserve more fuel; Tracy had to pit only twice during the 232-mile, 225-lap race. For the 2000 match, rule changes supposed to slow the cars down and create more chances for passing were bound to alter the race. CART had mandated the use of four different rear wings for the various road, street, oval, and superspeedway courses. The Handford device altered the wings used on speedways and oval tracks, and each produced different levels of downforce and aerodynamic grip. The new wing configuration produced more drag on the car and made it virtually impossible to run a race at Milwaukee with just two fuel stops, unless there was an unusually high number of yellow caution periods. Drivers' opinions of the new wings were mixed. Franchitti didn't like them, but Tracy thought his Honda Reynard was a bit faster and better to drive on the Milwaukee track because of them. In early practice, he was fifth fastest and qualified in sixth spot.

In a reversal of his previous races, Tracy qualified better than he raced at Milwaukee, finishing 15th, out of the points.

His finish was due in part to the black flag that continued to flap over him. A late entry into the pits caused him to cut across the blend line, and he was therefore forced to take another drive through the pits. Tracy insisted that only two wheels had been over the line, which is acceptable, but race marshals disagreed, saying that all four wheels had been over the line. Allowing his feisty side to show itself again, Tracy was angry at officials as he served the penalty and after the race, insisting he'd done nothing wrong. Then he had a meeting with Barry Green and came out of it admitting his mistake. Perhaps it was more a motivational seminar than a meeting. Perhaps Green had pointed out that Tracy had done well in the previous races, and still held the early championship lead despite the black flags, and that it wasn't in his best interests to upset officials and waste time arguing over something trivial. He needed to admit the mistake and move on.

Move on Paul did, but the black flag still showed itself, this time because of another accident in which a pit crew member was injured. On lap 57 of the 84-lap street race near Detroit, Tracy struck fueller Jeff Simon as he entered his pit at a sharp angle trying to avoid Gil de Ferran as he exited from the adjacent pit. Tracy was initially called in for a stop-and-go penalty on lap 61, but on lap 68 he was disqualified from the race altogether when it was found that Simon had suffered four broken toes in the incident. "I'm really sorry for Jeff. He's a very important part of Team Kool Green and a big reason we're so fast on our stops. It's really tough to take especially when we were running such a great race," Tracy said. "We probably would have been third or fourth in the end result. When I was coming into the pits, it looked to me like Gil would pull out in front of me. I tried to avoid him getting into the pits and then couldn't stop in the box, running into my crew guy."

Despite earning just three points in the previous three races, and no points at Detroit, Tracy still held a slim lead in the championship race with 59 points, five ahead of Jimmy Vasser and seven ahead of Roberto Moreno. It was now time for Paul, as the teams headed onto two temporary street circuits in Cleveland and Toronto for the halfway point of the season, and before them the storied road course in Portland, to get a firm grip on the FedEx championship.

But Portland proved to be another disappointment, and Tracy dropped out of the race with mechanical problems and slipped to third place in the standings. Portland must have seemed like a comedy of errors for Team Kool Green — that is, if it saw any humour in the race. Bad luck continued for Dario Franchitti, and this time more of it rubbed off on Tracy. The mess began on turn one of the first lap when Kenny Brack tapped Franchitti from behind as he tried to manoeuvre around Roberto Moreno and the two Penske cars. Franchitti was sent spinning, and several other cars, including Tracy's, were caught in the melee. Franchitti sat in his car while the mess was cleared away, and safety crew members then pushed his car into a shortcut area and told him to go around the crash scene that way. Then he was assessed a drive-through penalty, which CART officials later admitted was a mistake. During the incident, Tracy bent his car's left rear toe-link, which later broke when he brushed the wall, ending his day. Franchitti soldiered on to finish ninth.

Cleveland was an even bigger disappointment for Team Kool Green. After winding his way around a first-lap incident that involved several cars colliding and spinning as their drivers scrambled to enter the first turn on the wide airport track, Tracy dropped out on lap 41 of the 100-lap race after his gearbox self-destructed. "As cars started bouncing off each other, I worked my way through the accident," said Tracy. "Then I got a good run off the corner, and I was able to pick up 11 positions. I was really happy after that. We were getting great fuel mileage, and I started thinking about finishing first or second. Unfortunately, the gearbox went away, and I parked the car." Franchitti's car suffered the same fate on lap 94.

Racing in Toronto's Molson Indy has always been a homecoming for Tracy. His early season success and the disappointments of his past few races increased the attention of his die-hard fans, who'd long harboured the hope that he'd win a CART championship. Many thought that 2000 was his year. When Tracy won in Toronto in 1993, his star rose much higher among dedicated fans of the sport, and casual followers became familiar with him simply because of the attention he received from the local media for a week that July. In previous seasons, especially in 1998, fans couldn't rightfully say that Tracy had a shot of winning there, but in 2000 they believed that, if he was going to turn his season around at its halfway point, Toronto was the place to do it. After all, this was the only place on the circuit where he was truly the "local hero." "No matter how many times I've been racing in Toronto, I still get that special feeling knowing that I'm back home seeing a lot of familiar faces and meeting with Canadian racing fans," Tracy said before the race. "One of the highlights, of course, was winning there in 1993."

In 1999, Tracy finished second in Toronto in a race that his teammate, Dario Franchitti, won, and Paul used the momentum of that finish to set the stage for a series of solid results that put him in third place in the championship standings. In 2000, he was hoping to do likewise. "Last year was almost like a dream year for Team Kool Green in Toronto, with Dario and I pulling off a 1-2 finish. We not only want to defend our championship in Toronto, but we want to get back to the kind of success we were having in the series earlier this season."

It looked as though that success would elude Tracy as Friday qualifying went about as well as his qualifying had gone all season. A heavy rain during the first 30 minutes of the qualifying session washed away the hopes of Tracy and fellow Canadians Patrick Carpentier and Alex Tagliani. All were part of the first group to qualify, and Carpentier ended up 18th, Tagliani 22nd, and Tracy 16th. Both of the French Canadians complained that the system of two groups of qualifiers, based on the previous race's results, was unfair, particularly in this case since most drivers started with cars set up for dry conditions, then switched to set-ups for wet conditions, only to have the weather clear during their final laps. An upset Tracy got out of his car after qualifying, hopped on his scooter, and hightailed it back to his trailer without speaking to the media or fans. It looked like it was going to be a long weekend.

One of the reasons Paul was so upset, according to a statement he issued later, was that he'd spun the car on the slick track during the qualifying session, and the team hadn't been able to repair it. Heading down the Lakeshore Boulevard straightaway, he'd spun the car backward into the wall. The backup car had been brought in, and, while Tracy wasn't happy with its performance either, he'd decided to use it for the rest of the weekend. "It's a shame because we were really making some progress with the setup of the car, but that all went out the window with the rain," he said.

On Saturday, Franchitti held the provisional pole until he slid into a tire barrier on a flying lap and dropped back to fifth spot on the grid. Helio Castroneves took pole position. Tracy slid back to 12th spot, and that's where he started the race. Once all the fanfare was over — the parties, the tributes to Greg Moore, and the hundreds of fans, technicians, and actors who trailed Sylvester Stallone and his film crew — it was time to actually drive some cars. Tracy had now dropped down to fifth place in the championship standings and knew he needed a consistent performance in Toronto.

On the start, Castroneves braked badly, and the resulting confusion caused Franchitti and Montoya to collide near the end of the straightaway, taking both out of the race. Tracy brushed the wall while trying to pass Gil de Ferran and Oriol Servia after the first restart and drove the rest of the race with a bent suspension and a damaged right front tire. But his tenacity and patience paid off as he followed Michael Andretti and Adrian Fernandez across the finish line. "It was almost disastrous at the start," he said following the race. "I hit the wall and bent the suspension, and I had a problem with the right front tire. It would build up too much pressure, so I had to be really careful. It was a handful all day, and I'm glad we were able to come home in third."

As the trophies were handed out on the podium and fans lingered after the race, Tracy, in a burst of national as well as commercial pride, echoed the words of the race's main sponsor by taking the microphone and saying, "My name's Paul, and I am Canadian," much to the delight of fans and, of course, Molson.

On the oval at Michigan Speedway for the next race, on July 23, Tracy had clearly become more accustomed to the high-speed track since he first raced there and crashed in 1992. He qualified on the pole and in the process set a track record with a speed of 236.700 mph. He told a press conference that during qualifying his car had reached 248 mph. "It's fast; it definitely gets your attention," he said. Andretti qualified after Tracy with a speed of 235.356 mph, followed by Castroneves with a speed of 235.479. The times were set while a full field of cars was on the track, and there were many NASCAR-style drafting opportunities, in which cars tailgate each other and then shoot around each other in bursts of speed. All three drivers raised concerns about the speeds and urged engine manufacturers to reduce the horsepower, an idea that Honda's Robert Clarke called "irrational."

Those qualifying speeds turned into spectacular racing on the speedway in a race that featured 52 official lead changes and 162 lead changes on the track. In the end, Tracy's pole position wasn't of much benefit, though Paul did lead the race twice at about the three-quarter mark. The race came down to a drag between Montoya and Andretti, with Montoya edging out the veteran. Tracy finished seventh and now sat third in the championship standings with 80 points, behind Andretti and Moreno.

"We had four straight podiums going into Chicago last year, and the Chicago race interrupted the streak, so we're looking to make amends this time," Tracy said as he approached the Target Grand Prix in Chicago. "Despite having to retire about halfway through the race last year, we were competitive, and I enjoyed running on the new oval. You can do a lot of things on that track. There are wide passing lanes and plenty of opportunities to go wheel-to-wheel." The passing lanes weren't wide enough in 2000, and unfortunately the "wheel-to-wheel opportunities" involved his teammate. On the 76th lap, Tracy and Franchitti collided and took each other into the wall and out of the race. Both drivers were unhurt but suffered embarrassment over the incident, which could easily have been avoided. At the end of the race, Tracy was classified in 19th spot, didn't gain any more championship points, and slipped from third to fifth in the standings, while Franchitti remained in 11th spot. The incident was reminiscent of the St. Louis race in 1998, where the two also came together.

Frustrated and disappointed team owner Barry Green wasn't happy with his drivers. "Obviously, I'm very disappointed," he said following the race.

> *We were in the race with both cars. Paul had just lost a few spots for whatever reason. He got a bit anxious when he saw a hole to get one of those spots back. He got alongside Dario, and I don't think that Dario saw Paul. It's not a good day. I keep reminding my guys that there are two green-and-white cars out there, and they need to take some consideration that they're teammates. It's tough, though, because I've asked them both to race hard.*

Tracy agreed that Franchitti hadn't seen him because he'd been occupied trying to make a move on eventual race winner Cristiano da Matta.

> *Dario had got around me, and I was trying to get the position back. I made a move on him, but . . . he didn't see me coming. I was down on the edge of the apron,*

and we just barely touched each other. It was just a racing incident. It's frustrating because Dario and I have got together a couple of times. But it hasn't upset the team or our program. It cost us some points today, but there's a lot more races down the road. We'll just regroup and become a stronger team.

Outwardly, Franchitti agreed that the accident was just that, even though he'd had a lousy season until that point and had qualified relatively well for the first time in 11th spot on the sixth row. "Paul and I discussed it, and it was just one of those things — it was a racing incident. Paul and I will look at it on tape later and talk about it a bit more," he said. "It's a shame because we had a really good race car. I'm pretty upset for everybody on Team Kool Green. I didn't see Paul coming down the inside. I don't know how far down the inside he was at the time. It's just really unfortunate that both cars were put out of the race that early."

Clearly, the team needed some good luck, but it wasn't to come yet. On August 13, the Penske cars of Gil de Ferran and Helio Castroneves executed a sweep of the Mid-Ohio race course at the Miller Lite 200. Tracy went out of the race after colliding with Tony Kanaan and Cristiano da Matta.

However, as if Tracy had struck a deal with every other driver in the field that the Road America race would belong to him, he stormed back into the championship hunt for the 14th round of the 2000 season. Scenic Road America near Elkhart Lake, Wisconsin, has been called Mecca to road-racing fans, and Tracy has always been comfortable running on the 14-turn, four-mile, winding course with a storied history. His early qualifying didn't go well, and he sat in 13th place on Friday night after letting a wheel slip off the track and slightly damaging his car. On Saturday, however, Tracy managed to jump into seventh place on the grid. "The track conditions weren't great — it was a little slippery out there — so I'm pretty happy with where we are on the grid," he said. He admitted his mistake from the day before, saying he thought the car was good enough to put him in fifth or sixth spot. Meanwhile, Franchitti was enjoying some good fortune of his own by taking pole position.

Race day dawned with some great summer weather for racing, but a black cloud descended on Tracy as his car rolled into line to take the green flag. As he powered up the hill to the main straightaway, the engine died. He quickly fell to 23rd place and frantically radioed his team to figure out what to do. He admitted after the race that he was trying to keep his cool and fight back the feeling of panic, but it wasn't working. A sensor had stuck open, causing the engine to die, so just as anyone would reboot a computer Tracy had to reboot his car. His team gave him a sequence of switches to flip inside the car to shut down the sensor and reset the engine to get the car moving again. Although it took about 25 seconds to perform, it seemed like an eternity to Tracy as he watched the field disappear ahead of him.

If Tracy wasn't keeping his cool, Barry Green was. After the field roared off, and while Tracy was getting ready to rejoin the race, Green got on the radio. "He said, 'Don't lose your patience. Run it like qualifying. Run it as fast as you can as long as you can. We'll make three pit stops, so don't worry about the fuel,'" Tracy told the Associated Press. "After that, I just got into a rhythm, into a zone, and just kept going faster and faster and faster and getting better and better mileage."

And what a zone it was. While the race turned out to be a tough one for most of the other drivers — just 11 finished of the 25 who started — Tracy was on a tear. He began making up nearly a position a lap, and, by the time he made his first pit stop on lap 15, he'd moved up to 11th place. But Alex Tagliani was also on a tear and was in the lead. By the time Tracy pitted again on lap 31, he'd worked his way up to sixth place. On lap 36, he moved up to second place. Tagliani had returned to the front after pit stops and after giving up the lead momentarily, first to Montoya and then to Moreno. Luckily for Tracy, Tagliani's gearbox failed, and Paul took the lead. He gave it up eight laps later when he made his third and final stop on lap 45. When he came out of the pits, he found himself in fourth spot; however, after stops by Adrian Fernandez and Kenny Brack, Tracy moved into second place behind Moreno. When Moreno made his last pit stop, Tracy pulled away and made his dash for the checkered flag. He won by 7.450 seconds over Fernandez in a race run entirely without a full-course caution period. Tracy's dash to the flag turned out to be exactly that — Paul crossed the finish line and then ran out of fuel and coasted to a stop on the track. After jumping out of his car and waving to the crowd, he jumped back in to be towed to victory lane by a safety truck. "I didn't know how low we were on fuel, and I don't think the team knew either," he said after the race. "We just drove hard to the end. It's always satisfying to win, but today was one of the most satisfying. Wins that come when you really do it with everything stacked against you, it's that much sweeter."

After scoring his 17th win, and his second of the season, Tracy was tied with Danny Sullivan for seventh place on the CART winners list. It marked his first permanent road course victory since 1994. "What a great drive," said Barry Green to the *Toronto Star*. "What an effort. You can never, ever count that man out." The win moved Tracy to sixth place in the championship standings after the top two drivers in the championship race, Michael Andretti and Gil de Ferran, went scoreless at Elkhart Lake. After the race, Andretti had 125 points, Moreno 112, de Ferran 106, Fernandez 103, Brack 102 and Tracy 100.

Coming off the resounding win at Road America may have made Tracy's contract negotiations with Team Green much simpler. Paul was approaching his option year in 2001 and had expressed an interest in staying with Green, but that didn't stop other teams from pursuing him. So-called silly season was in full bloom. It's the time, usually around the three-quarter mark of the season, when drivers jump to new teams, sign new contracts, or get cut from their current teams, and drivers hoping to break in begin banging on doors. Silly season is also when most of the rumours about who's going where begin to circulate. Tracy had experienced some of his best seasons so far with Green and was widely expected to continue his association with the team. Under the guidance of Barry Green, and with the mental discipline taught by Tony Cicale, Tracy had seen good results on the track.

While Paul wanted to stay with Green, he was also being wooed by Player's Forsythe Racing, which wanted to replace Patrick Carpentier, who in turn was rumoured to be looking for a spot on the Newman-Haas team. Because Player's Forsythe is the only Canadian team in CART, it was interested in grabbing a Canadian driver to lead the team to a championship before it is forced out of auto racing altogether in 2004 by Canadian laws that will prevent the sponsorship of sports and cultural events and groups by tobacco companies. The Canadian connection, and the fact that Tracy has won races, while up to that point, Carpentier hadn't, were primary motivators for Player's, but signing Tracy also made sense from a business point of view. Imperial Tobacco, the maker of the Player's brand of cigarettes, is owned by British American Tobacco, as is Brown & Williamson, which makes the Kool brand. Plus, while Player's would still be restricted when it came to marketing and promoting its driver, having a recognizable and colourful winner such as Tracy on its team would go a long way toward raising its profile in Canada. And Player's Director of Operations Neil Micklewright was said to like Tracy's driving style and believed that Alex Tagliani, Player's number-two driver, was very much in the Tracy mould. Of course, Carpentier was left hanging. Tracy was looking for a three-year deal and had spoken to Player's Forsythe but said after Road America that he wanted to stay with Green. But he added that, if Green decided it didn't want to keep him around and decided to sell his contract to Player's, and if that was in the best interests of the parent company, then he would gladly make the move. But Tracy got his wish and signed a four-year contract with Team Kool Green.

Franchitti, on the other hand, had made no secret of his desire to compete in Formula One, and he wanted to do so sooner rather than later. He tested with the Jaguar team during the season, and Team Green stated publicly that it had allowed Franchitti to go, mainly to keep its driver happy. Franchitti himself remained tight-lipped about the test and his performance lest he upset his current boss. He hoped to replace driver Johnny Herbert, who was retiring from F1 (and reportedly was seeking a CART ride), but the job went to Brazilian Luciano Burti, even though Jaguar's Jackie Stewart was Franchitti's mentor. Some suggested that Ford Motor Company, which owns the Jaguar brand and the Jaguar team, was trying to distance itself from Stewart after some poor results in its first few seasons and was sending a signal that changes were afoot by not hiring Franchitti. The Scotsman ended up signing a one-year deal with Team Green.

Just before the Vancouver race, Tracy said he wasn't comfortable with the route that some drivers take to shop themselves around and didn't want to do that at the end of every season. He didn't like the rumours and gossip and backroom dealings that his father had revelled in earlier in his career. He wanted now what he'd always wanted: to get into a car and drive and let someone else worry about the business. He wanted security. "Barry understood that and made it happen," he told the *Toronto Star*. "It just gives me peace of mind. Some guys like Dario like to be in the rumour mill; throw their names out there. I'm not like that. For me it's an uncomfortable feeling, trying to shop yourself around, having meetings and sneaking out of buses."

But Player's didn't give up easily. The team pursued Tracy until the previous race at Road America, when Gerry Forsythe still thought he had a chance to land the Canadian. But what sold Tracy finally was Green's willingness to match Player's offer. "I didn't care either way," he said.

> I told Gerry, "If Barry wants to sell my contract to you and it's in the best interest of BAT, I have no trouble driving for you." My position on it was whatever's the best for the company. Whether they wanted me at

Player's or whether they wanted me at Kool. The ulti-
mate decision came down to my team and my sponsors,
and they did not want me to go no matter what the
cost. That's a nice feeling to have them say that. Both
Honda and Kool said there's no way they would let me
go to another team.

Tracy said being locked in to a four-year deal — worth U.S. $20 million — wouldn't make him complacent. Instead, he believed he'd thrive knowing his future was secure because Green, Honda, and the team had faith in him. While his first season with Team Kool Green, in 1998, wasn't a good one, filled with infractions and crashes, in 1999 Tracy made it to the podium seven times and won twice — his way of repaying Green for the faith he'd placed in him.

Had Tracy made the move to Player's, he would have displaced one of his friends. Patrick Carpentier won his first CART race in 2001 in Michigan. After breaking his wrist near the start of the 2000 season, he missed the first three races and struggled to stay in contention. His future was uncertain with Player's, and, while it was generally unsaid publicly, team management was criticizing Carpentier for not being aggressive enough, and the corporation was beginning to face some difficulties marketing two French Canadian drivers. Compared with Tagliani, Carpentier wasn't aggressive, but he battled with a poorly performing car all season, and, although not sliding out of a race in as dramatic a fashion as his teammate, he was doing his best to be consistent despite his three-race deficit. His team also left him hanging until it was clear that it was unable to sign Tracy to replace him.

As always, rumours persisted after Tracy signed the

contract with Green. The strongest rumour had Tracy signing his deal with British American Tobacco, Brown & Williamson's and Imperial Tobacco's parent company, and not with Team Kool Green. The theory is that signing with the parent company would make it easier to facilitate a transfer of Tracy from Team Green to Player's. While it may sound intriguing to some fans, it's just a rumour, says Tracy. "Ultimately, there's options in the contract, and Barry can let me go, and I can leave at times, but right now I want to stay where I'm at. I had an option to leave the contract last year, and I decided to stay with Barry and sign a new contract, so this is where I'm going to stay unless I have a reason to go somewhere."

Despite the politics of the racing world, the three Canadians, Tracy, Tagliani, and Carpentier, had become friends who were joined by their common enthusiasm for karting. Carpentier first heard of Tracy while the French Canadian was at the Spenard David Racing School at Mosport during the late 1980s. Tracy was in Indy Lights, and Carpentier knew of him because he was Canadian and because his reputation had preceded him. They didn't talk, Carpentier says, until he moved up to Formula Atlantic and then into CART racing in 1997. The buzz around Tracy grew when he signed with Penske because, as Carpentier noted, "he was kind of the first Canadian at that time to be running at that level, so it was pretty impressive." With Tracy's guidance, Carpentier and Tagliani, along with Jimmy Vasser, who also makes his home in Las Vegas, have all become hardcore karting enthusiasts. Carpentier said that every couple of weeks the drivers head to a kart track in Vegas that Bryan Herta owns for some "friendly" competition — at least that's the goal. "We call that 'happy hour,' and we put new tires on the kart at the end of the day," laughed Carpentier. In addition to the competition, the lifeblood for race drivers, they enjoy tinkering with the karts and using the time spent in them to hone their reflexes and their driving skills and to keep themselves in shape. "We actually go in the spring and summer when it starts to get warm and they open the track at night," said Tracy. "Once the summer comes and we're home in the middle of the week, we'll go out at night. They open the track at six at night. We go out and run around in the karts until 11 or 12 o'clock." It's just one of the ways the drivers remain friends.

When Tracy was just seven years old, his father would drop him off at a kart on his way to work in the morning, leave him an extra fuel canister, and pick him — and the empty canister — up on his way back home. It was as a karter that he first displayed his distinctive driving style and mastered many of the skills he'd put to use on the champ car tracks. Some drivers leave karts behind as they enter the big leagues, but Tracy is one of the few who stuck with karting and even got some of his friends involved in it. His former teammate, Emerson Fittipaldi, in fact returned to karts in 1982 after leaving Formula One. "I found I still had the motivation and the desire to win," he told *F1 Racing* magazine in September 1997. "I was 35 years old and racing against kids — 16-year-olds — and we had some great dices." At the age of 37, Fittipaldi won a superkart championship, proving that karts weren't just for kids anymore.

By the start of the 2000 season, Tracy's interest in karting had extended well beyond competing with friends for bragging rights, although it's clear Paul has a lot of fun doing it. He owns two karts, both six-speed models able to reach speeds of up to 100 mph, and he maintains them at his house in Las Vegas. His enthusiasm for karting is such that he decided to offer the kind of help to up-and-coming racers that his father had given him, but with Paul Tracy Karting he took the extra step and created an entire team. "I've always kind of been involved in go-karting, playing around with them and practising, and I wanted to start manufacturing karts and somehow be involved and sponsor some kids to drive," he said.

> I ran into an old friend of mine whose name is Mark Cartienren at a go-kart race two years ago. I hadn't seen him in 10 years, and he was importing karts and had just had a falling out with the company he was working with and was looking to do something new, and I was looking to do something, and we decided, hey, why don't we just hook up with a company, a manufacturing facility?

The two decided to strike a deal with a manufacturer in Italy. From hanging around karting tracks, Tracy knew several skilled teenagers in the Las Vegas area who were eager for a chance to race with the pros. "So we hooked up with a guy named Mike Wilson, who was a six-time world champion himself, and did a contract with him to build karts for us, and it kind of went from there," Tracy added. "We started off, and we struggled with some designs, and now things are starting to go. This year we've got three or four drivers that I sponsor, and they're all guys that are looking to go car racing."

Tracy is enthusiastic about karts, but he's more enthusiastic about helping out some young racers who wouldn't otherwise have the chance to compete and eventually move into the world of car racing. He likes to lend a hand and give some young people a push as they enter an extremely tough sport. Even though his father paid for much of his early racing career, Tracy knows how much money is needed and how important it is to get to know the people who will help one's career. The karters on Tracy's team range in age from 15 to 22 and hail from Arizona, Wisconsin, California, and Nevada. One of his racers won a scholarship to the Skip Barber Racing Academy in 2001 as well as a test in a CART champ car. During the 2001 season, his karters were to take part in about 13 races, including a five-race championship to be sanctioned by CART as well as a pro series. "I wanted to give back to the grassroots level," he said. "Help some kids out. Most of these kids are good drivers, and they just don't have a lot of money behind them. They don't have rich parents, and they're really good drivers."

Alex Tagliani was considered one of those kids not too many years ago, but he was now helping Tracy to bring the Quebec 2000 champion formula karter to compete in the 125-gearbox category in the Grand National race in Las Vegas. "When you win the championship, it's still really expensive — you need a kart, you need a trailer, to take part in testing for the event and qualifying," Tagliani said. "But just for that weekend, all the driver has to do is just show up with a helmet and gloves. It's really impressive to watch. It was very tough for me to do everything. I needed Paul's help to do it. He's Canadian, and he decided to provide a chassis to a Canadian driver." Tagliani was impressed that Tracy wanted to ensure that young drivers had the breaks he'd had and that he was willing to give something back to racing, knowing it was "very tough to get there." From their mutual interest in karts,

Tagliani and Tracy have become friends. The two met at a CART drivers' meeting shortly after Tagliani joined the Player's team. "I'd always been impressed by Paul, he's a very aggressive driver, I'd always liked aggressive drivers like Senna and like Zanardi," he said. "His reputation in Indy cars I already knew about, but I was impressed to be just sitting beside Paul Tracy. I was surprised. He was very easygoing, and I was really happy to get along with him very quickly."

Zipping around a track a few inches off the ground with just a helmet and gloves for safety equipment is what these guys do for fun and to blow off some steam that may have built up while they've been racing each other for real. But it's not just a casual thing either. The drivers try to make time in their schedules as much as they can to go karting. "Once every couple of weeks, depending on the number of races, [we'll be karting]," said Carpentier. "This winter I'm going to be there a lot more often, but we've got a lot more races during the season, plus last year we were allowed to do testing during the season, so time was limited a bit more. This year we'll be there a bit more. Jimmy Vasser goes there too, we all hang out. We always compete even if we don't want to," he laughed.

> It's pretty funny because we've got totally different go-karts, different engine packages, different horsepower, and we all try to set the best time. . . . Sometimes it's Jimmy that's faster, sometimes it's Paul, sometimes it's me. It's just fun, everybody says they're just doing it for fun, but they all put new tires [on] and less fuel in at the start of the day. We're competitive everywhere, and that's the way Paul is, he's hard to get close to, but once you know him he's very nice.

The competition helps to keep the four men friends, and that friendship carries over to their time on the CART tracks. When you're driving at 200 mph around a racetrack, you like to be sure that the guy who's trying to squeeze between you and a backmarker has the skills and the confidence to pull it off. And you like to be sure that, when you try the same move, the other driver won't be shaken by your pass and won't try to push you onto the grass or into the concrete. Still, they all know that friendship off the track is different than friendship on the track, when they're in the heat of battle. "Usually, Paul's pretty aggressive, but . . . pretty much all the time he knows who's around him and knows what's happening," said Carpentier. "If I'm making a pass, and I'm pretty much past, I think he's going to let me have it, but you've got to make sure you're pretty much past. I guess it's the same with pretty much everybody."

In both driving style and personality, the Player's drivers are almost complete opposites. Tagliani is the more aggressive of the two, like the eager kid who wants to be noticed and is hungry for his first win in the big leagues. Because their driving styles are similar, Tagliani has tried to learn from Tracy, watching tapes to see how he gains positions on a restart and how he manages a car on cold tires. "With his aggression, he always pushes the car to the limits," said Tagliani. A perfect example of how experience has enabled Paul to combine his aggression with a desire to win came at Road America, a race that Tagliani led until he was taken out of it by a mechanical failure. "He fell back while everybody was racing, and so Tony Cicale changes the strategy. To be able to do that, you need a driver that will respond," he said. "After the race, you can watch the tape and see where experience becomes a factor, but you need the skills to respond to that strategy." Tagliani doesn't believe that Tracy's aggression has hurt his career. He acknowledges that it may have cost Paul races, but his aggressive side has made him the driver he is today, and if Tagliani were coaching Tracy he wouldn't change a thing. "We're not playing piano, we're driving race cars." He echoed what other drivers have said: if he had a racing team, he'd want a guy like Paul to do the driving. They know he'll get up front and get some results, to hell with tire wear and to hell with fuel economy. Tagliani says that, like Zanardi, Tracy is one of the few drivers able to come from the back of the pack to the front and that a good team, like Team Green, is able to hone that ability. "What I like about Paul is he's very competitive. He and Team Green have been a good match."

The truth is, no matter how close Tagliani and Tracy become from their mutual love of karting, they still have to drive against each other on the track, and that isn't always easy. "I want to win, and I know that we're not going to be able to stay away from each other. But we're able to be friends and hang out together and talk about personal stuff," Tagliani said. "Paul knows that, whatever happens, the race stops when you drive past the checkered flag."

Carpentier is more laid back in his approach to racing, and his easy smile and calm manner hide a hard charger who can be aggressive when he needs to be. A charge sometimes levelled against him is that he needs to show that side more often if he is to become a champion. A husband and father, he always seems to be at ease, even when he's driving his hardest. He says that people who focus on Tracy's aggressiveness miss the point that his aggression wins races and that every team owner would take that kind of driver over someone who is more cautious. Like Tagliani, Carpentier believes that Tracy's presence on the CART circuit has made Canadian racers more visible to fans and made it possible for up-and-coming racers to move up in the sport. "He paved the way. It was so funny — I remember being at Mosport, and I don't remember who the guy was, but this guy said, 'Paul's not in shape, and he's never going to make it' to CART. I think he was in Indy Lights [at the time], and he made it against what everybody thought, and he made it to become one of the best ones."

Friends are hard to come by in racing, especially in the ultracompetitive world of Formula One; friendships are often stifled because of the intensely political atmosphere. Ferrari driver Rubens Barrichello commented on the differences between F1 and CART in an interview with on-line magazine *Inside F1* in November 2000: "At times it gets like that. But a good example of what can happen was at Indy when Paul Tracy, about whom some people say bad things, was sitting there with Max Papis and Tony Kanaan. They race each other, but they are there, and they are talking. In F1 we don't often get that chance."

Tracy can both race against and maintain a friendship with Jimmy Vasser. Native Californian Vasser has more in common with Carpentier when it comes to their driving styles, whereas Tagliani's style is akin to Tracy's in his early days. Vasser also has a cool, casual confidence that manifests itself on the track in his steady climbs to the front of the pack and his consistent wins on oval courses, prompting comparisons to the great Rick Mears. Like Tracy, Vasser is considered one of the veterans of the CART circuit, with nine wins and a

1996 CART championship to his credit. Vasser also makes his home now in Las Vegas and, due to Tracy's influence, has become an avid karter. But their friendship extends back to their early days in racing's minor leagues. "Paul and I came into CART about the same time, he was the Indy Lights hot shoe, and I was the Atlantic guy winning races, so we were kind of parallel — except I started out with the underfunded team running year-old cars, and he started out racing a Penske, so we were kind of at opposite ends of the grid early in our careers." Vasser witnessed the Tracy verve and knew the Canadian admired drivers who drove flat out as often as they could. After a particularly hard run, Vasser was given the Tracy seal of approval. "Early on in our relationship, it wasn't the first time I met him, I had met him beforehand, but I raced up in Canada in Formula Ford 2000, and we hung out a little bit, and I did a couple [of] one-off races," Vasser said. "But I did a race where I started at the back in Phoenix in 1991 in my Atlantic car and was in the front in, like, six laps, and I ended up falling out with a broken half-shaft. And after the race, he came up to me and told me I was his hero, so I always remember that. Because I was leading the race when I went out, and he thought it was cool."

That incident aside, Vasser and Tracy were usually at opposite ends of the spectrum when it came to driving styles. Throughout his career, Vasser has been an example of consistency, a driver who can make his steady way through a pack and who is capable of coolly taking on the wiliest of drivers on a high-speed oval. He's also something of a rarity among professional athletes in that he speaks his mind without resorting to clichés, and he will point out a fellow driver's mistake on a track as quickly and as honestly as he will his own. Like Tracy, he takes his career seriously, and he's a fan favourite, especially when he was paired on the Target Chip Ganassi team with Italian Alex Zanardi. Vasser's fan club web site is filled with photos of race fans — many of whom are women — grinning next to a smiling Vasser, often caught in the paddock on his way to or from his car.

His relationship with Tracy has grown over the years, and the two men have become close. Until the 2000 season, Vasser's last win came during the 1998 season, and Jimmy spent some time being overshadowed by teammate Juan Montoya, who replaced Zanardi and who, like Zanardi before him, has taken a spot on the Williams F1 team. While Vasser was toiling in Montoya's shadow, some observers wondered if he'd lost the spark that carried him to the '96 championship in the same season that saw his first win after four years of trying. Vasser says that the spark is still there and that he and Tracy are actually getting closer in their driving styles. "I think before he was more of a wild man and a hard charger; I've always been kind of the patient one, maybe a little more apt to wait," said Vasser.

> And I think now our driving styles are a lot more similar; they used to be a little more diametrically different; now I think our driving styles are very similar. Paul has been a little more patient as of recent races, and I've been a little more aggressive. He's still probably the one that's throwin' his car in there and taking a little more of a chance than I will, but, who knows, maybe we'll still keep developing in the same direction and be even closer together.

As for the wild-man image, Vasser sees it as something that Tracy, while he fought against it initially, has grown into, and he's now comfortable wearing the mantle of rebel. "Well, usually where there's smoke there's fire. Maybe it's been exaggerated a bit, but he's certainly looking to get the bad-boy image with the goatees and Harleys and stuff. So maybe it's something that at first he didn't like, and now he likes to be the bad boy, the intimidator, if you will."

The four men have managed to maintain a friendship based on a mutual respect of abilities and a mutual interest in karts, cars, and racing. While they know that tempers can flare in the heat of battle, they realize that the best way to resolve an on-track dispute is to talk about it briefly and then move on. "It's not hard," said Vasser. "I think we all realize competition on the track is one thing, and out of the car you spend so much time, and the guys that get along seem to gravitate towards each other. It's just like any other friendship in life."

Tracy has found kindred spirits outside racing as well. One is Oakland A's right fielder Jason Giambi, who shares Tracy's love of motorcycles. Their friendship was put in the spotlight when they formed a bet with one another in 1999 that each would perform a public stunt. Giambi's would come after he hit his first home run of the season, and Tracy's would take place after winning his first race of the season. So, when Giambi cracked his first home run, he tore around the bases as fast as he could and then dove headfirst into home plate. "He did it, and the pitcher got pissed off at him because it's like mocking him," laughed Tracy. "So next time at bat the guy hit him. He threw the ball at him." Tracy's part of the deal was to do "some wrestling dance." As soon as Paul took the checkered flag in Houston, and just after he completed his victory lap, he leapt from his car, did a swinging two-step, and then struck an Atlas pose. He was captured on many cameras and was filmed by a surprised ESPN crew just before the broadcaster had to cut away because it was running out of time. His fans, of course, loved it, and his photo graced the drivers page on the CART.com site for several months.

Winning at Road America and securing his future with Team Kool Green must have given Tracy the feeling of a conquering hero as the series made its way to the streets of Vancouver for round 15 of the 20-race season. Overall, his season had been one of more ups than downs, and it would be hard to top the dominating performance he'd put on at Elkhart Lake. Winning was on his mind, but the memory of a lost friend lingered over Vancouver more than any other track or city on the circuit.

Moore never won his hometown race, and organizers were expecting some fans to stay away from the 2000 event because they were still mourning the loss of their hero. Leading up to the race, there was a golf tournament to raise money for the Greg Moore Foundation, set up after the driver's death to distribute money to various charities and groups that Moore supported. A Greg Moore Achievement Award was to be announced along with the presentation of the Greg Moore Pole Award. And in a ceremony near the start-finish line, which was emblazoned with the word *courage* above the driver's name and number, number 99 was set to be retired from use by CART. It joined number 14, worn by all-time CART victory leader A.J. Foyt as the only numbers to be retired in CART history. Tracy, of course, along with Carpentier and Tagliani, still carried the memory of Moore whether they wanted to or not. Carpentier was Moore's team-mate when Greg died, and Tagliani was his replacement.

The Molson Toronto Indy was the first of the two Canadian races, and Moore's memory was invoked there by the media, fans, and CART officials looking for an appropriate way to provide closure to his death. For his own tribute, Tracy drove the Toronto course wearing a helmet designed like the helmet Moore had worn with the late driver's name prominently displayed on the front. The helmet was designed by Troy Lee, and Tracy auctioned it off before the race, raising $45,000 for the Greg Moore Foundation. Moore's father, Ric, was at the race and presented Helio Castroneves with the first Greg Moore Pole Award.

What Tracy remembers most about Moore is his sense of humour. Greg was already seen by many as the stereotypical race car driver — handsome, charming, cool, and cocky — yet all the drivers who spoke about him after his death remembered his sense of humour. Moore and Tracy didn't always see eye to eye when Moore first entered the CART series. As a matter of fact, they clashed on the track regularly. Both were aggressive drivers and appeared to be fearless. Moore was clearly trying to make a name for himself, and his driving demanded that other drivers take him seriously. His entrance into CART was similar to Tracy's — he expected to run at the front immediately. Moore broke Tracy's Indy Lights wins record the year before they started racing together in CART. Tracy mentioned that

> *I didn't really know him all that well up through Lights but would see him here and there and say hello, and I got to know him better and better when he was in Indy*

cars because we were around each other a lot more. In Indy cars, your schedule's real busy, so you don't get to pay attention a lot to what's going on in the other formulas other than the results. So I got to know him when he got to Indy cars pretty well.

Tracy recalls hanging around with Moore during race weekends and on those evenings before races when the drivers with motorhomes would hang out at the tracks waiting to go racing the next day.

The last couple of years, we'd hang around a lot together at night. He had a motorhome, I had a motorhome, we'd be parked pretty close to each other, and I was good friends with Steve [Challis], Moore's race engineer, and there's not really much to do at night when you've done all your activities, and we'd just hang out in either person's motorhome, and we'd just bullshit around and talk . . . to each other about what we were going to do the next day.

He was funny. Really had a good sense of humour off the track and was funny to be around. Always chasing girls. He'd always have new girlfriends.

With his sense of humour and charm, Moore brought all the drivers together in a way that hadn't been done before. Given the highly competitive nature of racing, few of the drivers were really friendly with each other before Moore came along. Part of that had to do with age and the fact that the CART schedule was shorter and less intense, which meant fewer demands on a driver's time away from the racetrack.

Drivers such as Mario Andretti could easily head home after a race and be with their families. And, during the peaks of their careers, Andretti and his fellow racers were older than the current crop of CART drivers. In the 1990s, sponsors' demands increased, and drivers spent much of their time at a track racing or testing or doing promotional work. While they were still at work, Moore helped to turn many of the drivers into an expanded circle of friends, Tracy said.

> *A lot of drivers were pretty close with him because he was really friendly and outgoing, and he was a great competitor. He wasn't stuck up at all. He enjoyed what he did, and he had a great time with the people he was doing it with. He was competitive on the track and a guy that you could race with, but you know, when the helmets came off, he didn't carry that competitiveness on a personal level. . . . He could go out and have fun, and . . . that kind of rubbed off on a lot of people.*
>
> *When I started, guys were really competitive towards each other. Nobody spoke to one another. When I started, it was guys like Emerson, Rick, Bobby, Mario, those guys hardly ever spoke to each other, or they never hung around each other and go out to a bar or go out to eat together. Nothing. That's kind of the way it was. Michael's that way. He's not one of the guys that's going to go out and have a beer with a guy he's racing against. You can see that in his personality.*
>
> *When Greg came in, it was still kind of that way a little bit, and he kind of made a group of friends out of everybody. A lot of the younger guys that came in — me, Dario, Max, Jimmy, and Tony Kanaan — we all*

got really kind of close with each other off the racetrack. That made it a lot more fun 'cause, you know, you're living your life on the road in kind of a circus, and it can be pretty lonely.

During early qualifying in Vancouver, things were finally looking up for both of the Team Kool Green drivers. Franchitti ended the day holding the fastest lap with a speed of 104.993 mph on the 1.781-mile street course, giving him the provisional pole. As of Friday night, Tracy was in third spot with a speed of 104.294 mph. On Saturday, Tracy improved his time and moved up to second place on the grid, within 88/100ths of a second of Franchitti, who hung on to the pole position with a speed of 105.989 mph. For Franchitti, earning the pole in Vancouver, home of his good friend Moore, was a welcome respite from a season of disappointment. For his efforts, he received the Greg Moore Pole Award, presented by Moore's mother, Donna. "I really wanted this Greg Moore Pole Award trophy," said Franchitti after qualifying. "Greg's mom, Donna, told me on Thursday night, 'I want to present you with the trophy.' I said, 'Why don't you?' I was pushing hard the whole weekend; I really wanted this. The car was very good today, and I know we'll have a good race car for tomorrow. This weekend has been just a great team effort by everyone at Team Kool Green." Tracy was pleased with his qualifying performance at a track that has been tough on him in the past. And he liked the changes made to the track from the previous year. "I like the new layout, it's much better than the old layout," reported the *National Post*. "I have good speed here. It's not as tight, doesn't have so many hairpin turns, and it's a lot wider than it used to be." He added that the track, criticized in its early days, now compared favourably with some of the other street tracks that make up the CART circuit. "They're all bumpy, but you just set the car up with softer springs, and after a while you don't even notice the bumps anymore."

When race day dawned, some fans painted their faces blue and white, the colours of Moore and Team Player's, while others adorned themselves in the green and white of Tracy and Kool Green, and they all listened to hockey great Wayne Gretzky holler "Gentlemen, start your engines" to begin the 90-lap race. At the start, Franchitti took advantage of his pole position and led the race for the first 40 laps, keeping Tracy at bay by as much as nine seconds. Franchitti led until he relinquished it to third-place starter Gil de Ferran for laps 41 and 42, taking it back again and holding on to it until lap 52. That's when his season-long bad luck returned. The two Team Kool cars pitted on the same lap for their second refuelling and tire change, one behind the other. As Franchitti attempted to pull away from the pit, he stalled the car, allowing Tracy to leapfrog ahead and pull into the lead.

That's when team orders came into play. In 1999, the Kool Green cars finished the Houston race one-two, with Tracy in the lead. When Franchitti finished the season tied with Juan Montoya for the championship, he ended up the loser because he had fewer wins than the Colombian. Had he, Tracy, and Barry Green agreed before the race that he should win it because his shot at the championship was on the line, he may have taken home the big prize. Green wasn't willing to let the same thing happen again. Going into the race, he instructed his drivers that whoever was in the lead coming out of the last pit stop was not to be passed by his teammate. His decision shows he respects his drivers' abilities and isn't willing to institute the driver rankings that are common in CART's closest competitor, Formula One. In that series, drivers clearly have number-one and number-two status, with the number-one driver often getting preferential treatment. Green could easily have decided that Tracy should set the pace and lead the pack because he was closest to the top of the championship. But Franchitti had the pole, and three-quarters of the way through a dreadful season the Scotsman desperately needed a boost. So Green decided the race should unfold as uncertainly as all the others, letting Tracy, like any other driver, fight for the right to rest in the winner's circle. But for a problem with his car's rev limiter as Franchitti tried to leave the pit (drivers are required to keep to a speed of 50 mph in the pit lane; while the Honda-powered cars use a rev limiter to maintain the speed, Franchitti prefers to rev his engine much higher and maintain the speed with the accelerator), the win likely would have gone to him.

Franchitti took the loss like a true sportsman. In the closing laps of the race, though, he drew as close as possible to Tracy's rear wing, prompting Paul to anxiously and excitedly ask his boss over the radio if Dario remembered that they had a deal. "I knew I wasn't allowed to pass him," said Franchitti.

> I was playing with Paul a little bit, and I think he was getting a little heated for a little bit, but he knew I wasn't allowed to pass him. I was giving him pressure, just keeping him honest. An agreement's an agreement. I'm at peace with that.
>
> I'm a little disappointed. I really wanted to win this one today, but it's better to have a one-two finish for Team Kool Green than to have another Chicago incident. The

atmosphere on the parade lap was unbelievable. People were going crazy, and I'm not even from here. They really went crazy when Paul came around. I think it was an appropriate tribute to Greg. It was a party atmosphere, and, let's face it, Greg was a party guy. I'm going to take Mr. Tracy out tonight and show him a party.

Tracy admitted after the race that Franchitti had the strongest car and set the pace throughout the afternoon. "When I pulled out, I saw them [the pit crew] pushing his car. I could say I was happy and also disappointed because Dario was the measure of the field today. I don't think I would have been able to beat him outright today." Tracy showed his elation after a few days of remembering the loss of Moore by performing a series of tire-smoking doughnuts in front of most of the 63,938 fans. And then Mr. Tracy was ready for a party.

I think Dario and I are going to have quite a celebration tonight. We've got to look at this as a team effort. To win races at this stage, you've got to have everything go right, no mistakes. At the end, I think I could've probably pushed harder if I had to, but I didn't need to do that. I think to win the championship, and to beat people like Michael Andretti, you're going to have to take the bull by the horns and get after it. You're not going to be able to just cruise around and collect points. Now that we've gotten back in the championship, we're not going to change the way we're doing things.

The race for the championship was now tighter as the teams packed up and headed to the Shell 300 at Laguna Seca

Raceway in Monterey, California. With 120 points, Tracy was now six points behind championship leader Michael Andretti. Adrian Fernandez was just three points behind Tracy, due in part to his third-place finish in Vancouver and a series of other strong finishes. Tracy qualified poorly at Laguna Seca, in 13th place, while Franchitti would begin the race in third spot. The reason, said Tracy, was his inability to get in at least one fast lap. On his first attempt, he found the track to be very slow, and after a tire change he went back out onto the track only to have the session red-flagged twice because of on-track incidents. In one, Team Player's driver Patrick Carpentier's Ford Reynard left the track and slid backward through a gravel trap — which was supposed to slow him down — and struck a barrier, which then catapulted his car backward over a fence, where it landed upside down. Carpentier crawled out from under the car and, with a strained neck, got into his backup car and gamely came back onto the track to qualify 18th. Anyone who'd ever questioned his desire to win needn't have. Tracy's race didn't go much better than his qualifying. Paul complained of a lack of passing opportunities throughout the afternoon on the 2.238-mile road course. He managed to work his way up to ninth place before going off course while trying to pass Oriol Servia during the final laps. "Servia was holding me up so much. He was driving into the turns real deep and taking it easy cruising up the hill. I caught him going up the hill and drove under him but couldn't stop," Tracy said. "It just wasn't much fun today." The finish put Tracy back into third spot in the championship race, now led by second-place finisher Gil de Ferran, whose teammate, Helio Castroneves, won the race. Andretti dropped to second place in the standings.

The trip to Madison, Illinois, for the Motorola 300 at Gateway International Speedway started out promising for Tracy, but in the end he met with disappointment again. This time his qualifying wasn't to blame: he and Franchitti qualified side by side in the second row. Tracy managed a lap of 25.500 seconds around the 1.27-mile oval in the shadow of St. Louis with an average speed of 179.294 mph. His goal going into the race was not necessarily to win it but to run near the front and collect some championship points. The race was 236 laps long, and Tracy got off to a good start and ran third most of the afternoon. Franchitti retired from the race on lap 62 when he lost fourth and fifth gears. On lap 208, Tracy was still running with the leader, Juan Montoya, and appeared to be set to finish at least second when his gearbox gave out. He was about to downshift coming into turn four when it broke, and he subsequently went high on the track, into the grey, less-travelled area, and brushed the wall, bringing out the race's only yellow flag. Paul had the car inspected in the pits and returned to the race, but he gave up because a suspension arm had been damaged. "All we were looking for was a solid finish. But now we'll pack it up and head to Houston," Tracy said. Carpentier finished second, matching a career-best finish at the same race in 1997 and in 1999 in Vancouver. The win for Montoya put the Colombian back into the championship race, albeit now in eighth place, with de Ferran maintaining his grip on top spot. Like Tracy, Andretti failed to score any points and dropped to third spot, while Tracy slid back to fourth place.

At Houston, Tracy pulled out a respectable fourth-place finish after starting ninth in a race that Jimmy Vasser won. Tracy finished behind de Ferran but ahead of Andretti, who ended the race two laps behind, moving Tracy into second spot in the standings and within striking distance of the Brazilian.

After making the long trip to Surfer's Paradise on Australia's Gold Coast for the October 15th race, all the CART drivers were rarin' to go, as witnessed by the melee of the first lap, when several cars collided going into the first turn. When the checkered flag fell, five of the series' top contenders had failed to score any points. Adrian Fernandez emerged safely through the rubble to take the win, earning 21 points and moving into second place in the championship. The Surfer's Paradise race was a raucous affair that included five caution periods, which consumed 19 of the 59 laps, before the race was halted by the two-hour time limit six laps short of the planned length. Just 13 of the 25 starters finished the race, and 7 of the 13 went out due to contact with a wall or other drivers. The first-turn incident removed Montoya and Franchitti from the equation and damaged de Ferran's car, leaving Tracy to take the lead, which he held through 11 laps until his engine acted up, and he spent some time getting it restarted in the run-off lane in turn three. He came back in 21st spot and began what had become for him a characteristic charge through the field, actually taking the lead on lap 37 while still on pit road. He remained among the front-runners until he was shunted off the track by young Spanish rookie Oriol Servia's Toyota Reynard. Servia, who finished ninth, appeared to go too fast into the chicane and didn't leave any room for Tracy. While it would have been presumptuous of Tracy to assume that Servia should let him past, Servia could have been more sporting when he realistically had no chance of winning the race. Seventhgear.com correspondent Tara Munger caught up with Servia and Tracy at a party following the race. She pointed to Tracy's conduct following the incident as another example of his newfound maturity.

> *Now, had that been Paul Tracy of last year, he would've gotten out of the car and thrown a punch. I went to a party that night, and both Oriol and Paul were there, and when Oriol got there I said "What were you thinking? It's a wonder you didn't get slugged." And he kind of laughed and joked, and Paul was standing not too far away, and he overheard us and kind of hit him on the back, and Paul looked, not happy with him, but he smiled and turned around and started talking to me, and I just kept thinking, boy, what cool that takes, because that's championship points, and that's really heated, and had that been Paul a year ago he would've been in his room still pouting, or he would've swung.*

Servia's driving didn't sit well with Jimmy Vasser either, and he had some harsh words for both Servia and Christian Fittipaldi. "Some guys were driving like they had their heads up their butts," he told the Associated Press. "They drive like they don't want to finish, so they don't."

It was fitting that a series that had come down to a five-way battle for the championship would be postponed by an unusual West Coast rainstorm and marked by a pace car accident and the return to California Speedway in Fontana for the first time since the death of Greg Moore. "If we have a great race on Sunday, and there are no incidents, it would be the best gift we can give Greg," Patrick Carpentier said before the race. "I'll say a little prayer for Greg when I drive past that spot on the back stretch." For Carpentier, the return was made worse by his crash at Laguna Seca (near the spot where Penske driver Gonzalo Rodriguez was killed when his car flipped upside down in 1999), and he admitted that the first couple of laps around Fontana would "feel weird." Tracy had made peace with Moore's death before coming to California, preferring to concentrate on the championship battle that lay ahead.

Before the race, there was an eerie reminder of just what can happen on a racetrack, even if you're not one of the 25 men regularly employed to drive at 200 mph. Canadian racer Andrew Bordin, a Formula Atlantic driver who was looking for a CART ride for the 2001 season, crashed while driving the pace car, a $120,000 Acura NSX. Bordin was driving passenger Yoshimichi Inada, senior managing director of Pioneer Electronics (then the sponsor of Cristiano da Matta's car), at the time. Bordin lost control of the car heading into turn two and slammed backward into the wall. Inada was airlifted to hospital with head injuries after being unconscious at the scene; it was later found that he had a fracture at the base of his skull and a dislocated shoulder. Bordin was also taken to hospital and underwent surgery to repair the fracture and dislocation of the fourth cervical vertebra at the base of his neck. In the weeks following the accident, he publicly expressed doubts about ever racing again.

As had happened several other times during the season, Tracy's qualifying didn't go well. He was pushing for pole position, and the one point that went with it, to give him an edge heading into the race. Instead, he had to settle for ninth after a poor gear selection prevented him from getting up to peak engine rpm. "The gearing I ran just wasn't right, and the rpms were way down, and that cost us a bunch of power," he said. "I thought we should have run at least what Dario did or better, but it didn't work out that way. I'm a little disappointed." To capture the championship, Tracy had to win the race, which would be difficult, considering that de Ferran, Brack, Andretti, and Fernandez had the same hope. Tracy was tied with Brack for third spot in the standings, 20 points behind de Ferran. Paul would have to win the race, and de Ferran would have to finish out of the points. But, with de Ferran grabbing the extra point for winning the pole, Tracy's chances to win the Vanderbilt Cup became much more of a long shot. Still, Paul remained hopeful. The lure of U.S. $1 million for winning the race had clearly become stuck in his mind despite his lacklustre qualifying effort. He'd dyed his hair green for the race and was wearing a helmet adorned with green dollar signs.

The race got off to a great start, with teammates de Ferran and Castroneves swapping the lead as if they were running in a 125-lap NASCAR shootout instead of a 500-mile marathon. Franchitti worked his way up to third spot. Then on lap 23, Tracy's hopes of winning the race and the championship were dashed. His engine exploded. "I don't really know what happened," Paul said. "There was no warning. We were just cruising, kind of taking it easy, and all of a sudden we lost the engine." Ten laps later, the race was halted as the rain came down. The track would remain silent for nearly another 24 hours until the race could be run in full on a cool but dry day. Christian Fittipaldi came away with the win and a cheque for $1 million, and Gil de Ferran gave Roger Penske his eighth champ car series title.

Before the 2001 season began, Tracy's engineer, Tony Cicale, left Team Kool Green to join the Player's Forsythe team. He would work with Alex Tagliani, fulfilling almost the same role as he had for Tracy. Cicale believed he'd done all he could for Tracy and was about to reenter retirement when he was approached by Player's. The money was much better than what Green could offer, and Cicale couldn't turn it down. It was time for the teacher to leave the student and for the student to chart his own path.

Tracy was disappointed to see Cicale leave; he knew it was for more money and because Cicale thought they'd both learned all they could from each other. "At the time that I joined the team, I wasn't having a very good time," Tracy said.

> *I was uncompetitive, struggling with the car. My confidence was down, and he rebuilt all of that and made me kind of see things in a different way. Maybe to have a little bit less expectations of having a perfect car and dealing with things in a different way, and I think that we reached a point where we both learned from each other. . . . It's not a one-way street, and he was ready, he felt that he had done enough for me, and I had done enough for him, and he was basically going to stop racing. Then he got an offer from Player's that he couldn't refuse.*

Tracy sees the chance to work with his new engineer, Steve Challis, as an opportunity to learn something new. He's fond of saying he likes to "reinvent" himself. He's done so with different hair styles and colours and by racing with different teams, and now he was applying that term to his mental approach to his job.

> *Now I've got somebody else to work with, and I think I'm seeing things, trying to do things, in a little bit different way because, you know, in life you've got to reinvent yourself all the time. You can't do things the same way over and over and over again, or else you'll never progress. You know, when I joined Green, I was doing things the way that Penske was doing it, and it wasn't working, and they brought in Tony and tried doing things a different way, and I learned a lot from that, and now I'm working with somebody else who has a different philosophy on how to do things. So I think it's good.*

Journalist Gordon Kirby has seen Tracy's private and personal ups and downs. Kirby has been covering auto racing since 1973 and has written for publications such as *Autosport, Championship Racing,* and *Road and Track,* among others. He's also been a fixture at CART races since the series began, and the Toronto native has known Paul since they met at an Indy Lights race that Tracy was competing in (it was a support race for the Toronto Molson Indy). Kirby was covering the race and wanted to write a profile of the winner for *Autosport.* Tracy won the race, and Kirby did the profile. Like most others who saw the young Tracy drive, Kirby was struck by his aggression and what seemed to be raw talent. He recalls sitting with Bobby Unser and watching Tracy during the race as Unser hooted and hollered nearly every time Tracy passed by, the Indy 500 great enthusiastically telling Kirby that this was a kid to watch.

Kirby believes it's that aggressive side of Tracy that has prevented him from reaching his peak as a driver and winning the CART championship. "I like Paul a great deal," he said, adding that the fan in him wants Tracy to succeed. But ". . . he'll do something, he'll get too emotionally embroiled about things, and he'll start going backward. He's never totally become a real mature person." That lack of maturity, Kirby maintains, stems from Tracy's difficult relationship with his father.

Despite his personal difficulties with his father and his own divorce and subsequent remarriage, Paul has tried to be as much of a father as he can to his daughter, Alysha, and his son, Conrad James (C.J.). The children, ages eight and six respectively, live with their mother, Tara, in Arizona. They attend a private school, and neither is allowed to miss classes, but during the racing season Tracy is able to fly there and spend a few days at a time with them. Paul bought a go-kart for his son — he keeps one at his house and one at Tara's home — and he says C.J. is already developing a taste for karting, while his daughter is a little more hesitant. Simply because he doesn't live with the children, he likely won't be as much of a dominating presence as his father was in his own youth, but he also won't discourage either child from pursuing racing as a career. He's aware of the dangers of the profession. "I don't have a problem with that. I mean he [C.J.] likes to go-kart. He likes to drive it, and my daughter likes to drive it too, but she's kind of hot and cold on it. Sometimes she likes it, and sometimes she doesn't, but he really likes it, so, if it's something that he wants to do, that's fine with me."

By the end of the 2000 season, Tracy had separated from his second wife, Liisa. He moved out of his Las Vegas home briefly and into Jimmy Vasser's house. Tracy said that, while going through the split was difficult, he benefited from the different perspective of Vasser. "He's a guy I've known a long time, and he said, 'If you've got a problem, my door is open.' Staying with Jimmy just gave me a different way of looking at things. . . . At the same time, we were both struggling, and both of us began to pick up our performance." At the time, Vasser was told by Chip Ganassi that he wasn't renewing his contract, leaving Jimmy to look for another ride.

As Paul entered the 2001 season, he believed he'd actually become the "new" Paul Tracy whom fans and racing pundits have been hoping for since he joined Team Kool Green. He's comfortable with who he is, and, unlike during his time with Penske, he's not trying to be someone he's not — he's not trying to fit into someone else's mould. He's also much more conscious of the members of his team and their roles in his success. Now he's a team player with a clear focus on his own goals. A combination of maturity and painful experience has brought him to this point. He's acknowledged his own shortcomings and knows what he must do to improve them. He says he's no longer interested in speaking out about perceived slights or problems with the rules.

I see there is some inconsistencies in the sport. Sometimes guys are penalized for things, and you know everybody's doing the same things. Everybody blocks, and everybody holds people up, but some people are penalized for it, and others aren't. I don't speak out about it anymore, I just try to deal with it. I try not to get into any trouble anymore. I do my best not to get impatient. I've learned now that it's the better way. Ultimately, if you get aggressive and try to muscle somebody else out of the race, you can take yourself out as well. The last two years, when I get stuck behind somebody, I'll just take a deep breath and try to relax and not get impatient.

As for his personal style, the hair colour, the wrap-around sunglasses — all that won't change, Tracy said. He was glad to step out of what he called the restrictive Penske regime, and he's decided never to put himself in that position again.

When I was with Penske, they didn't want to let me [grow a goatee.] They were very code oriented. You weren't allowed to have sideburns. You weren't allowed to have a goatee. Things like that, and it wasn't until I went to Newman-Haas I grew a goatee, and they kind of let me be myself there, and then when I came back to Penske I had the goatee, and I wouldn't shave it off, and that kind of irked Penske a little bit. He didn't want me to have it, and I wouldn't shave it off.

All rebel posing aside, the reason for the facial hair is more a personal issue than a battle with an authority figure. "I have a goatee 'cause I don't like the way my chin looks. I've got a long chin like Jay Leno, and I don't like the way it looks."

It's that streak of independence that keeps fans coming back for more.

A lot of people meet me, and they think that I'm this real roughneck, aggressive guy, and I'm really not that way. But you know CART *and the media kind of portrayed me as that, and if that's the way people want to think that's fine. I can't change people's opinion of me if they don't know me. Until they get to meet me and get to know me, I don't really care what people think.*

BIBLIOGRAPHY

Toronto Sun

Toronto Star

Associated Press

Canadian Press

Trillium Communications (producers of Television documentary, "Paul Tracy's Big Test: Racing with the Big Boys," 1992)

Maclean's magazine

Racer magazine

F1 Racing magazine

Championship Racing magazine

Autosport

The New Villeneuve: The Life of Jacques Villeneuve, by Timothy Collings

Road & Track

TSN

Montreal Gazette

On Track magazine

Champ Car

The Globe and Mail

National Post

Vancouver Sun
SeventhGear.com (online forum and chat room)
Time Magazine
Inside F1 (grandprix.com)

INTERVIEWS

Michael Andretti — Jan. 17, 2001

Zak Brown — Feb. 27, 2001

Patrick Carpentier — Nov. 27, 2000

Tony Cotman — Jan. 17, 2001

Ron Fellows — Nov. 10, 2000

Scott Goodyear — Feb. 22, 2001

Burke Harrison — Aug. 22, 2000

Jim Hancock — Dec. 28, 2000

Joseph Heitzler — Feb. 3, 2001

Gordon Kirby — July 15, 2001

Horst Kroll — July 13, 2000

Scott Maxwell — Jan. 11, 2001

Tara Munger — Jan. 3, 2001

Brian Stewart — Aug. 6, 2000

Alex Tagliani — Nov. 30, 2000

John Tracy (Uncle to Paul Tracy) — Dec. 15, 2000

Paul Tracy — Feb. 12, 2001, April 19, 2001

Tony Tracy — Aug. 12, 2000

Jimmy Vasser — Jan. 17, 2001

Alex Zanardi — Jan. 16, 2001

RACING WEB SITES

www.paultracy.com (official site, under construction)

www.cart.com

www.koolracing.com (restricted access sign-up required)

www.patrickcarpentier.com (official site)

www.indyracingleague.com

www.speedvision.com (in association with *Racer* magazine)

www.teamplayers.ca

www.andretti.com

www.jv-world.com (Jacques Villeneuve site)

www.penskeracing.com

www.newmanhaas.com

www.indyracingleague.com (official site of IRL)

RACING HISTORY

The 2001 season marks Tracy's 11th year on the Champ Car circuit and fourth consecutive season competing for Team KOOL Green. Since joining Barry Green's TKG outfit for the 1998 season, Tracy has scored five wins, bringing his career victory total to 18.

Three of Tracy's wins came during the 2000 season, when he scored dramatic come-from-behind wins at Long Beach, Road America and Vancouver. Tracy took the lead in the CART championship following his win at round two in Long Beach and held it through round seven in Detroit. He finished fifth in the final point standings, marking the fifth time in his ten-year career he finished among the top five drivers.

Tracy's other two wins for Team KOOL Green came during his breakout season of 1999. That year, Tracy scored wins at Milwaukee and Houston and earned a total of seven podiums to finish third in the championship.

Tracy made the jump to Champ Cars after claiming the Indy Lights Championship by winning nine of 14 races in 1990. In his rookie season in CART, he started one race with Coyne Racing and then joined Team Penske as a test driver in the middle of the season, competing in three more races. Working as a Team Penske test driver in 1992, he competed in 11 races as a substitute for the injured Rick Mears.

In 1993, his first full season, Tracy tied series champion Nigel Mansell for most victories with five. His $1.4 million in earnings at the age of 24 made him the youngest driver to top the $1 million mark in career earnings. That year, his peers voted him the Most Improved Driver after he led the most laps of any driver in the series, 757 of the 2,112 total laps. He earned 11 of his 18 career victories while with Penske.

In 1995, he won two races competing for Newman/Haas Racing before returning to Penske in 1996.

2000

- Won three races — Long Beach and consecutive triumphs at Road America and Vancouver — and garnered six podiums
- Started the season with three straight podiums and five consecutive top-10 finishes
- Fifth-place result in championship (134 points) marked the fifth time in his 10-year career he finished among the top five drivers, and the third time in the past four seasons
- Led championship from round two at Long Beach through round seven at Detroit
- Set a qualifying lap record in winning the pole at Michigan — his first career pole on a superspeedway
- Rallied from 17th on the starting grid to win at Long Beach and from 23rd on first lap to win at Road America
- Led teammate Franchitti in a 1-2 finish at Vancouver
- Started all 20 events and moved into ninth place on the CART career starts list
- Named to CART's All-Star Team for second consecutive year

1999

- Had 10 top-five finishes, including victories at Milwaukee and Houston
- Finished on the podium seven times, including a streak of four consecutive podiums at Toronto, Michigan, Detroit and Mid-Ohio
- Finished third in the standings with 161 points, tying his career best finish in the series (93 & 94)
- Led seven races (Madison, Milwaukee, Cleveland, Michigan, Mid-Ohio, Vancouver and Houston)
- Named to CART's inaugural All-Star team
- Voted "Most Improved Driver" by his peers

1998

- Joined Team KOOL Green
- Had eight top-10 finishes, including a season best of fifth in Japan, Nazareth and Mid-Ohio
- Led races at Japan, Milwaukee, Michigan and Fontana
- Finished 13th in standings with 61 points
- Won the Budweiser Accelerator Award in Cleveland, given to driver with the greatest speed improvement between his first and second qualifying session

1997

- Became first driver since Al Unser Jr. (1994) to win three straight events (Nazareth, Brazil, Madison)
- Won pole at Nazareth
- Set Milwaukee Mile qualifying record (184.286 mph) in claiming second pole of the season
- Missed Detroit race because of cervical muscle spasms associated with mild vertigo
- Became points leader following fifth event (Brazil), finally slipping to second place after Michigan (11th event)
- Finished fifth in standings with 121 points

- Also won the Omega Speedmaster Award at Nazareth and Milwaukee, given to the driver who clocks the fastest lap during the race

1996
- Returned to Team Penske, had first winless season since 1992
- Set track record at Nazareth and became first driver in Champ Car history to crack 190 mph on a mile oval (190.737)
- Won two poles, one of three drivers that season to win multiple poles
- Had six top-10 finishes, including a season best of third at Milwaukee
- Ranked third in the series with 214 laps led
- Missed two races because of a chip fracture sustained in a practice accident for the Michigan 500
- Finished 13th in standings with 60 points

1995
- Was sixth in points standings in only season with Newman/Haas
- Earned two wins (Australia, Milwaukee) in season's first seven races
- Grabbed points lead for first time in his career after Phoenix race
- Was runner-up at Road America, Mid-Ohio and Laguna Seca

1994
- Started all 16 races for Team Penske. Recorded wins at Detroit, Nazareth and Laguna Seca
- Won poles at Phoenix, Long Beach, Road America and Laguna Seca and set four new track records
- Despite collecting only two points in first four races, rebounded to finish third behind Penske teammates Al

Unser Jr. and Emerson Fittipaldi
- Earned first career oval triumph at Nazareth

1993
- Scored first career win at Long Beach, and reached the $1 million mark in career earnings after only 18 starts
- Ran his first full Champ Car season, winning five times (Long Beach, Cleveland, Toronto, Road America, Laguna Seca) and earning two poles (Cleveland, Road America)
- Tied for most wins that year with CART champion Nigel Mansell
- Led most laps (757 of 2,112)
- Named "Most Improved Driver" by his peers
- Finished third in points standings

1992
- Started season as a test driver for Team Penske, who would compete in a select number of races. However, due to an injury to teammate Rick Mears he subbed in seven races and then ran five races in the #7 Mobil Penske car
- Had six top-five qualifying efforts, including first career pole at Road America
- Made three podiums, including second place at Michigan and Mid-Ohio
- Led races on seven different occasions for a total of 128 laps
- Became the youngest driver to qualify for CART's All-Star event

1991
- Started first CART Champ Car race at Long Beach for Dale Coyne Racing
- Signed with Team Penske in mid-year as team test driver

- Qualified eighth at Michigan 500 but crashed on lap three, breaking his left leg
- Recovered from injuries in time to start at Nazareth and posted best finish of the year — seventh

1990
- Won Indy Lights championship by winning nine of 14 races
- Set single season record for poles (seven)
- Set four race records and six qualifying records
- Set a series record with four consecutive wins
- Awarded Bruce McLaren Trophy by the British Racing Drivers Club presented annually to the British Commonwealth's most promising driver

1989
- As Indy Lights sophomore, posted two second-place finishes and one third for eighth place in the standings

1988
- Spent early part of the year in New Zealand competing in International Formula Pacific (nee Atlantic) Series
- Won a pole and earned four podium finishes, including two wins.
- Tied for third place overall with David Brabham
- Entered American Racing Series (Indy Lights) Competition. Won first ARS event he entered (Phoenix)
- Finished ninth overall and led 74 laps in Indy lights

1987
- Competed in Canadian Formula 2000 and won at Mosport
- Also raced in SCCA Escort Endurance Series, Mosport's 24-hour event
- Raced in the FF2000 British Grandstand post-season

series
- Worked as test driver for Reynard Racing and General Motors

1986
- Won Budweiser 650 Can-Am race, setting record as the youngest driver to win (17)
- Competed in Canadian Formula 2000 and won at Sanair
- Also won two races at Mosport and one at Shannonville

1985
- Won Canadian Formula Ford 1600 Championship, setting record as the youngest driver to win (16)

1984
- Sixth in World Karting Championship

Information courtesy of Team KOOL Green (Drivers) Website.